Iowa
simply beautiful II

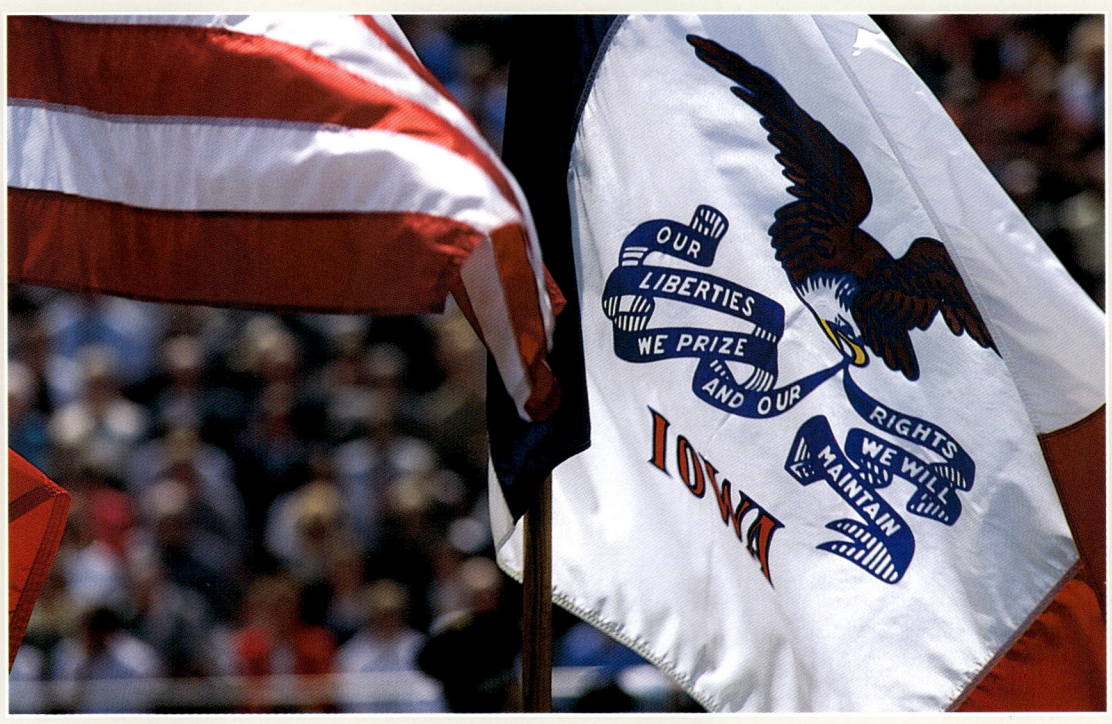

PHOTOGRAPHY BY
LARSH K. BRISTOL, KENT FOSTER, AND CURT MAAS

Right: Vibrantly colored hot-air balloons take to the skies above Indianola at the National Balloon Classic Competition. KENT FOSTER

Title page: The proud colors of the Iowa state flag. Iowa adopted the banner in 1921, seventy-five years after the state was admitted into the Union. LARSH K. BRISTOL

Front cover, inset: Stunning Iowa sunset. CURT MAAS

Front cover, background: Corn, the bounty of Iowa. LARSH K. BRISTOL

Front flap, top: Sunflower. KENT FOSTER

Front flap, bottom: Iowa State Capitol at sunset. CURT MAAS

Back cover: Marvelous pastel skies. CURT MAAS

ISBN 1-56037-270-2

© 2004 Farcountry Press

Photographs © by individual photographers as credited

This book may not be reproduced in whole or in part by any means (with the exception of short quotes for the purpose of review) without permission of the publisher. For more information on our books call or write: Farcountry Press, P.O. Box 5630, Helena, MT 59604, (406) 443-2842 or (800) 654-1105, or visit farcountrypress.com

Created, designed and published in the USA.
Printed in China.

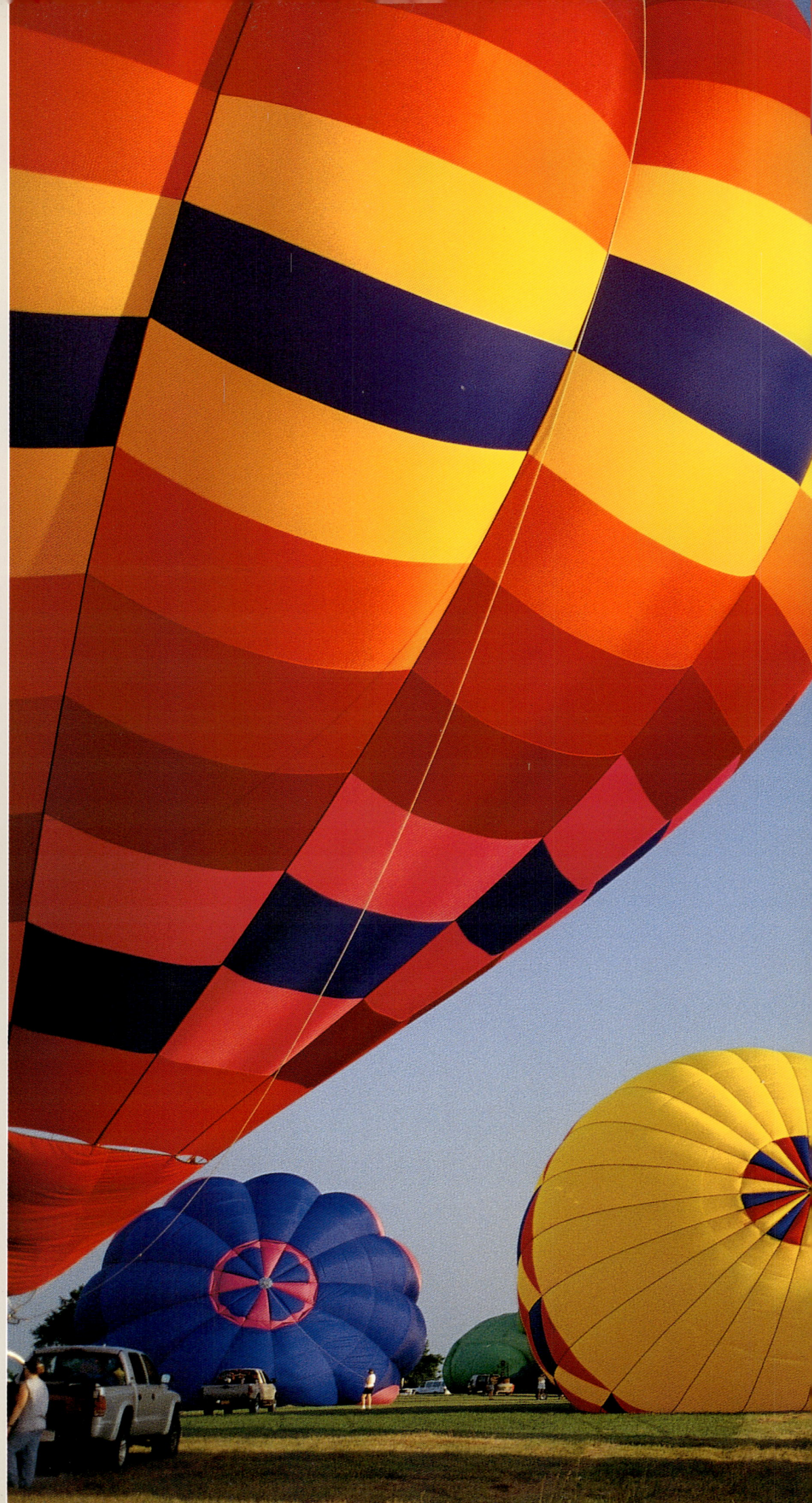

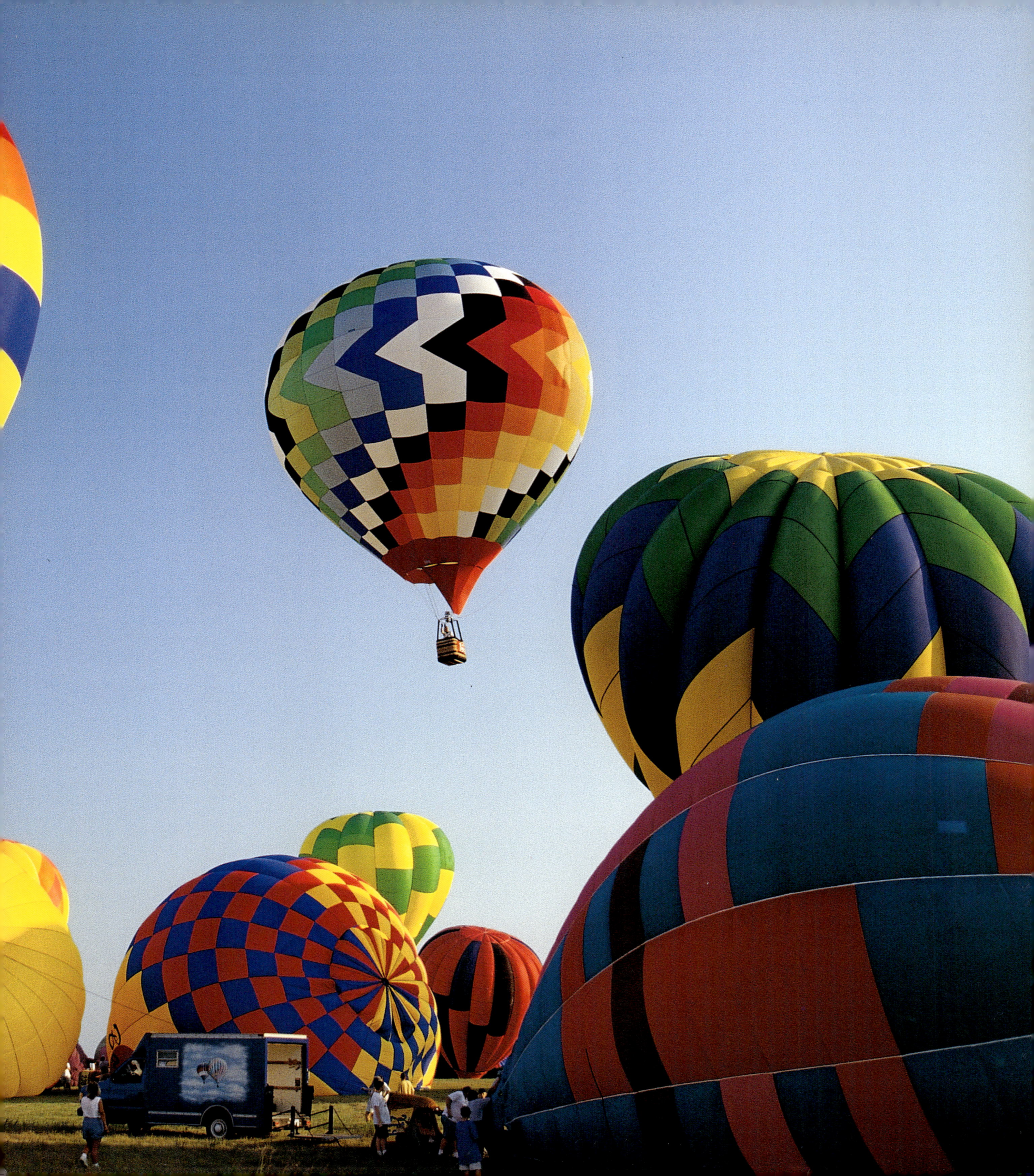

INTRODUCTION

Larsh Bristol's beloved northeast Iowa is a place particularly mysterious, and especially blessed. In many respects, it defies the flatland mythology of Iowa. There are few open fields as far as the eye can see. There are even fewer straight roads. And the wind, when it comes, does not whip the land flat. It whirls inside our rounded hills, and 80-year-old oaks groan in its grasp.

What is most commonly forgotten, in all the Iowa talk of farms and corn and extraordinary, ordinary people making a living the best they know how, is that Bristol's small stretch of Iowa is a lumbering, jumping, transitional batch of land thrown from the backyard of a thick and rolling Mississippi River. Northeast Iowa is a place where, historically, a water's wealth met, and married, the labor of land. It is precisely this unlikely union—of a river people's romantic heart and a farmer's resilient back—that founded the unique, and beautiful, soul of a place and its people.

For folks in Bristol's small river towns like Lansing and McGregor, among the many meanings of home are Friday night fish fries, a few days each steaming summer of mayfly mayhem, and creeping up behind combines and schoolbuses on fog-soaked October mornings. For "uplanders," those ground-driven Iowans miles off the Mississippi's banks, life is marked by rolling, gravel-roaded valleys, country churches, remants of rural schoolhouses, and fields where tractors dip dramatically more than do those of their western Iowa neighbors. In both cases, a people and a landscape are as bound as the thick twine holding a mid-August, square hay bale.

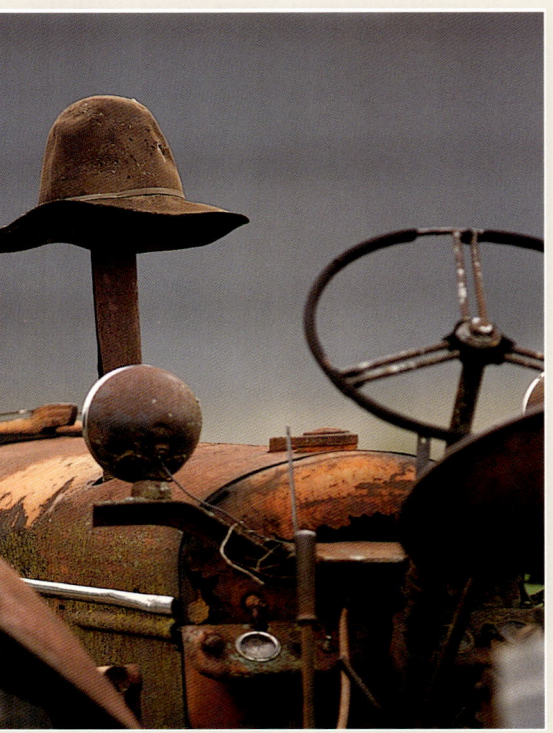

Larsh Bristol is a native Iowan, a rural Iowan, who has lived and worked on photojournalist jobs on the American east and west coasts and, in particular, spent 15 years shooting the red rocks and rolling sagebrush of his adopted state of Wyoming. In his younger years, he did not expect to wind up calling home a white and rambling frame farmhouse with a well-kept barn and a few horses in his backyard. That he has chosen to do so is a gift to both his fellow Iowans and those who choose to glimpse them from afar. Among Bristol's greatest gifts lie the capacity to harness natural light effectively and a journalistic knack for getting past the package of a place, or a person, straight into the heart of a matter, and back out again, so that the story may live on its own.

What is told in the following photographs marks a place in time that becomes timeless, and that is the best that can be said for any story—that it catches the heart, and is remembered for what it is. This volume contains the kind of photos people have come to expect of Bristol—fields, valleys, and rivers framed in all seasons, in the best that day's light had to offer. Yet there are new photographs as well, representing Bristol's increasing interest in the faces of northeast Iowans, their happiness and hardship, their farming past, and their determined yet changing future in tomorrow's world. They are photographs of a land and a people, at play, at work, and at rest. Rural Iowa, in the years to come, will continue to change, but these pictures, at least, have been grabbed and given, and in that there is the gift of peace.

— Tanya O'Connor

Having just returned from a trek to the Mississippi to catch a final glimpse of this year's fall colors, my mind is at peace with memories of the spectacular visions of fall in northeast Iowa.

I returned to my home of Iowa 6 years ago to be closer to my family and to find my roots again. Raising a child in the heart of America has very special rewards. Wholesome, down-to-earth values, beautiful countryside, and great people make a childhood in Iowa a lasting treasure.

It never dawned on me while growing up in Iowa how precious I would now hold the subtle characteristics of this Midwestern wonderland. Whether it be the gentle rolling hillsides filled with new crops, the faint mooing of cows, or just watching my son climb onto my neighbor's combine so he could ride along while the corn was harvested.

It has taken many years for me to realize the value of what has been right in front of me most of my life: the elegance of simplicity. To be back in Iowa has meant restoring the basic values of life, living with honest pleasures, and witnessing the

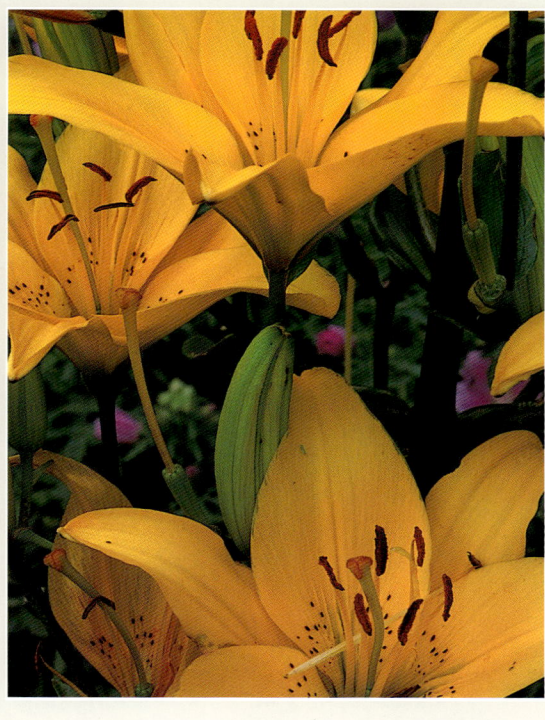

landscape forever changing.

I have traveled throughout the world and visited many countries, experiencing both their cultures and customs, and I can honestly say the hidden jewels that lie in this heartland are priceless. Many of these riches stem from within the people who live here and have deep roots—their family farms and a legacy of tending the land.

The value of the many heritages and cultures planted in Iowa are evident throughout the state. Every city, town, and village seems to possess its own unique personality.

I have only begun to capture the glory of our state and look forward to rediscovering the well-kept secrets of what makes Iowa such a great place to live. It's like finding a lost friend.

— KENT FOSTER

There's a sense of comfort and security in Iowa that I've never felt anywhere else. A sense of being home and belonging.

I think anyone from Iowa has the same feeling—whether they're coming back to live or just to visit relatives and old friends—there's an unspoken bond there.

Iowans also love their celebrations, whether it's Sauerkraut Days in Bouton, the Tulip Festival in Pella, Old Thrashers Days in Mt. Pleasant, or the granddaddy of them all, the Iowa State Fair, where corn dogs, snow cones, cotton candy, and fresh-squeezed lemonade are enjoyed by nearly a million visitors every year.

RAGBRAI (Register's Annual Great Bike Ride Across Iowa) is another huge event in Iowa. Thousands of bicycle enthusiasts come here from all over the country and the world to spend a week riding more than 500 miles from one end of the state to the other, enjoying the peace and solitude of the countryside and the charm and generous hospitality of every small town along the way.

The Iowa countryside is both serene and inspiring. Although we don't have oceans or snow-capped mountains, the blue skies are our "rolling seas" and the majestic hillsides covered with trees, crops, and grazing livestock are our "mountains."

I also can't say enough about the character, honesty, and friendliness of Iowa people. They are always willing to give a complete stranger a helping hand, a friendly handshake, and a sincere smile.

My good friend, Judy Harris Peek, also a native Iowan and who has recently returned after 25 years, describes it best:

"The people of Iowa absolutely love the seasons. They live by not only seasonal clothes but seasonal menus as well. Winter is for dining on soups, spring for emptying the freezer of garden produce, summer for grilling out, and fall for 'grill-gating' at the football games.

We have a wealth of elders who pass generations of knowledge and special secrets on down about everything: cooking and canning, gardening and quilting, as well as raising crops and livestock, or even running your own business. They're priceless.

The people of Iowa work hard, play hard, and are always there for their neighbors in good times and bad. And 'being in a hurry' in the rural community just isn't something that happens.

Iowa folks thrive on quality farming, education and a clean environment. The locals are friendly; my favorite Iowa custom is the 'hand-wave hello' as you travel along the country roads. These are the things that have triggered my senses and what being 'home' again is all about."

— CURT MAAS

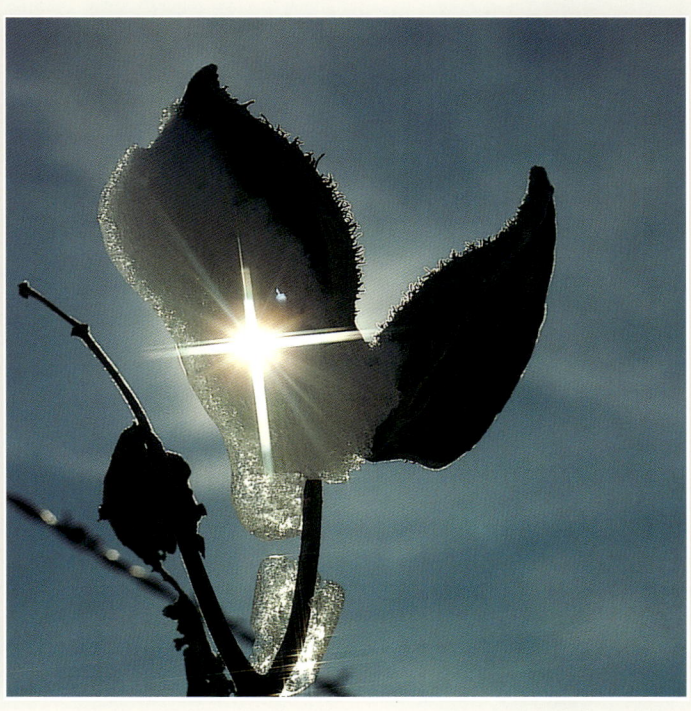

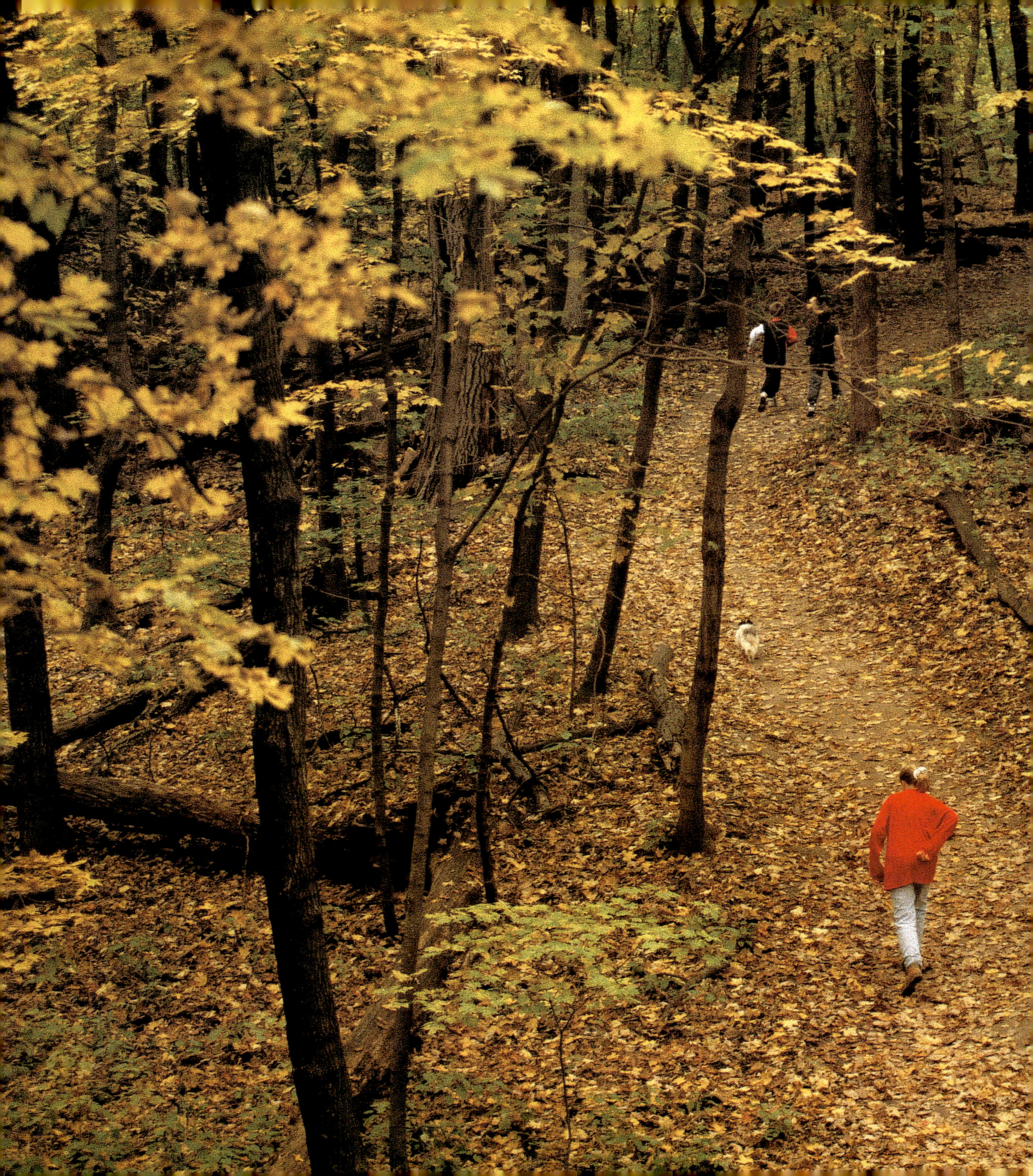

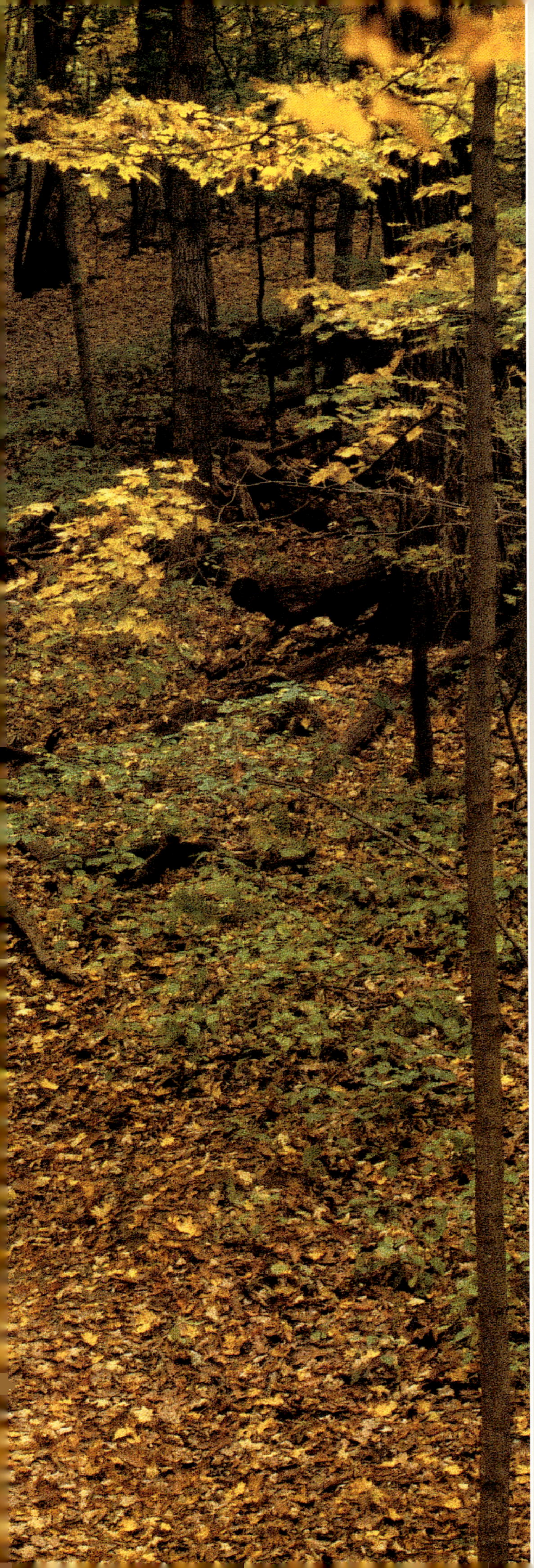

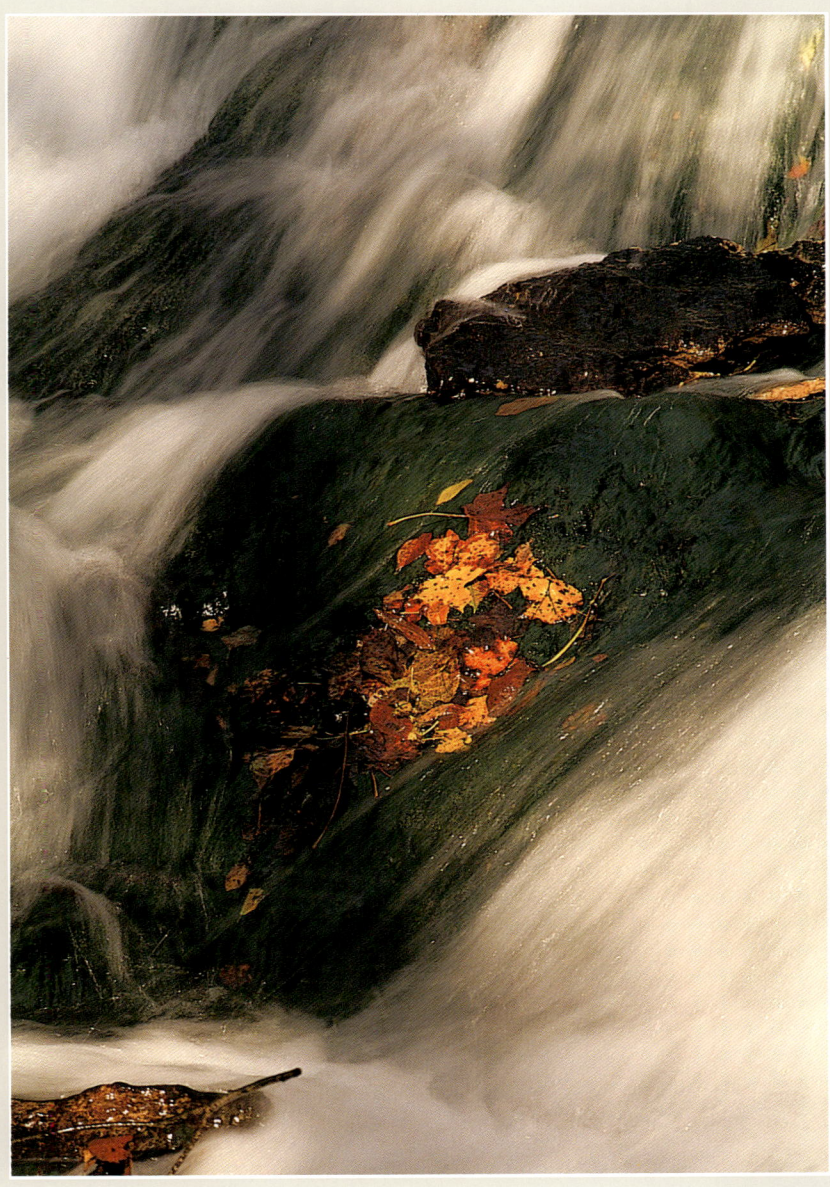

Above: Fall leaves ride the currents of a stream near Decorah. LARSH K. BRISTOL

Left: A gentle, leaf-strewn path through Pikes Peak State Park. CURT MAAS

Following pages: A cow moves tentatively into the fog of an Iowa morning. LARSH K. BRISTOL

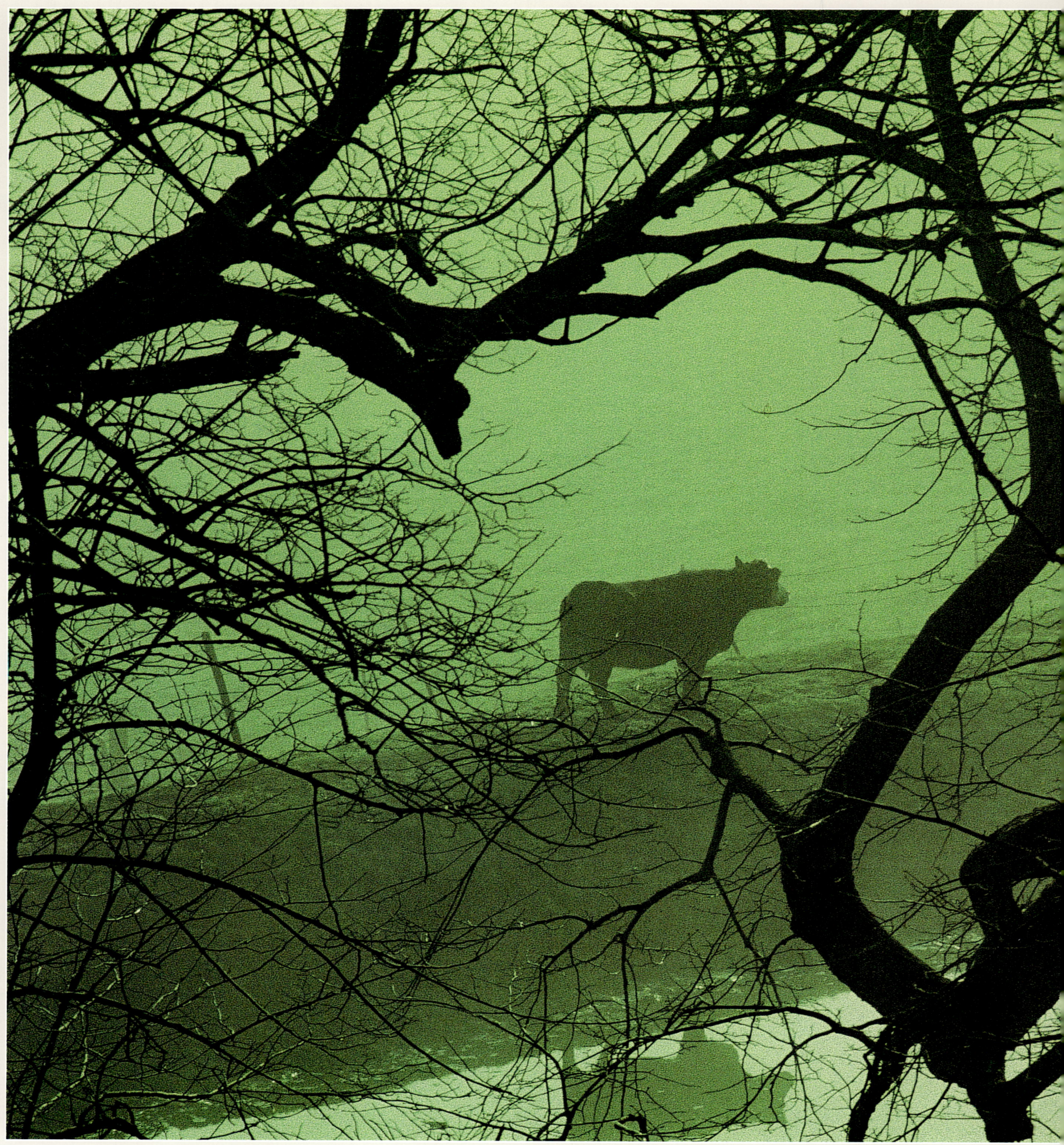

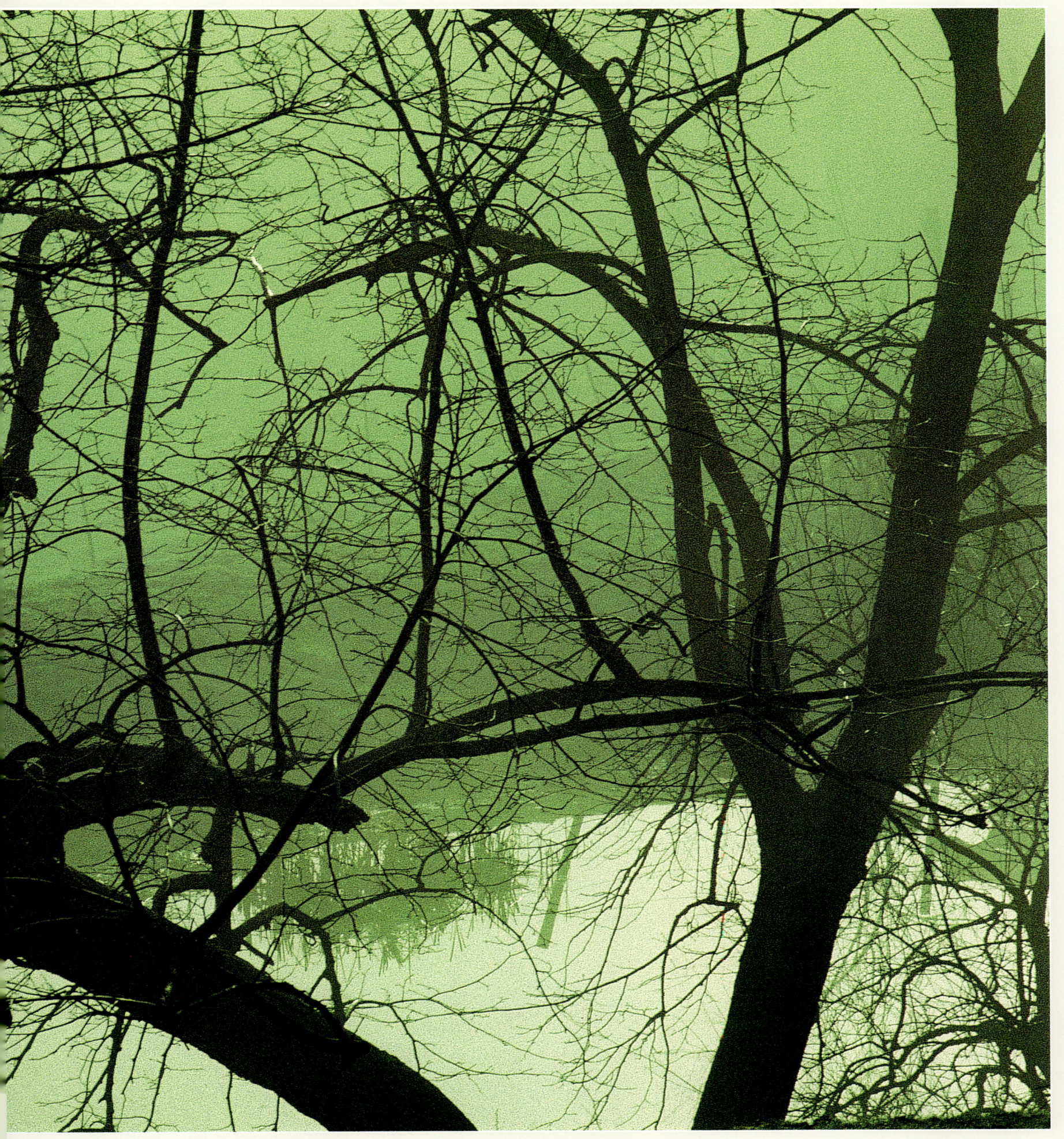

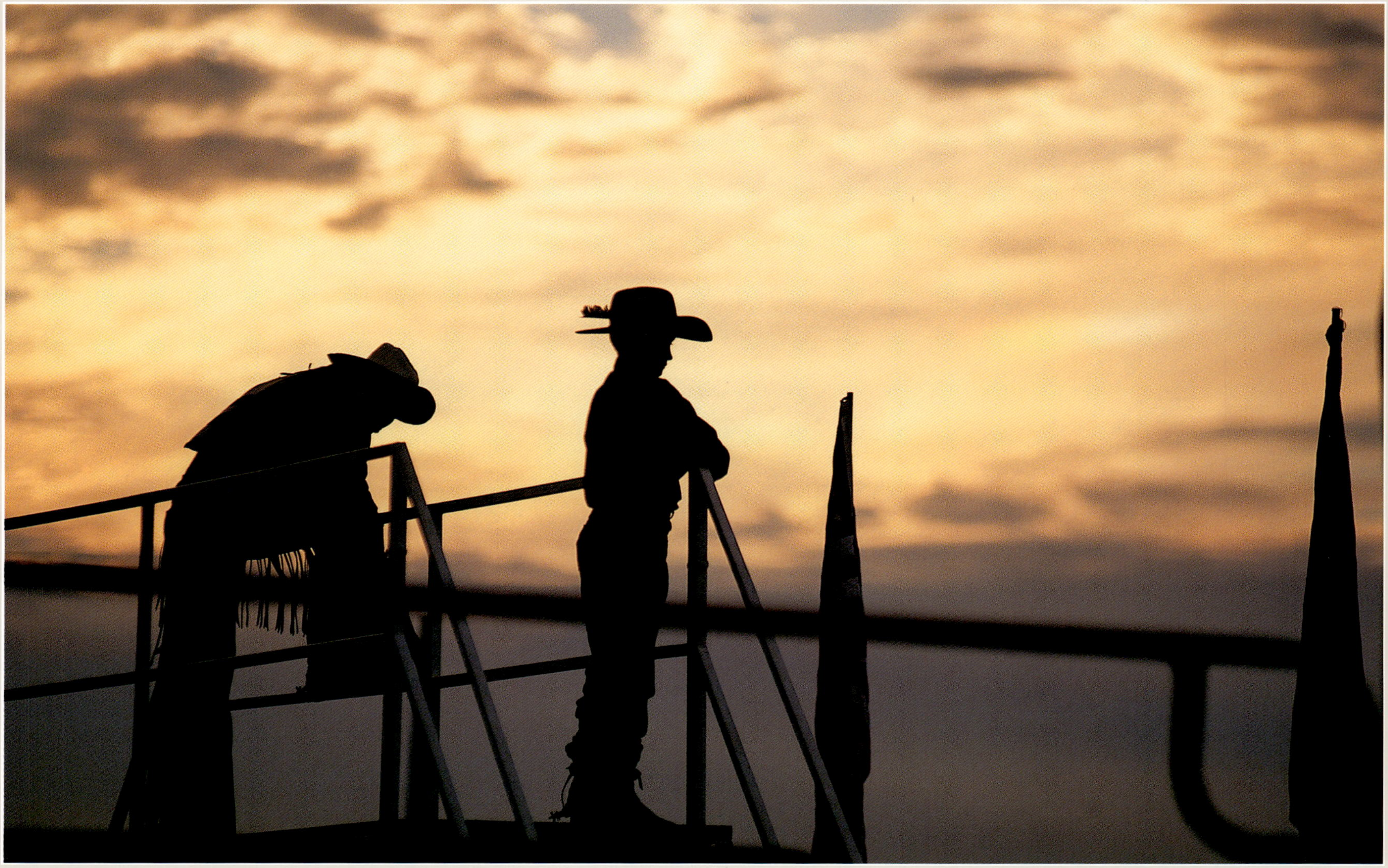

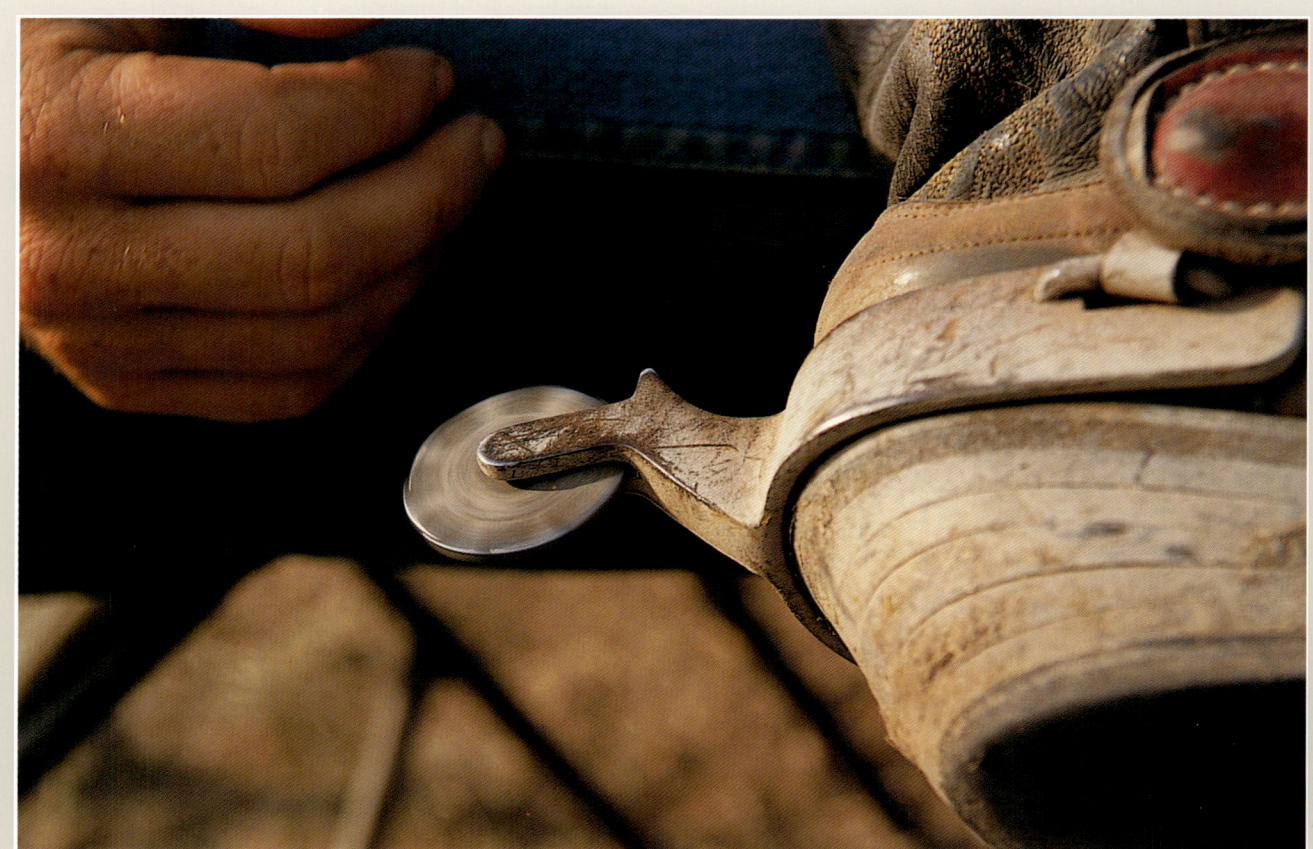

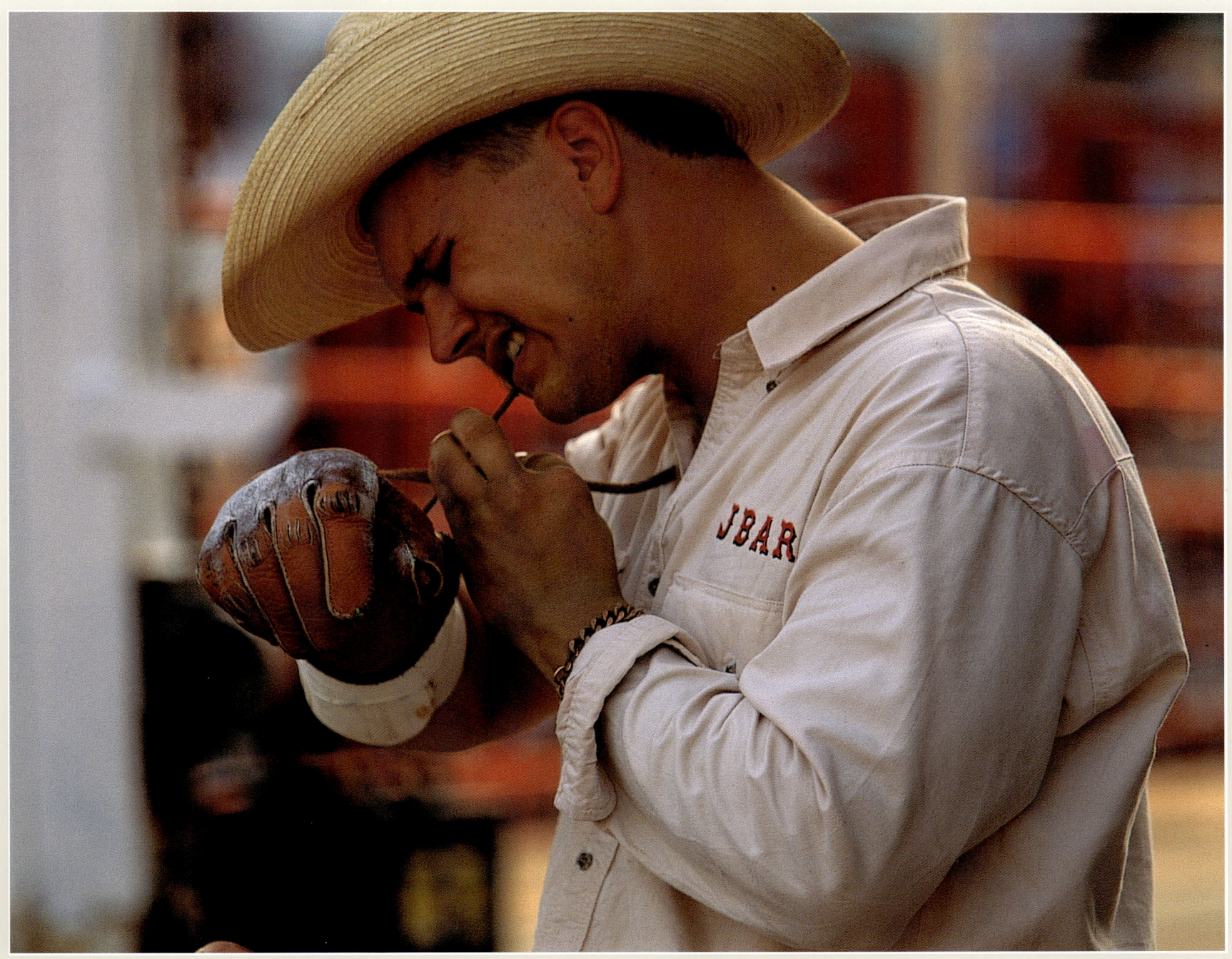

Above: A cowboy cinches up his glove in preparation for his ride in the Professional Rodeo Cowboys Association rodeo in Cherokee. KENT FOSTER

Facing page, top: Two young contestants survey the grounds at a rodeo in Fort Madison. LARSH K. BRISTOL

Facing page, bottom: A spinning spur, Fort Madison. LARSH K. BRISTOL

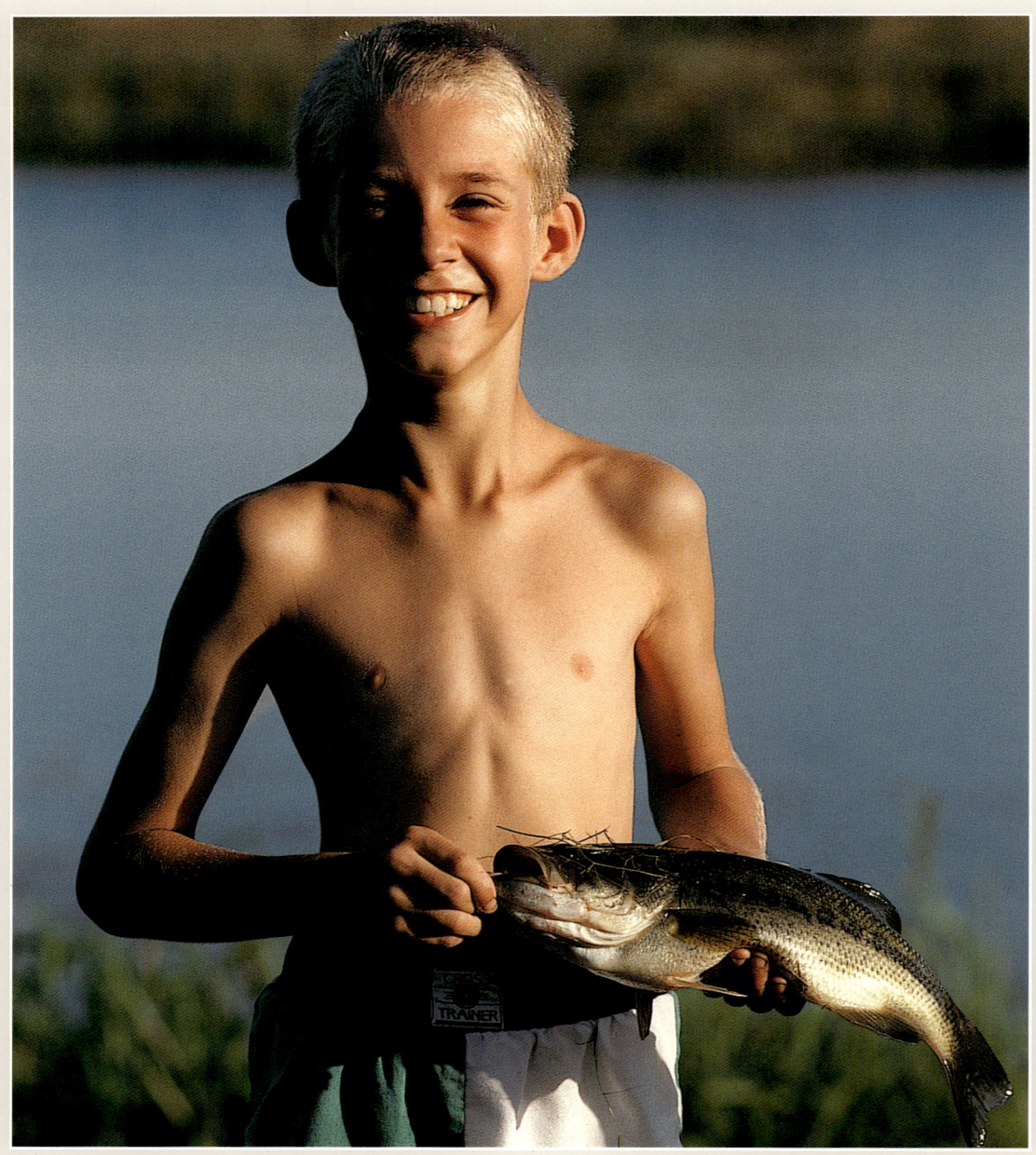

Above: A triumphant Iowa youngster shows off a largemouth bass caught at a farm pond near Cumming. CURT MAAS

Right: Reeling in the big one! CURT MAAS

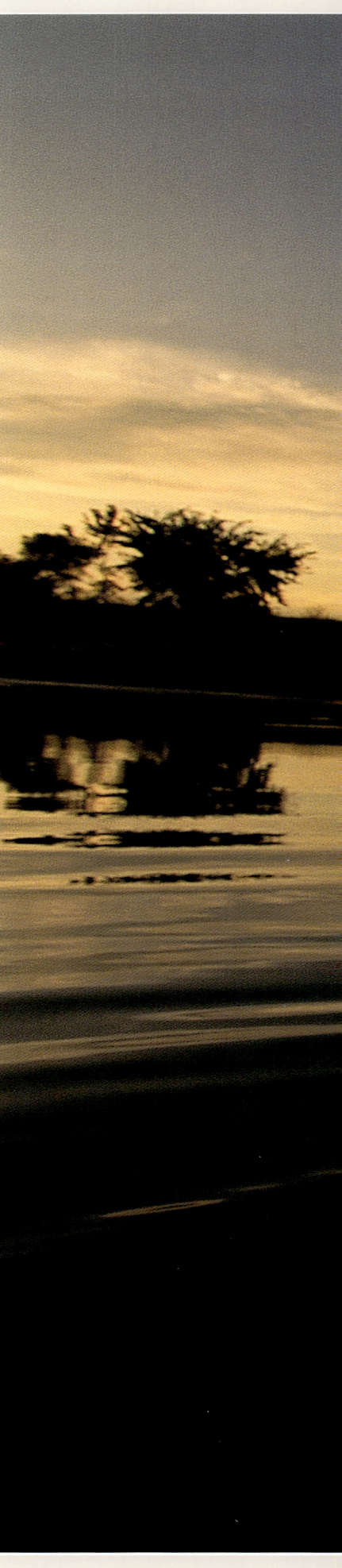

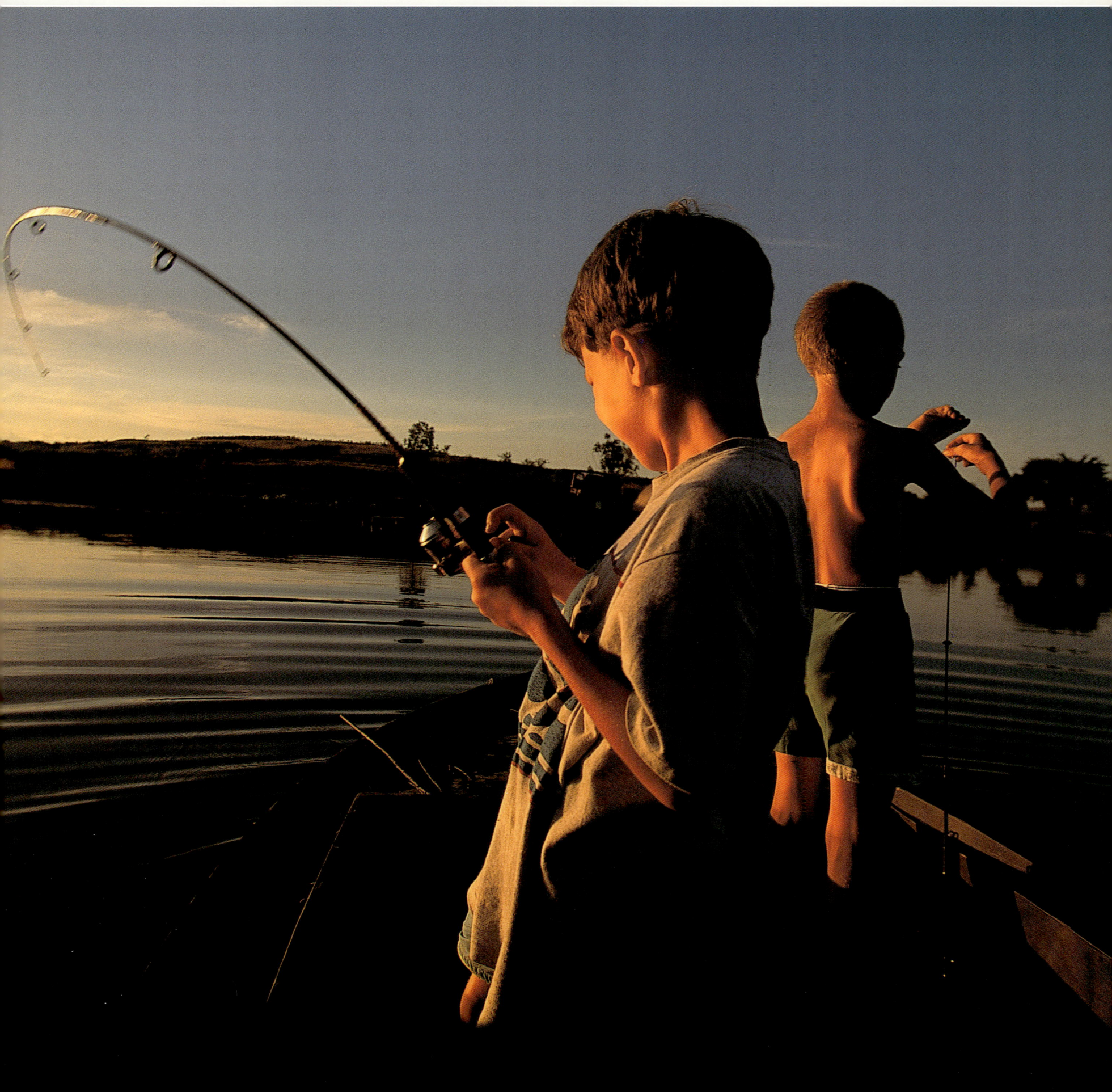

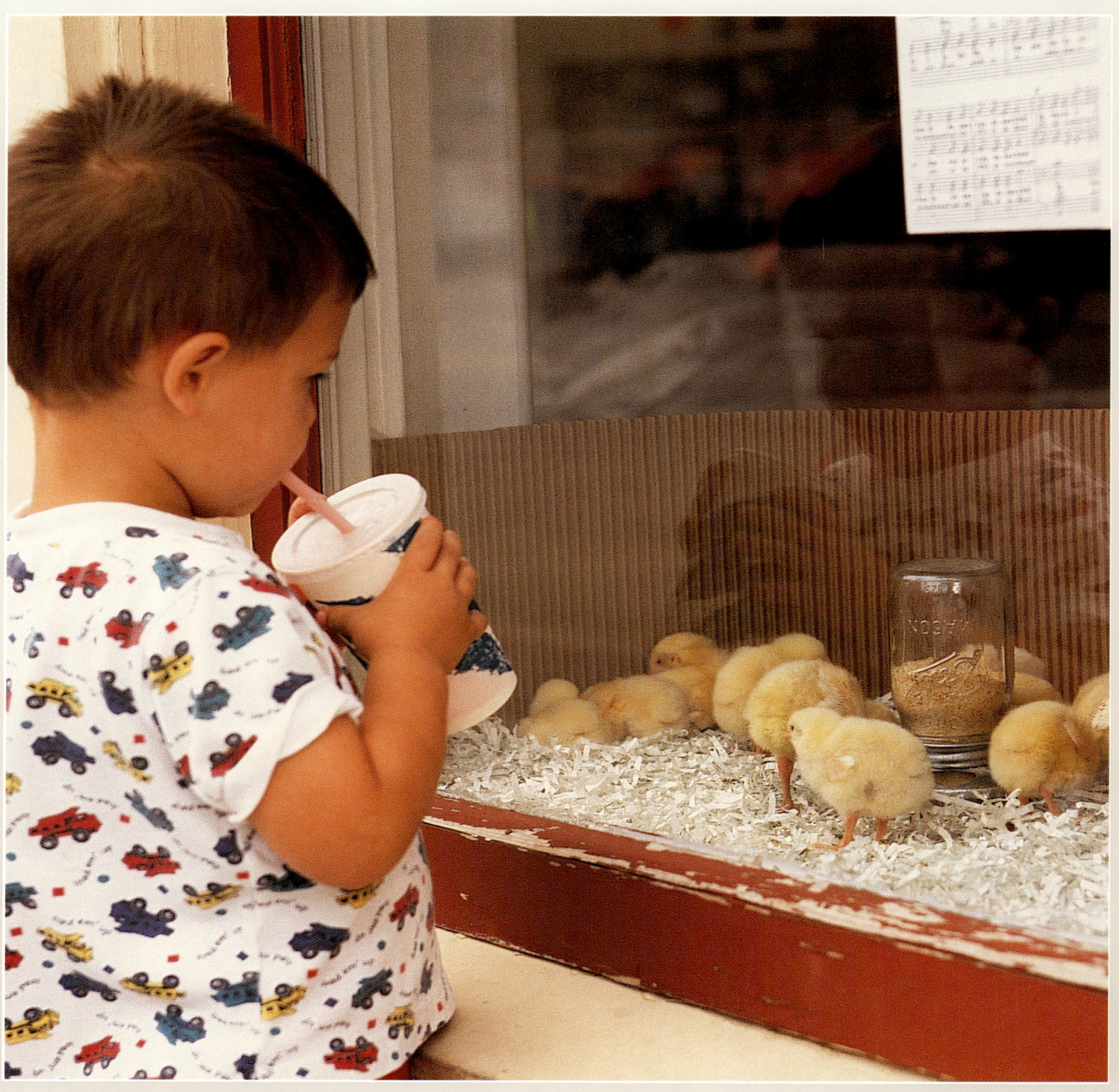

Above: A child gazes at some chicks on display at the annual Nordic Festival in Decorah. The festival began in 1966 and is held in celebration of the area's proud Norwegian heritage. KENT FOSTER

Facing page: Organically raised chickens at a farm in Algona. LARSH K. BRISTOL

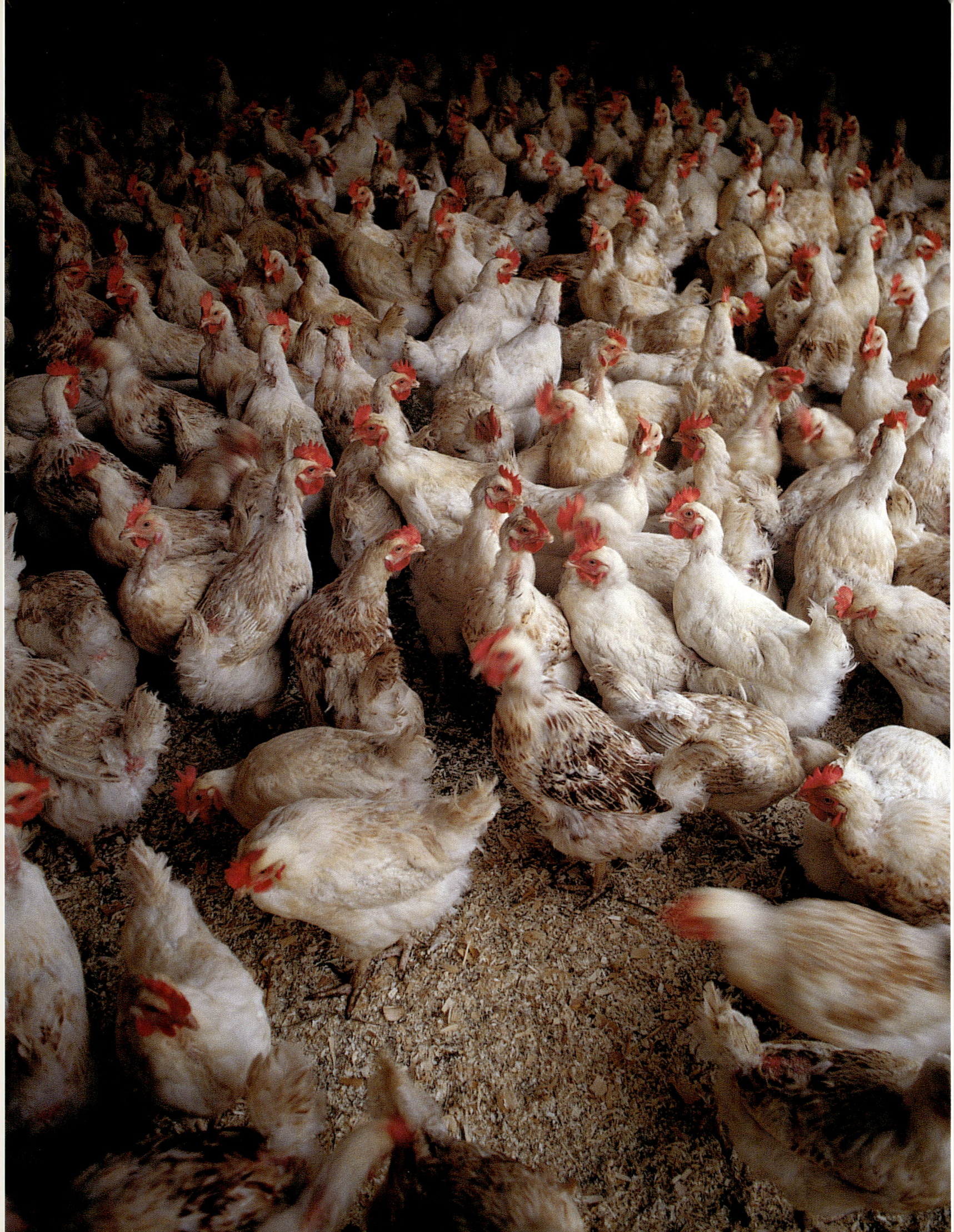

Right: Farmsteads with tassel-topped corn in the foreground—a classic Iowa scene. CURT MAAS

Below: Droplets of morning dew form on a corn stalk. CURT MAAS

Bottom: Corn silk crowns these ears of corn growing mid-season. CURT MAAS

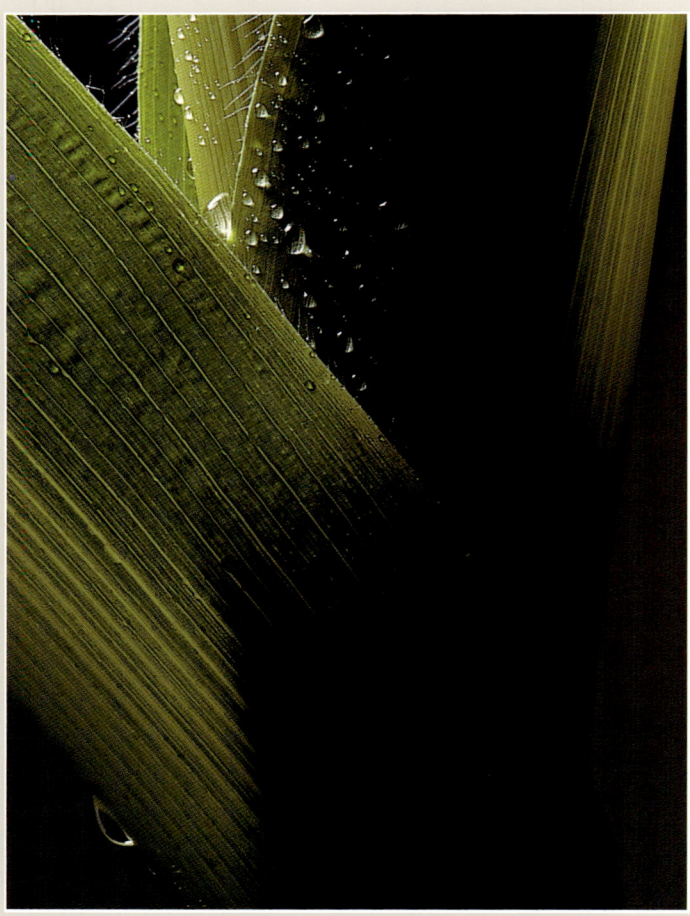

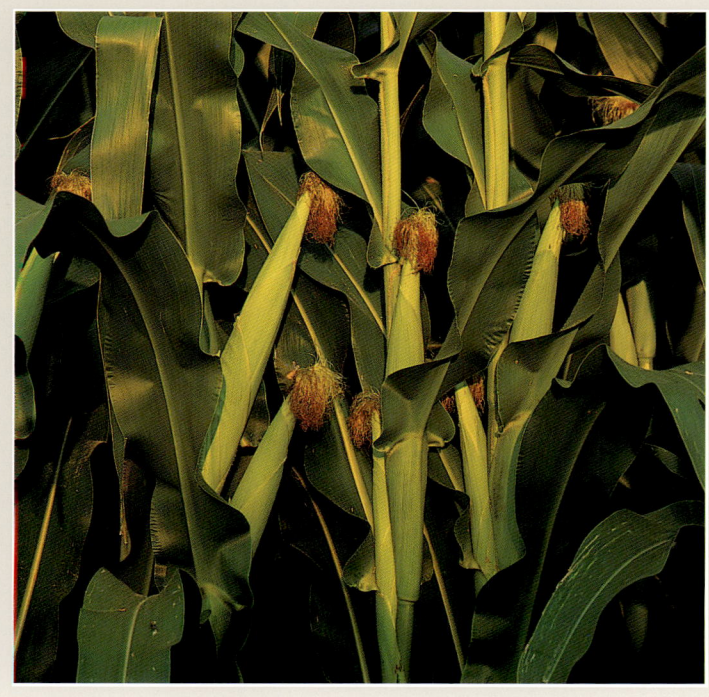

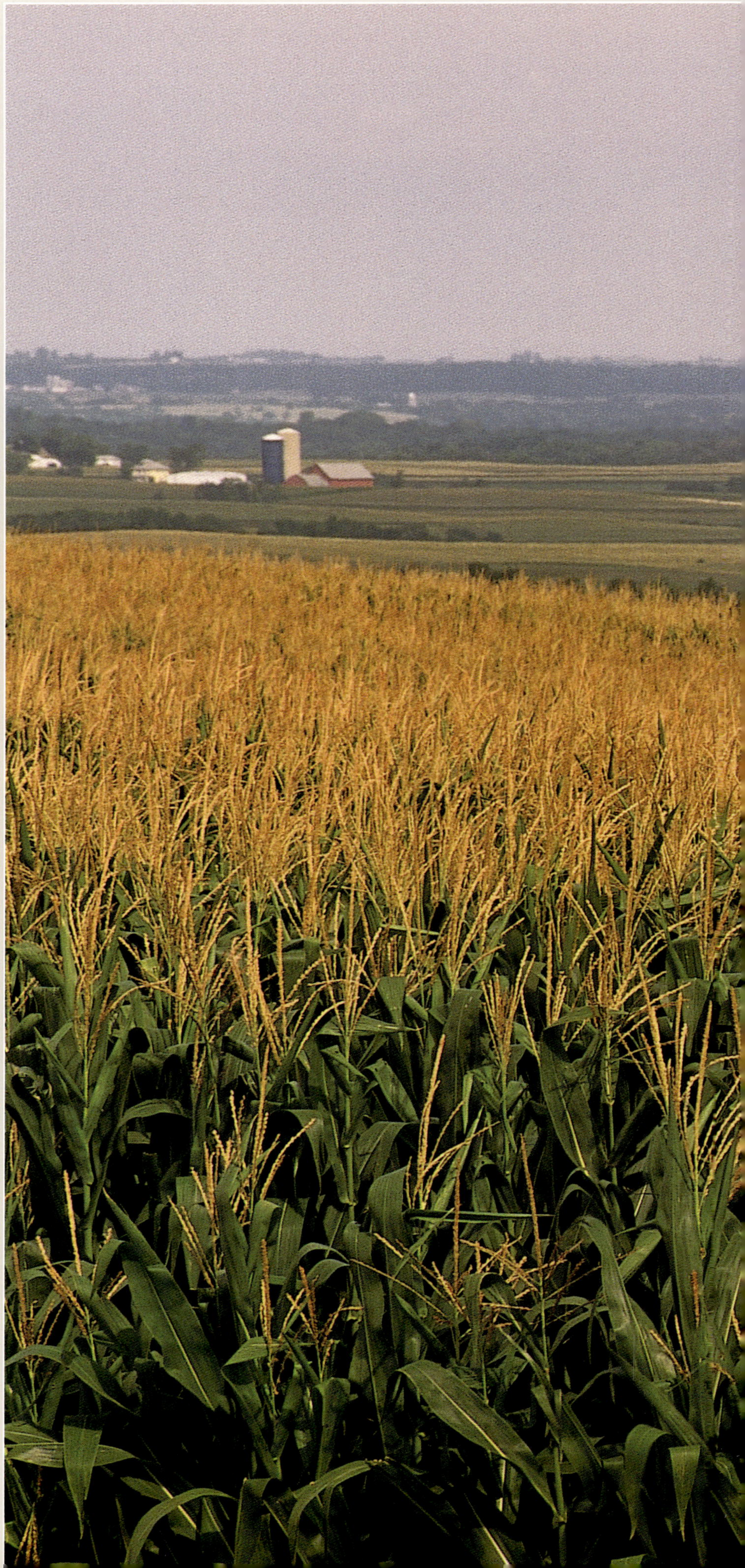

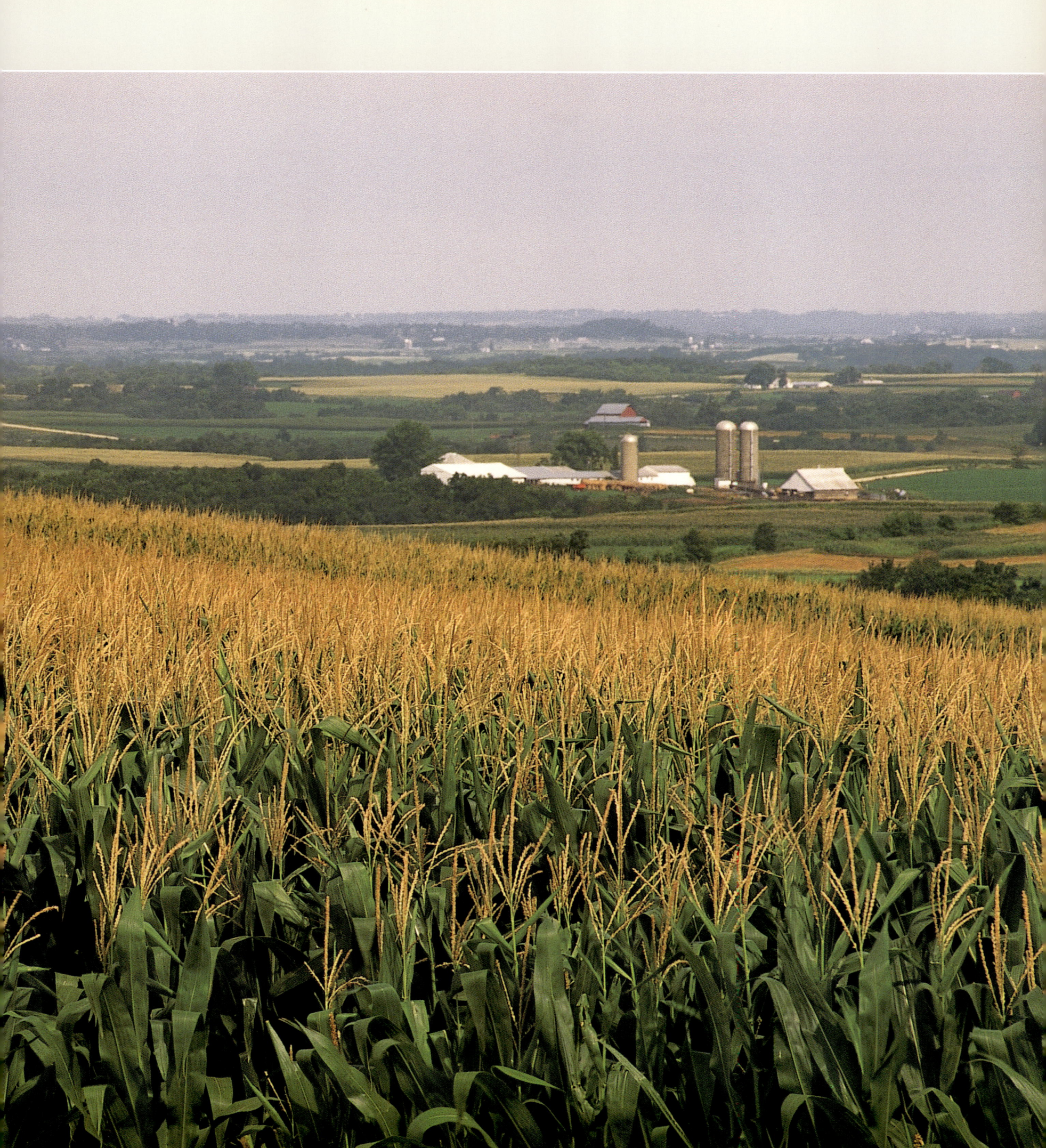

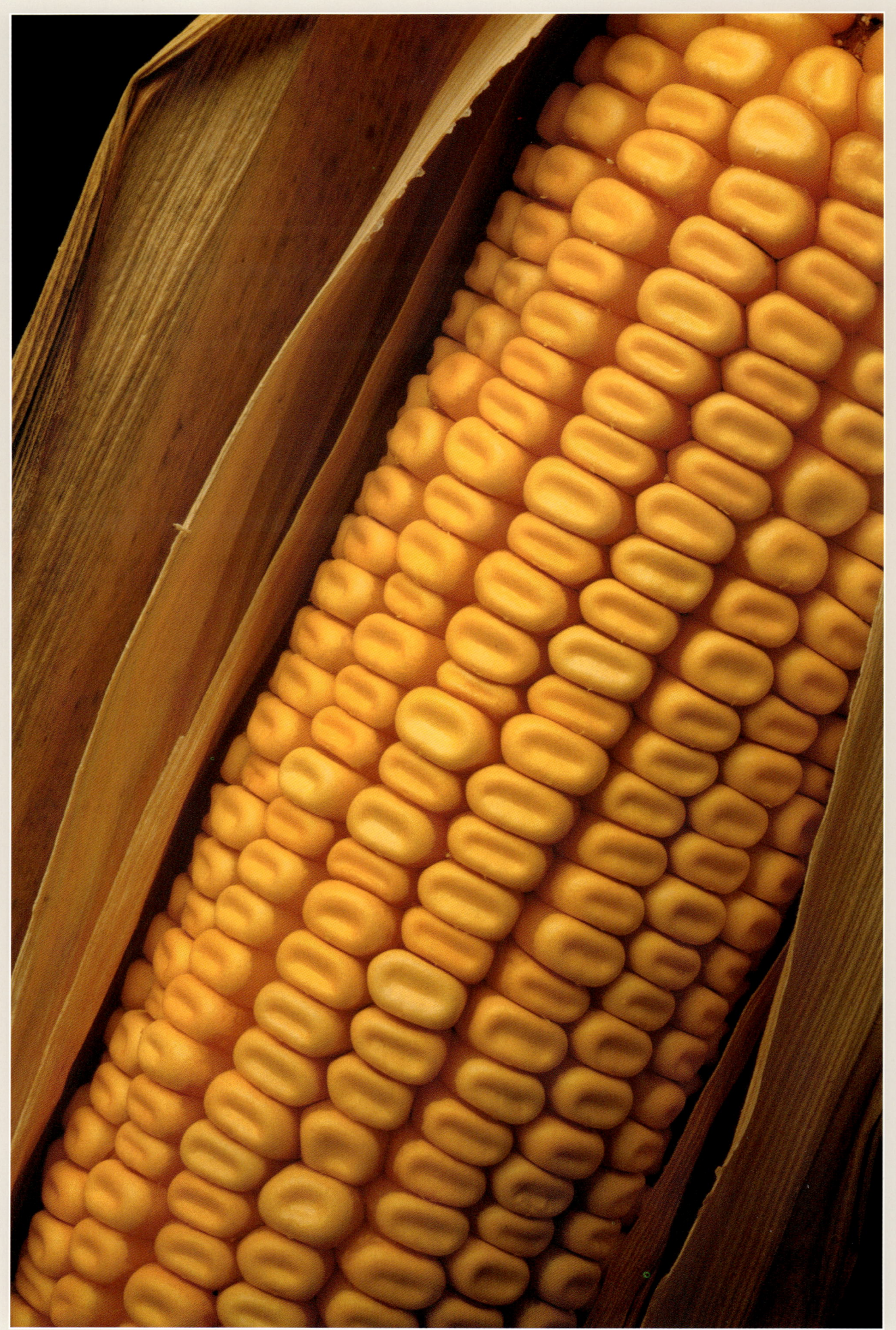

Right: Detail of a mature ear of corn. LARSH K. BRISTOL

Facing page, top left: Corn in a crib. LARSH K. BRISTOL

Facing page, top right: Corn is expelled from a combine onto a loading truck. LARSH K. BRISTOL

Facing page, bottom: Results of a successful harvest in central Iowa. CURT MAAS

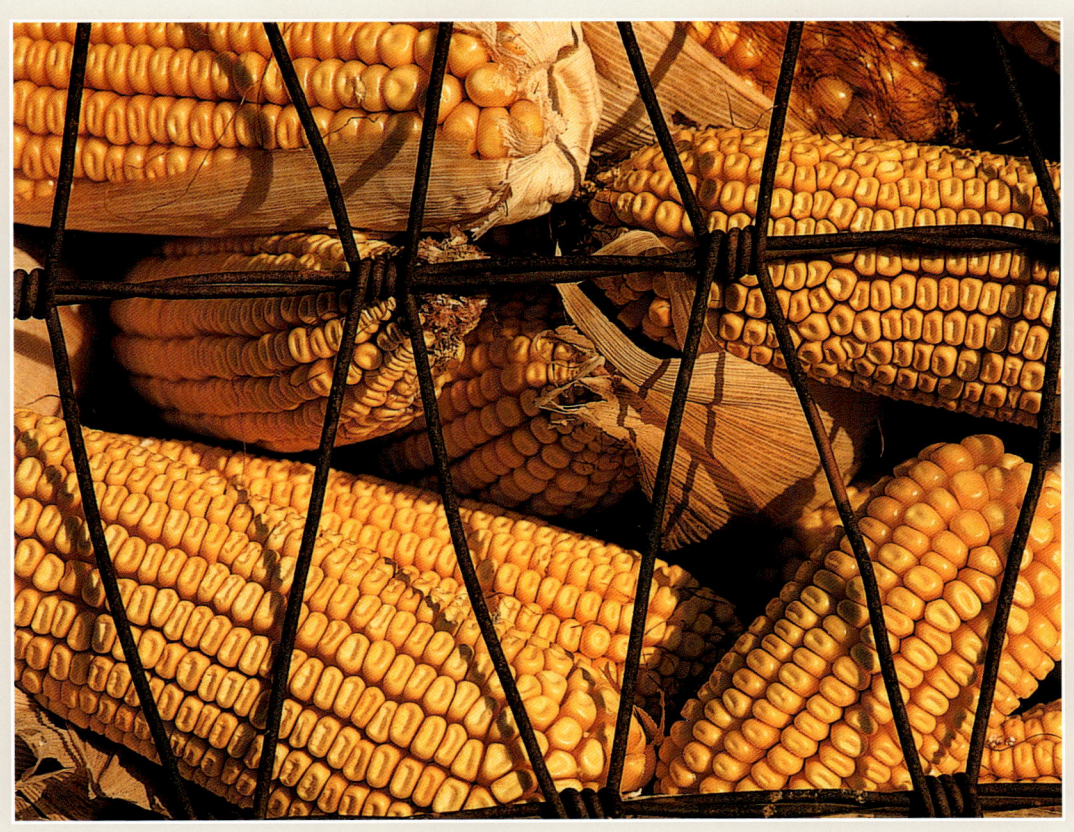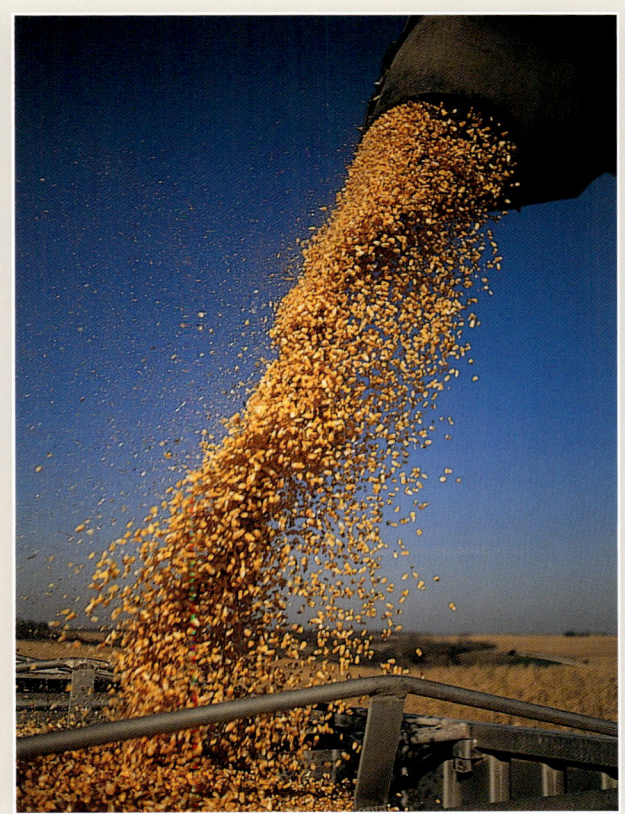

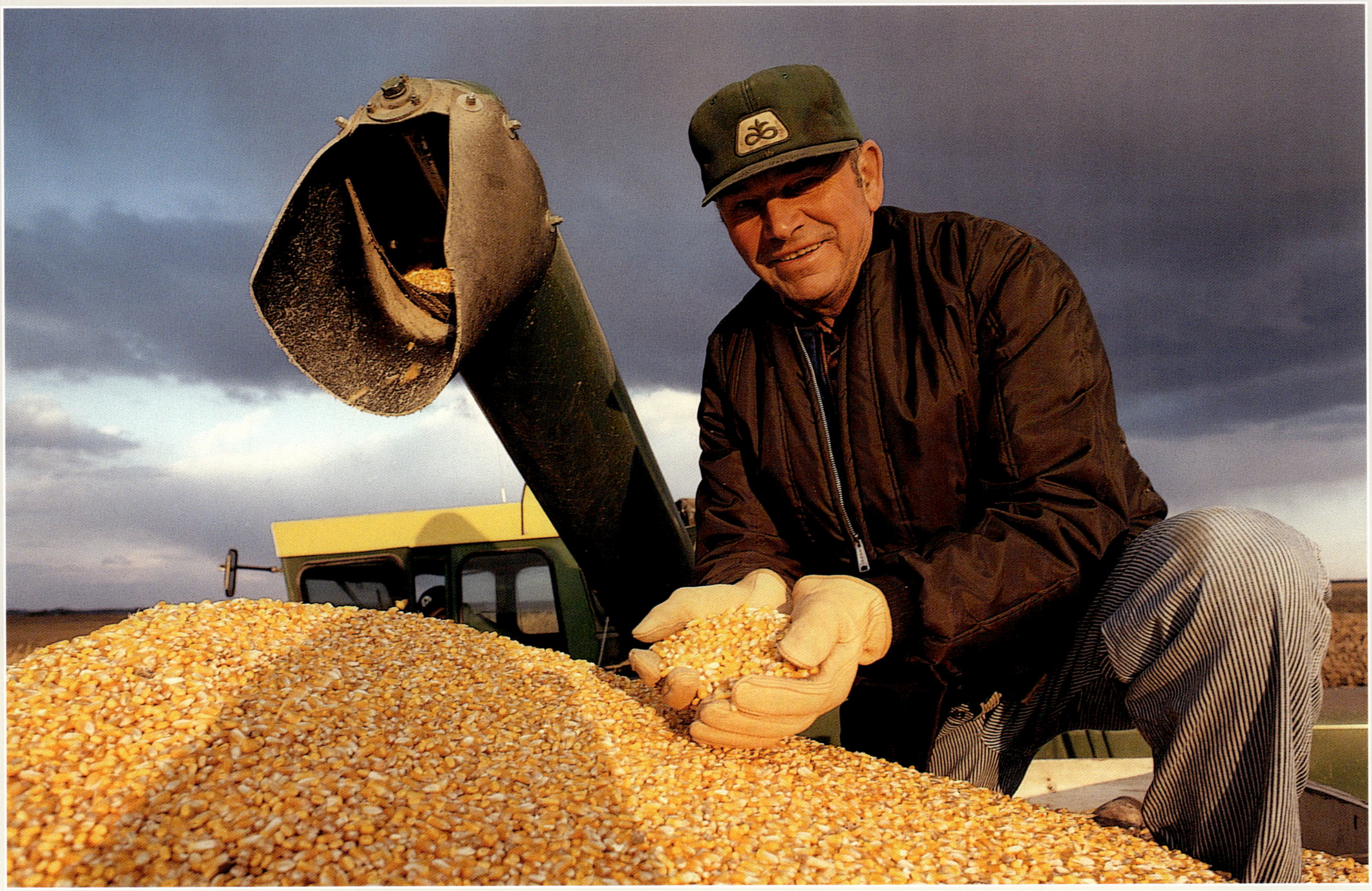

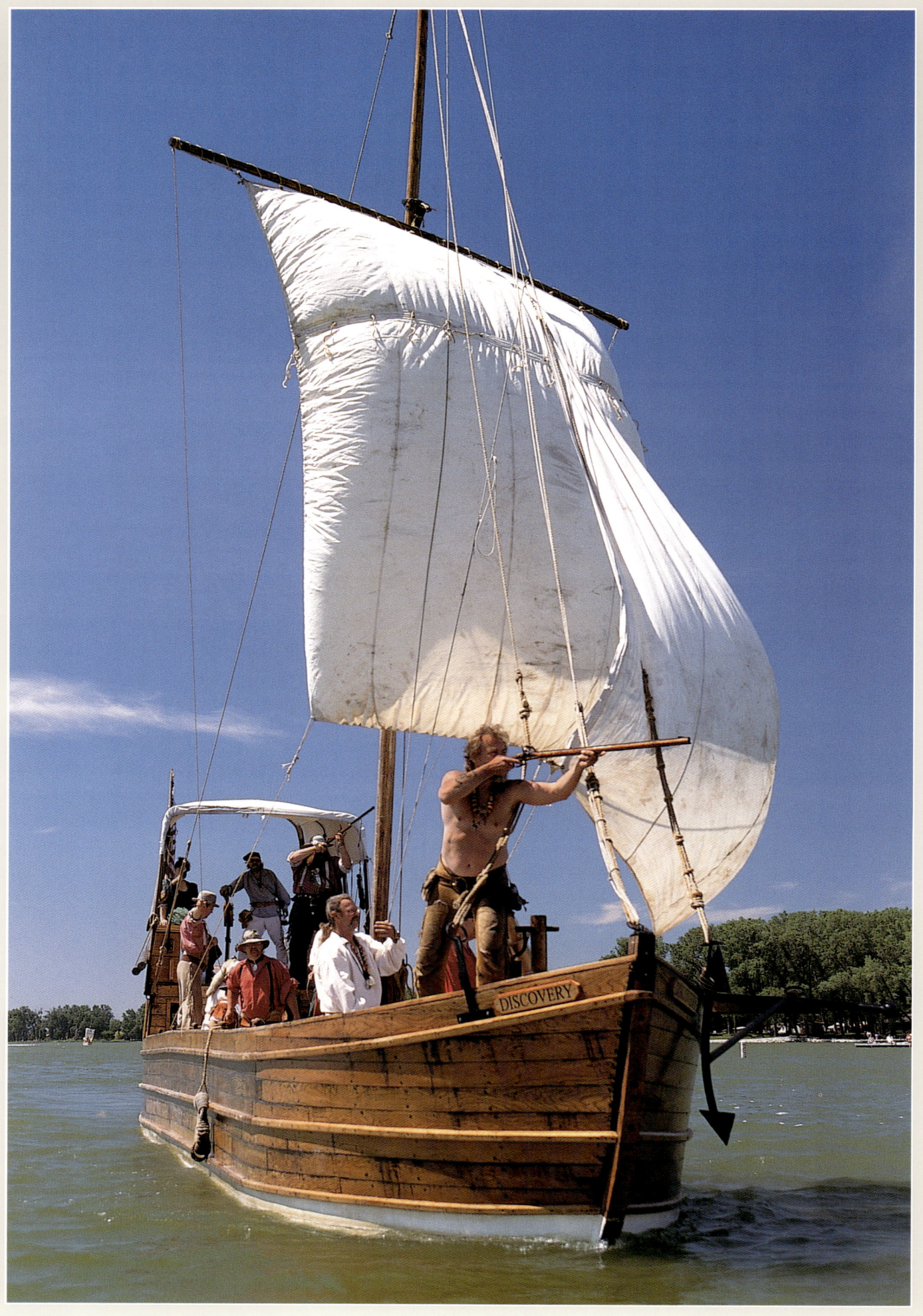

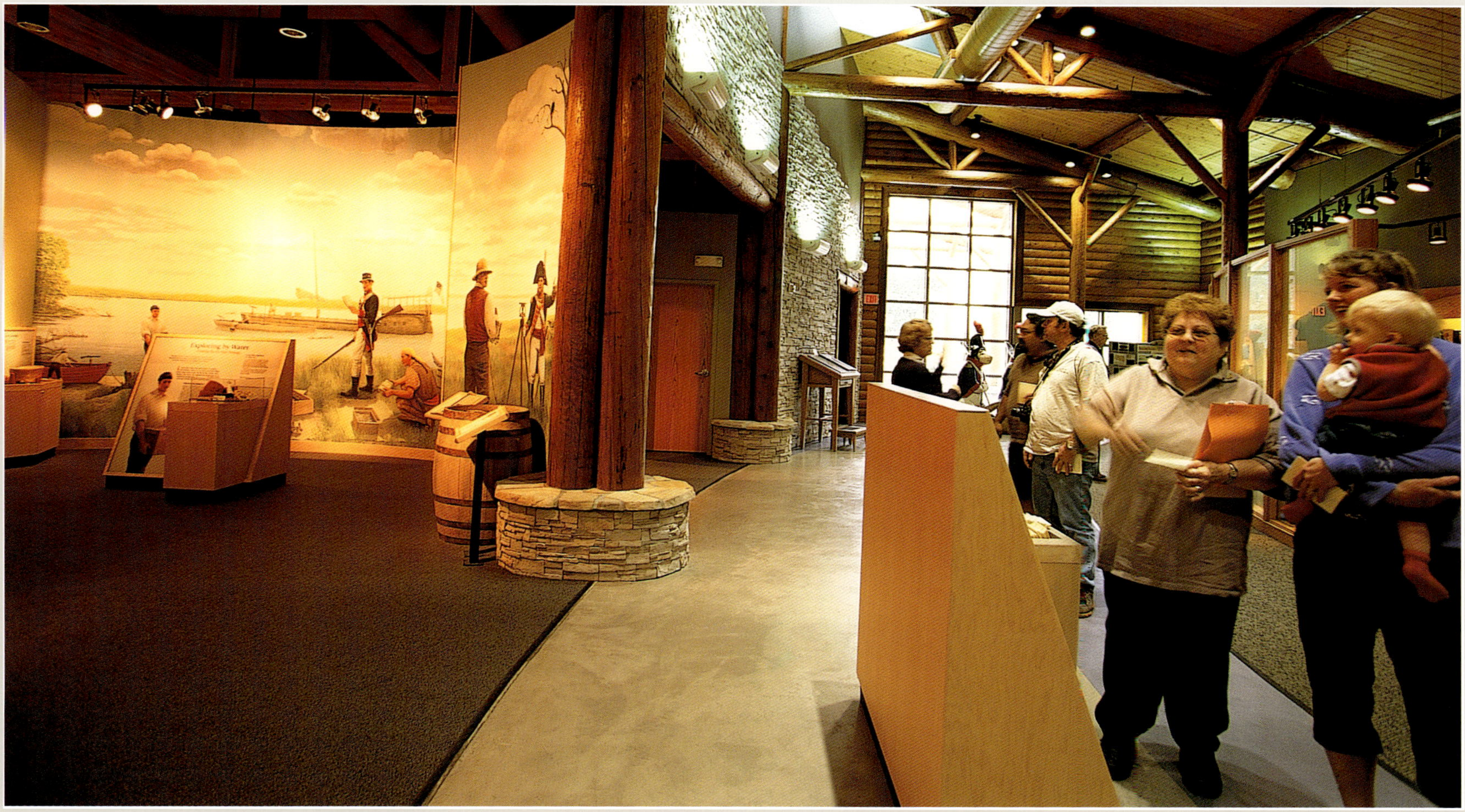

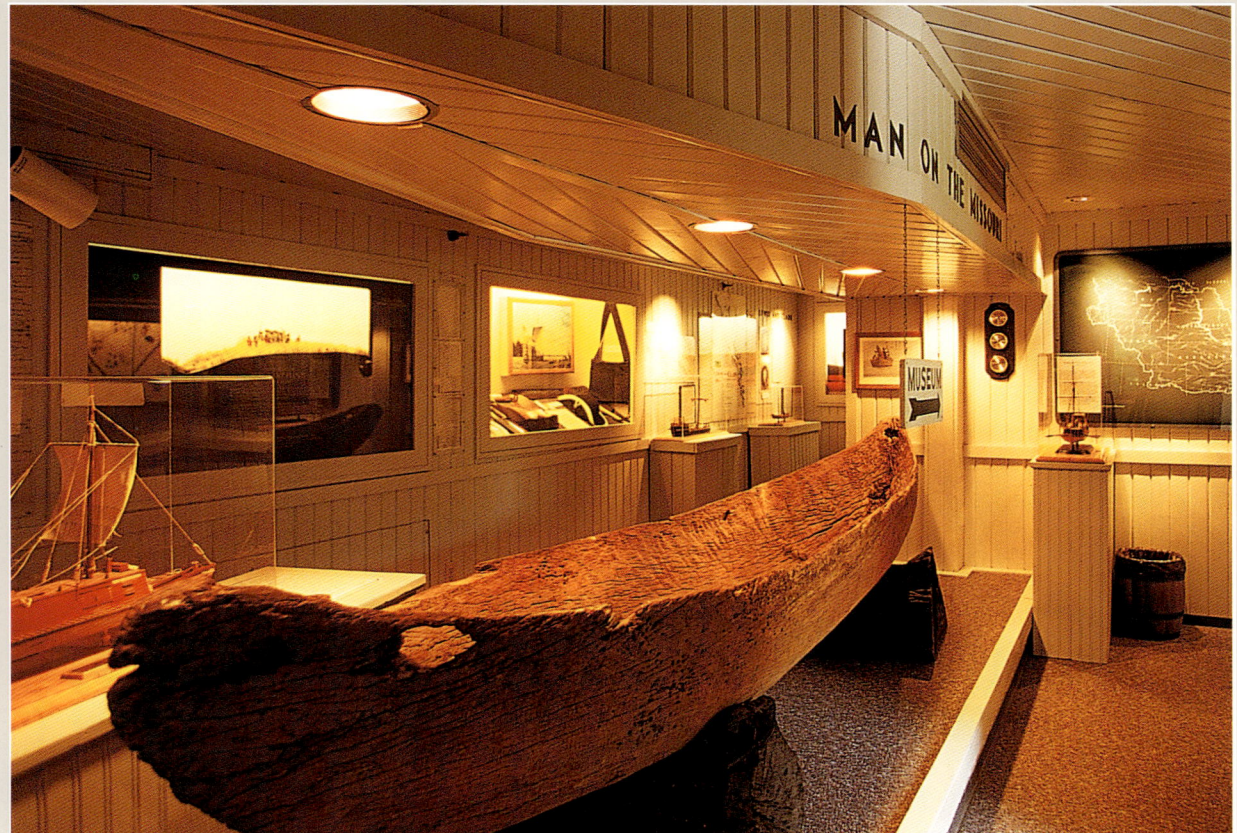

Above: Visitors learn about the Corps of Discovery at the Lewis and Clark Interpretive Center in Sioux City. KENT FOSTER

Left: A pirogue replica is displayed at the Sergeant Floyd Welcome Center and Riverboat Museum in Sioux City. KENT FOSTER

Facing page: Interpretive guides command a Lewis and Clark expedition keelboat replica during a festival at Lewis and Clark State Park in Onawa. KENT FOSTER

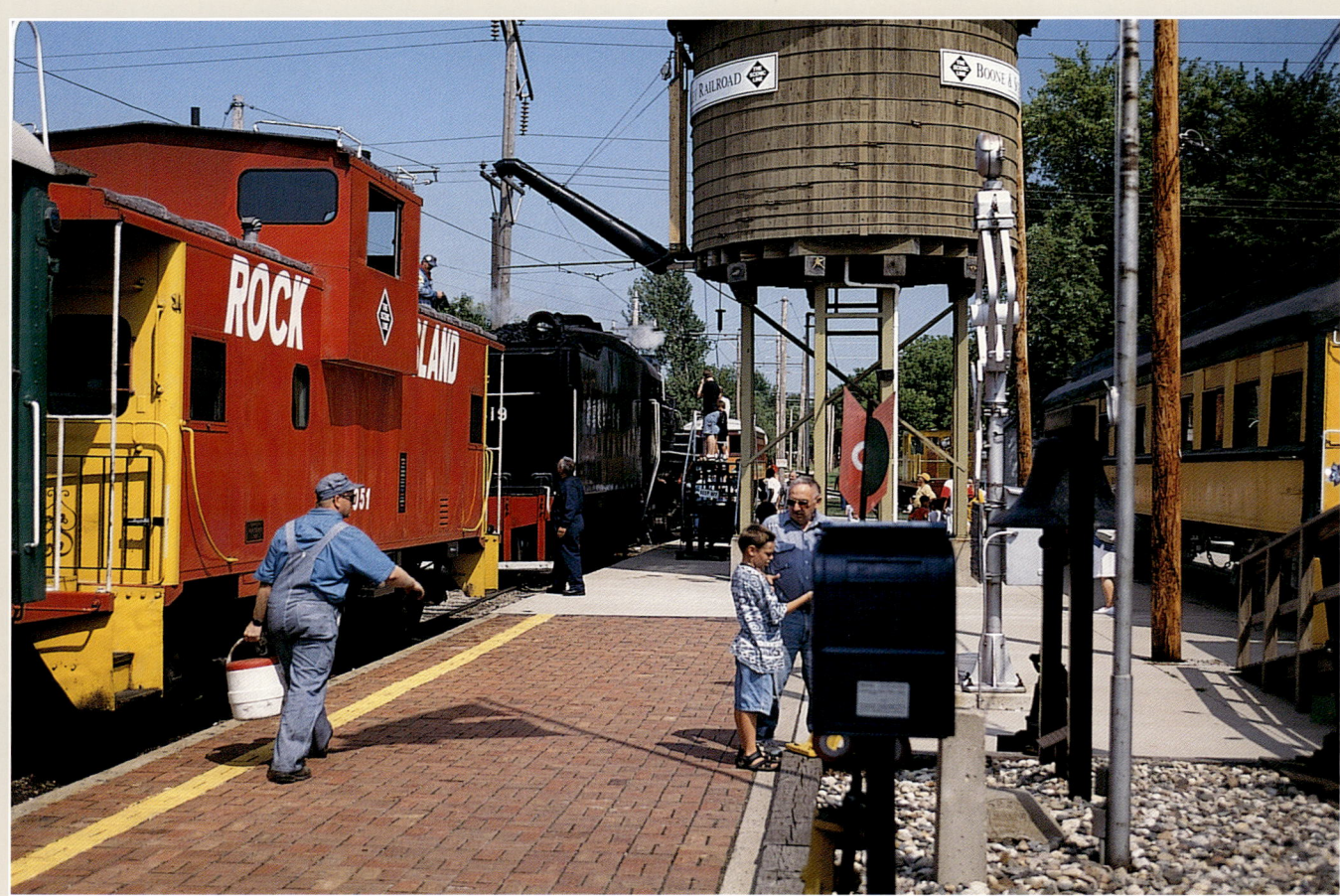

Above: Boone Scenic Valley Railroad Train Station. KENT FOSTER

Right: A steam engine runs through rural Boone. KENT FOSTER

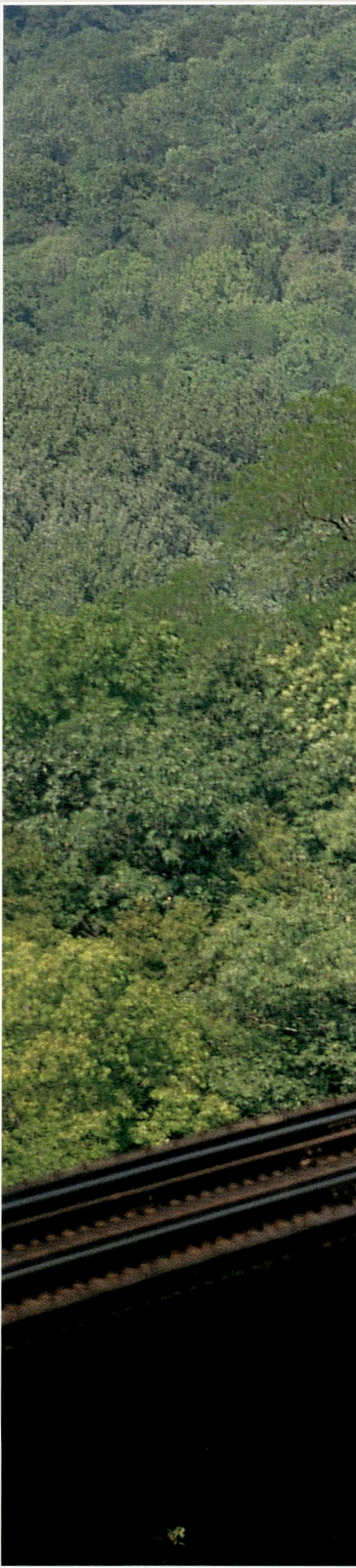

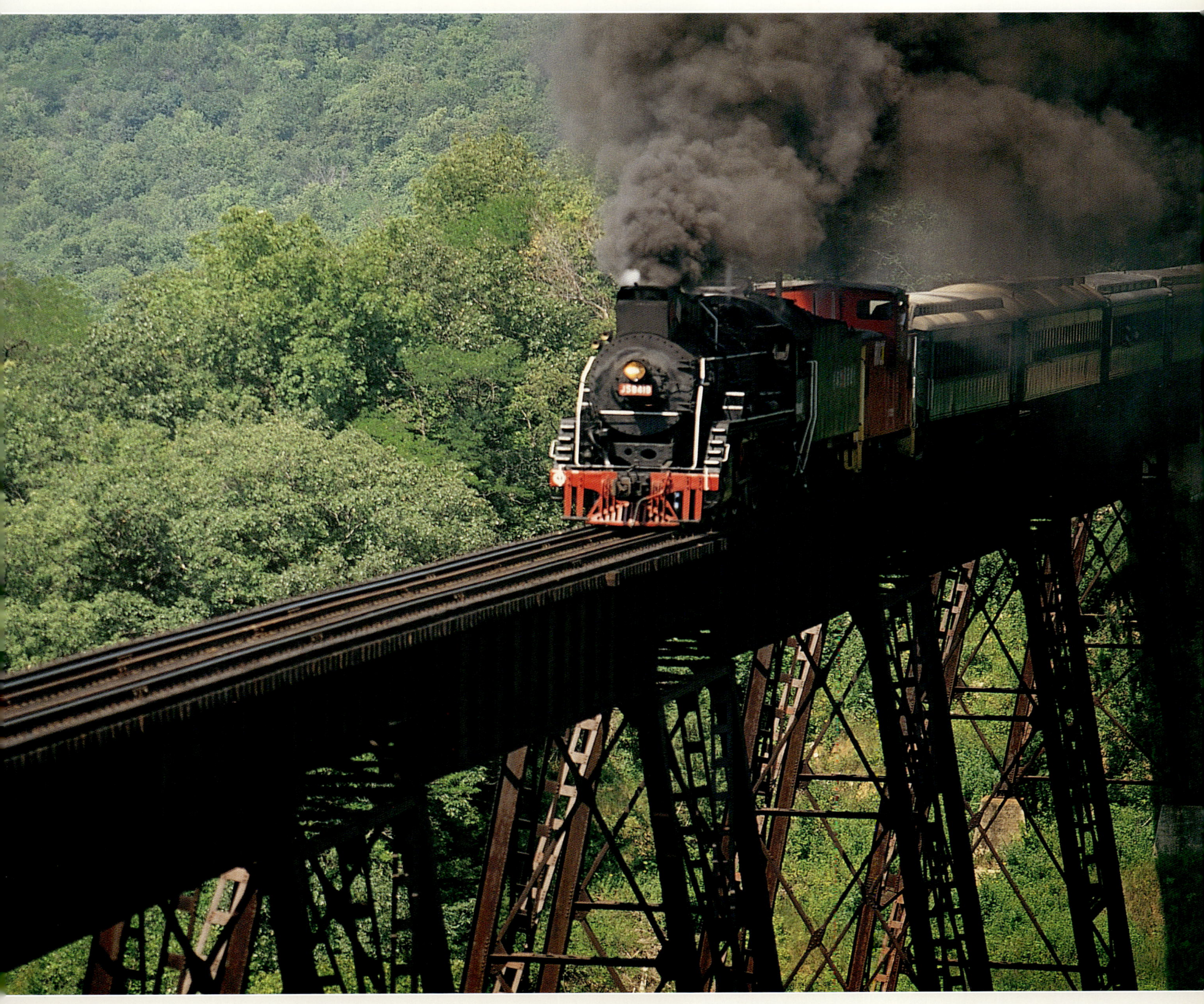

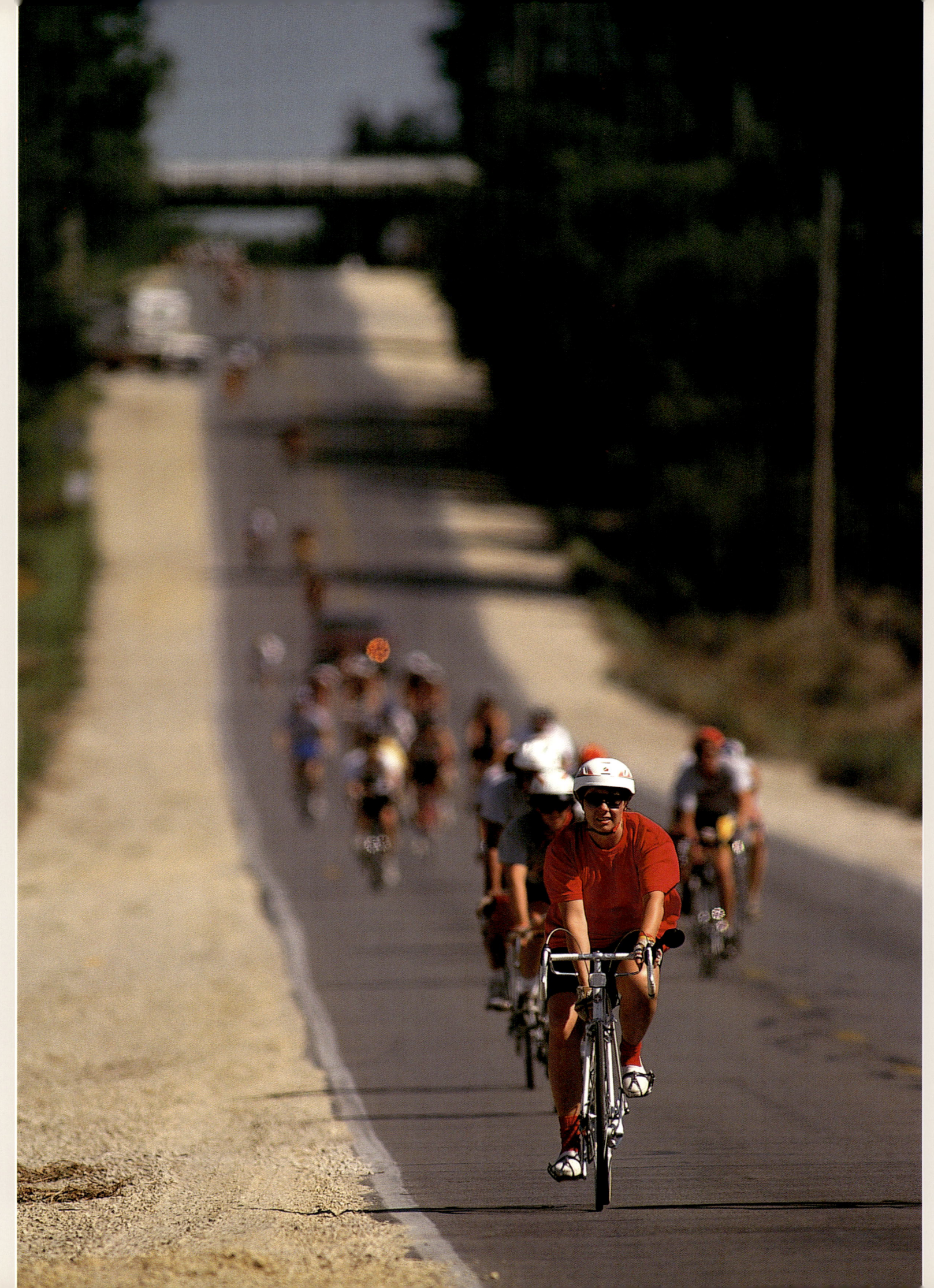

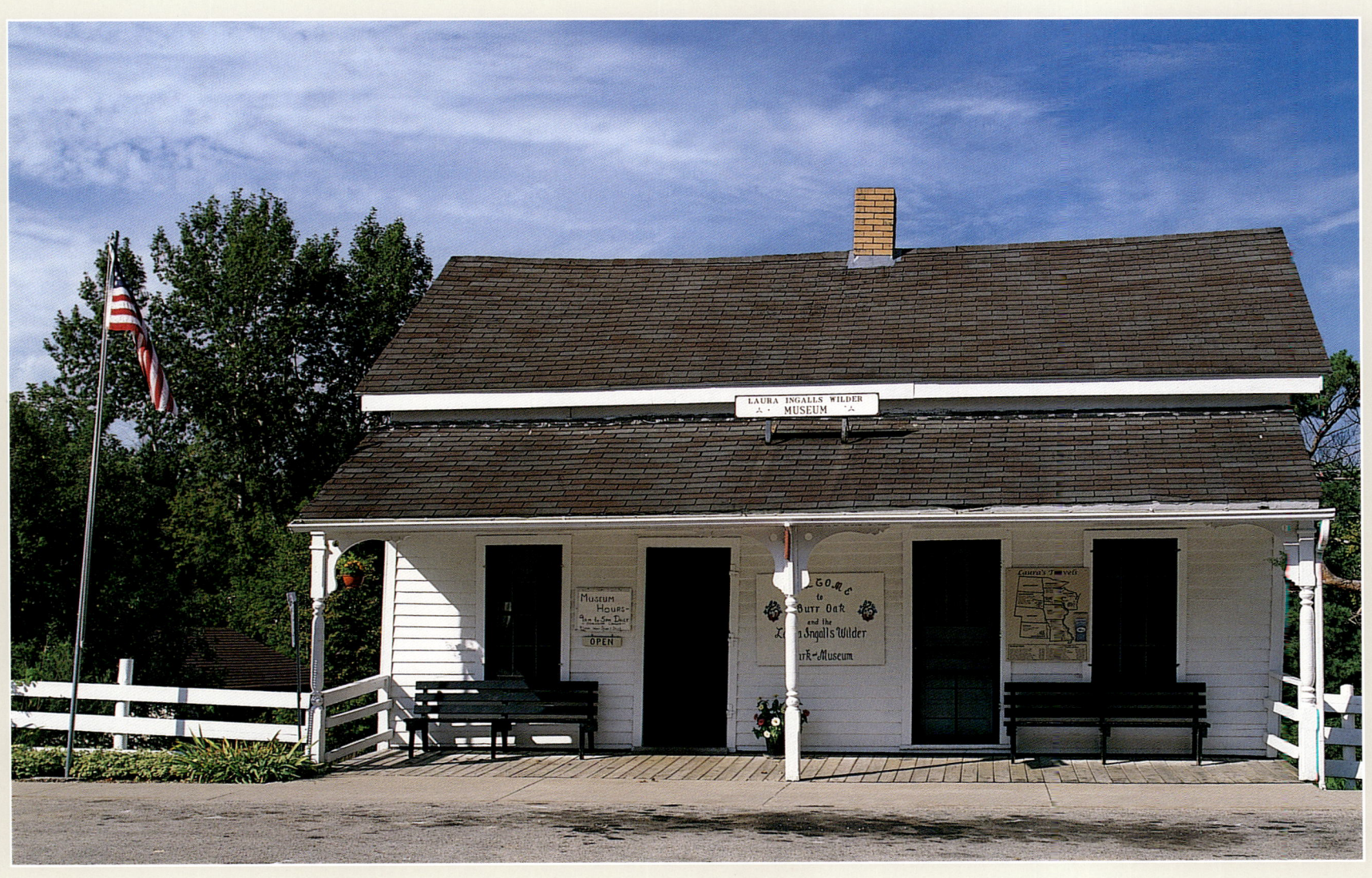

Above: The Masters Hotel at the Laura Ingalls Wilder Park and Museum in Burr Oak was once the home of the Ingalls family and is now on the National Register of Historic Places. KENT FOSTER

Facing page: Bicyclists take part in RAGBRAI, Register's Annual Great Bike Ride Across Iowa. CURT MAAS

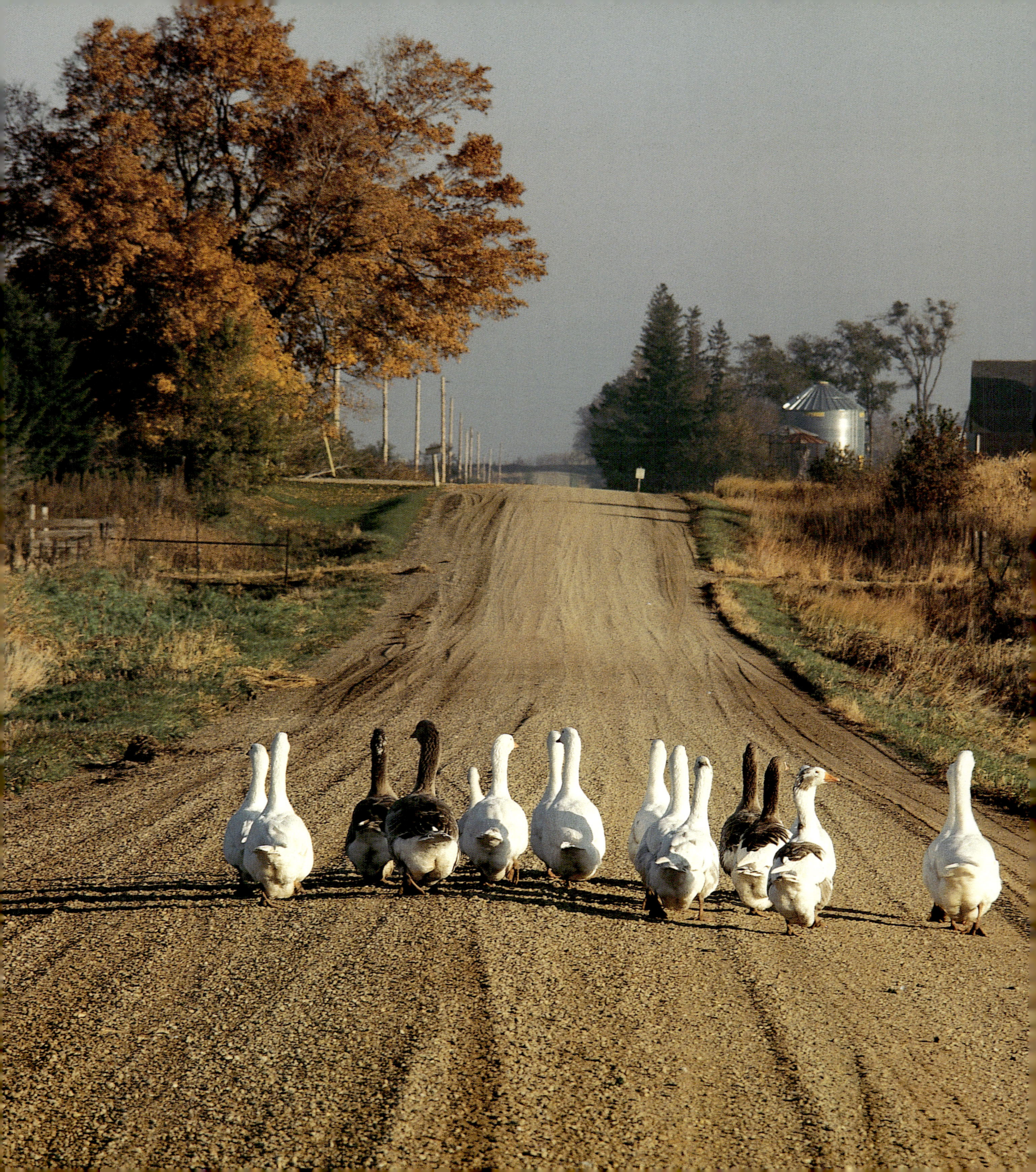

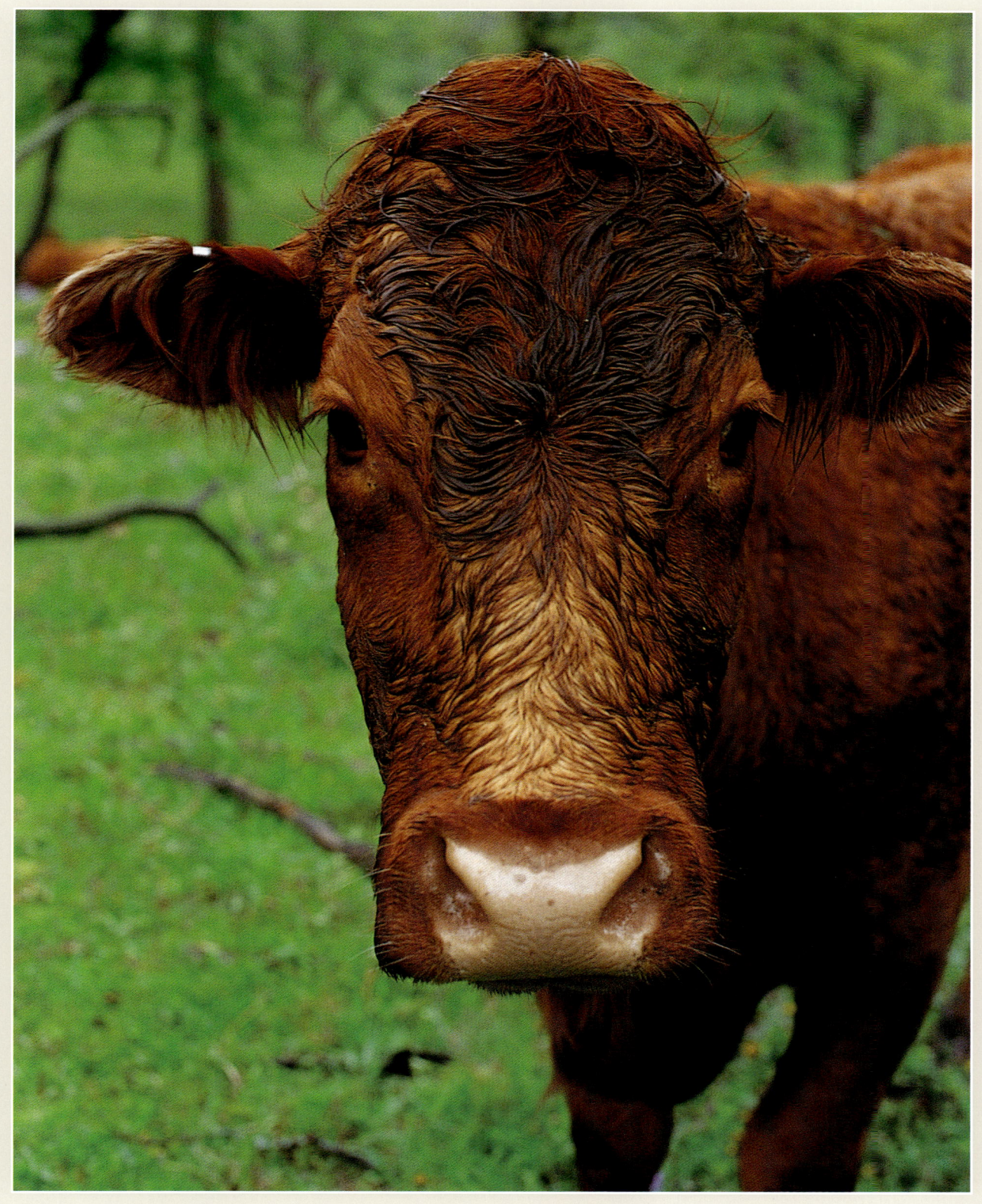

Above: A cow takes a break from grazing in the lush Iowa woodlands to step in for a close-up. LARS K. BRISTOL

Facing page: A gaggle of geese strolls down a country road near Garner. CURT MAAS

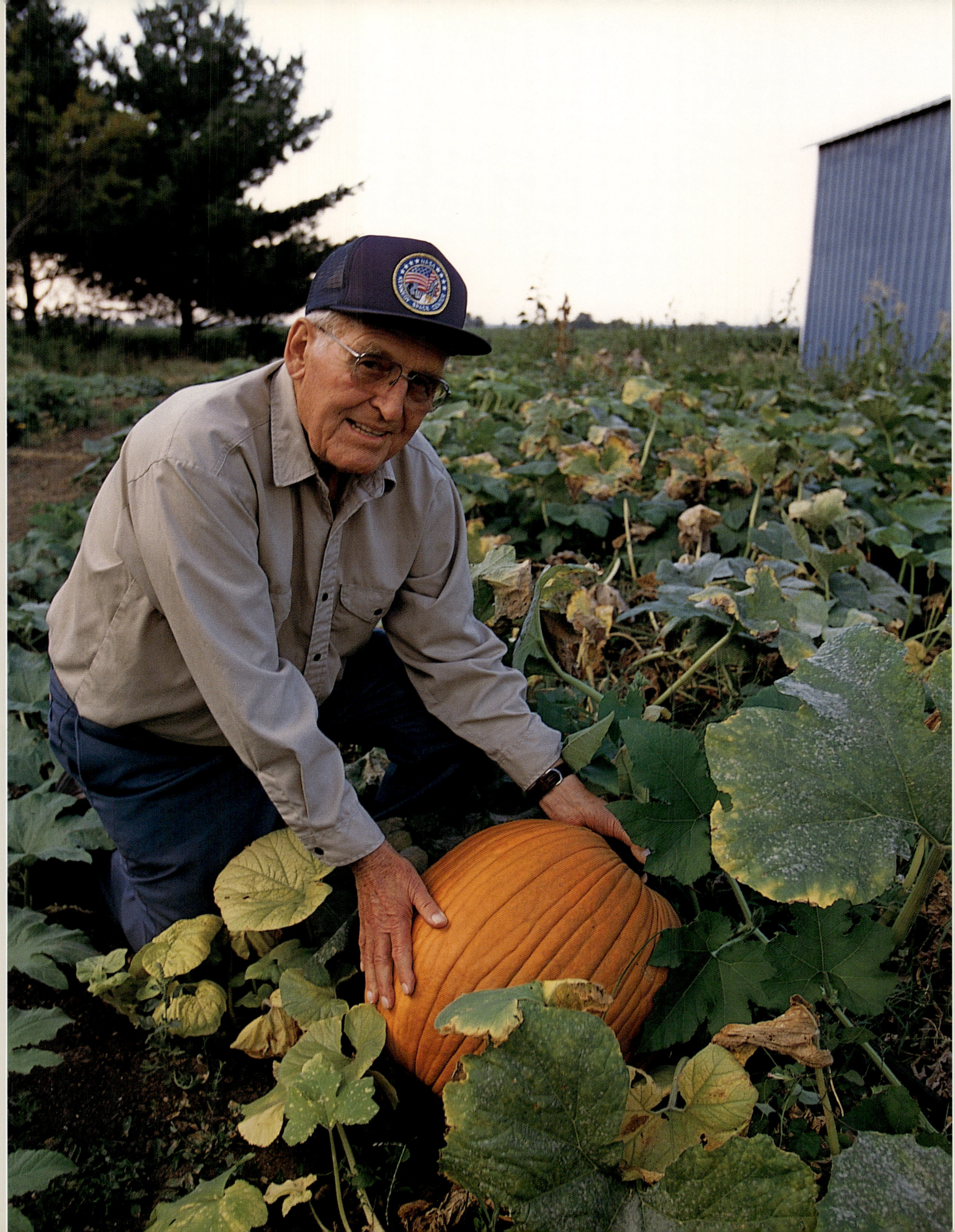

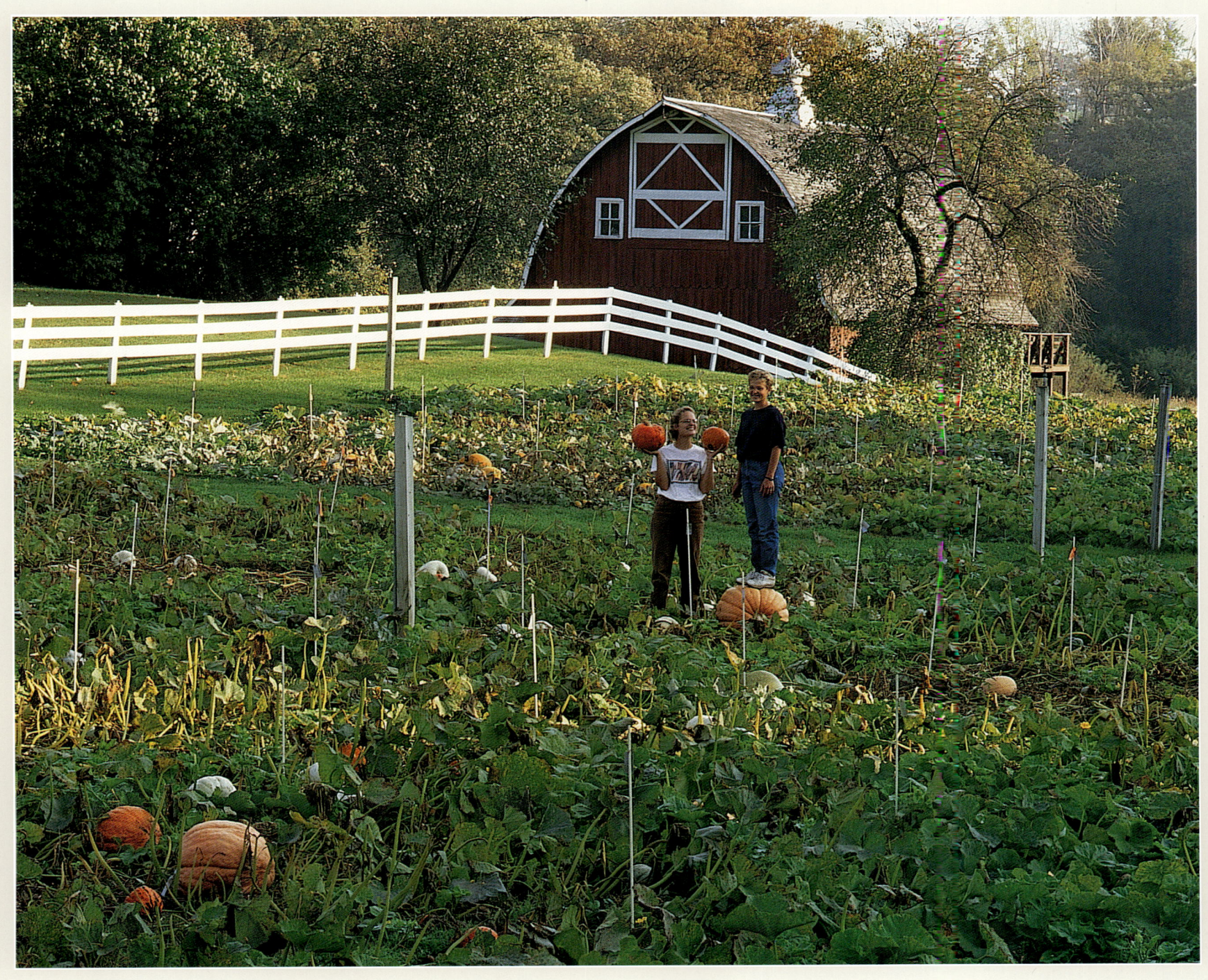

Above: Picking winners from a pumpkin patch at the Seed Sowers Exchange in Decorah. LARSH K. BRISTOL

Facing page: A farmer proudly tends his pumpkin patch near Norwalk. CURT MAAS

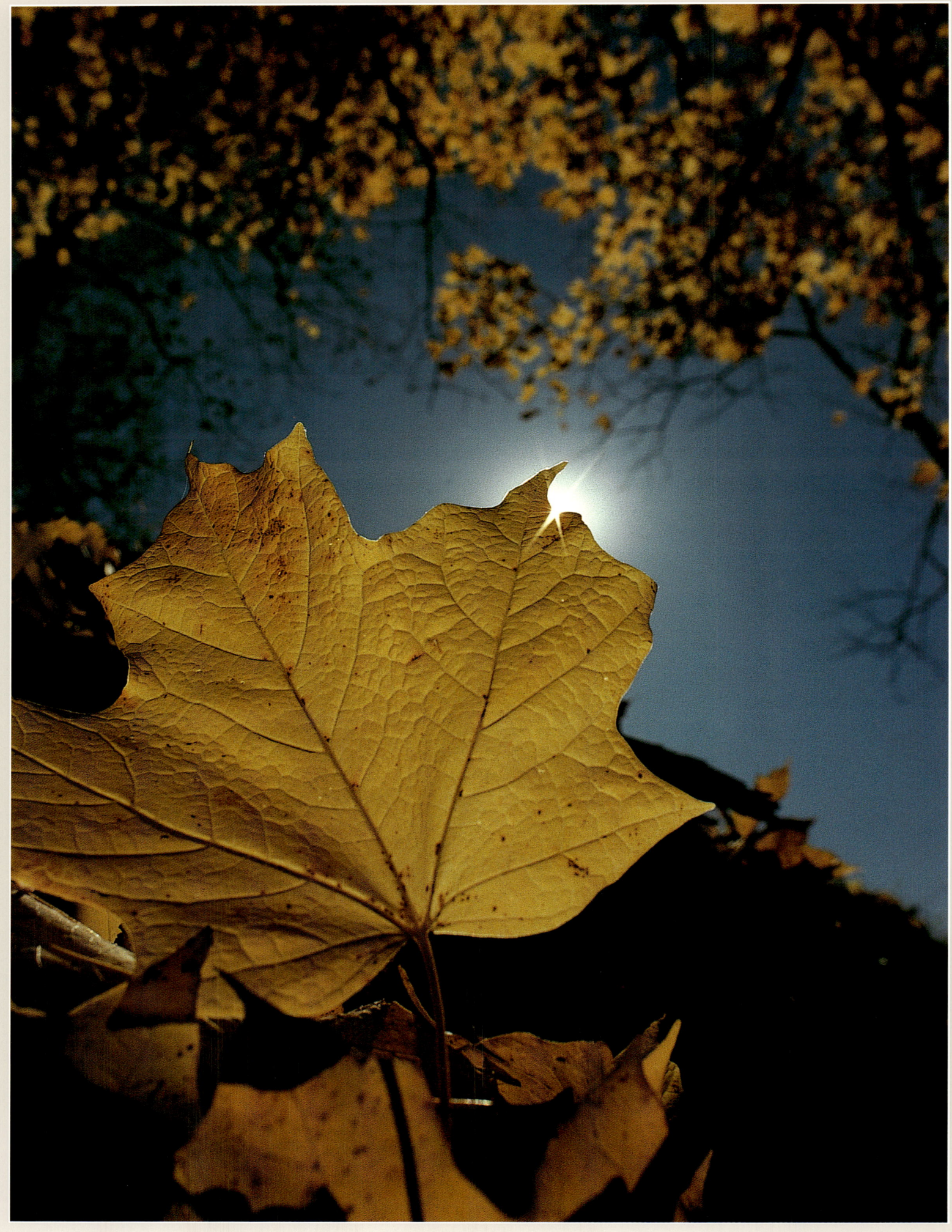

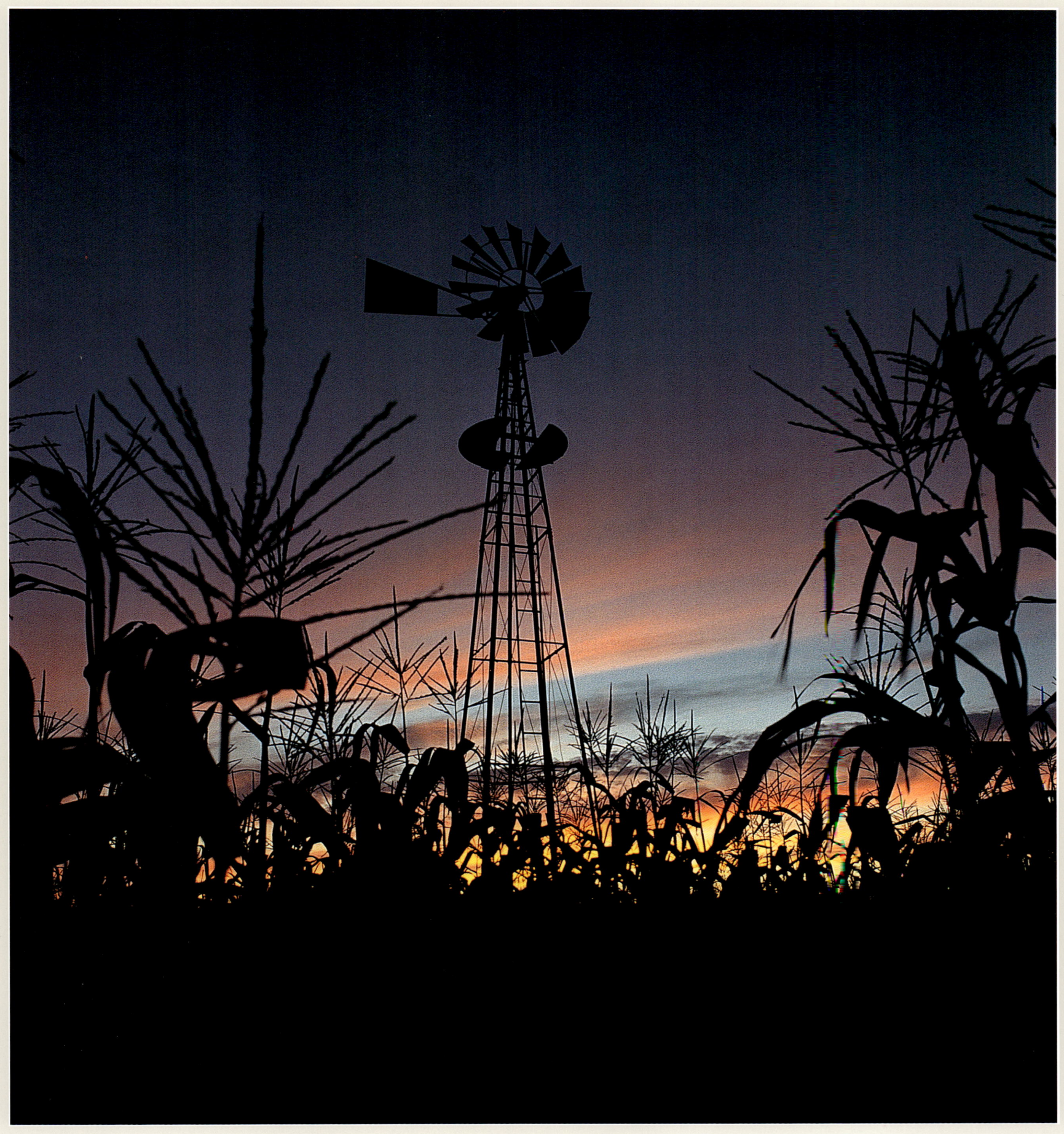

Above: The beautiful simplicity of a windmill and corn field silhouetted against a colorful midsummer sunset near Granger. CURT MAAS

Facing page: A maple leaf glows with crisp autumn sunlight. CURT MAAS

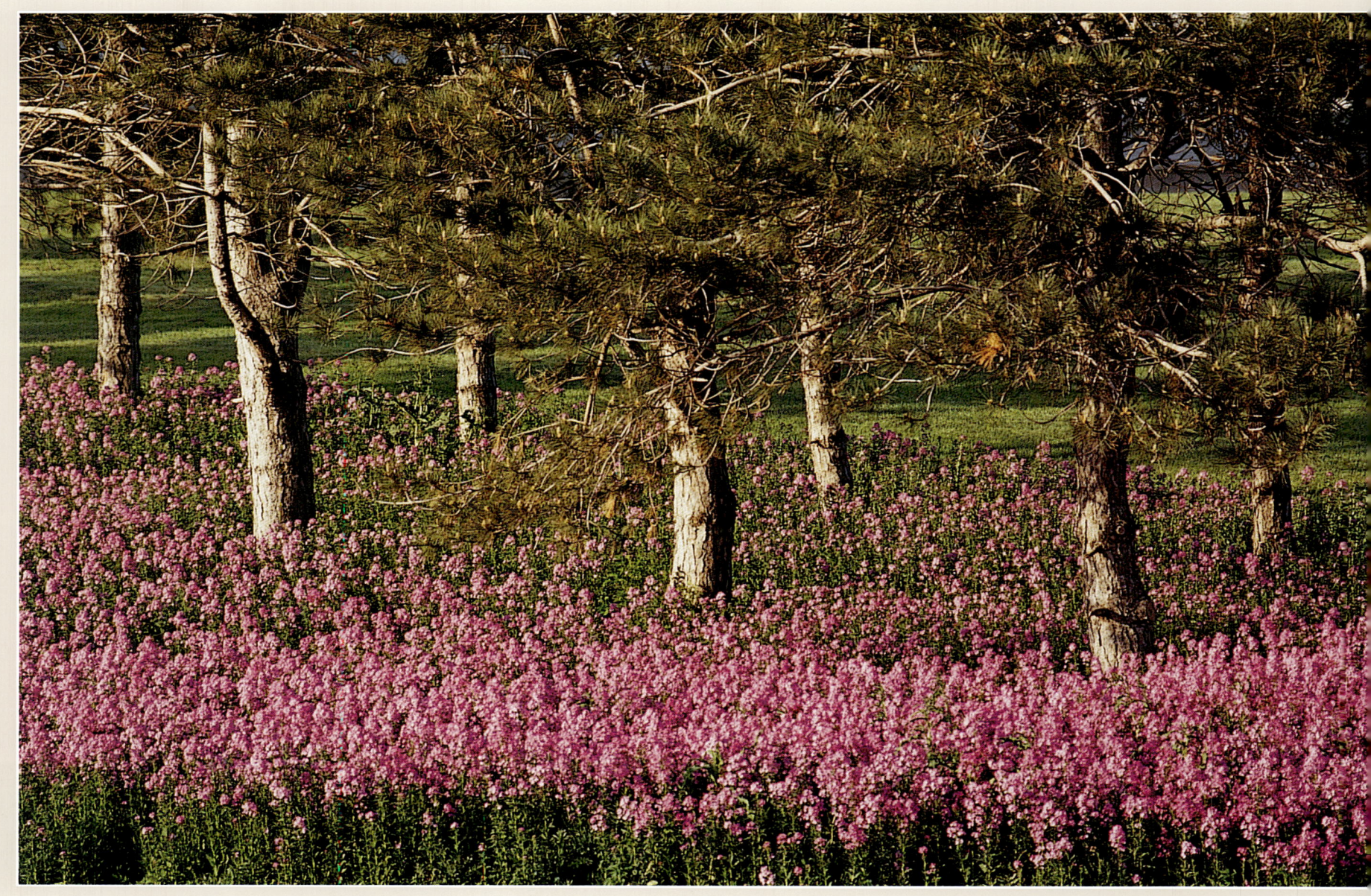

Above: A bed of bright-blossomed wild phlox flourishes among pine trees. KENT FOSTER

Facing page: Heavy with blooms, the branches of this crabapple tree promise a fruitful bounty. LARSH K. BRISTOL

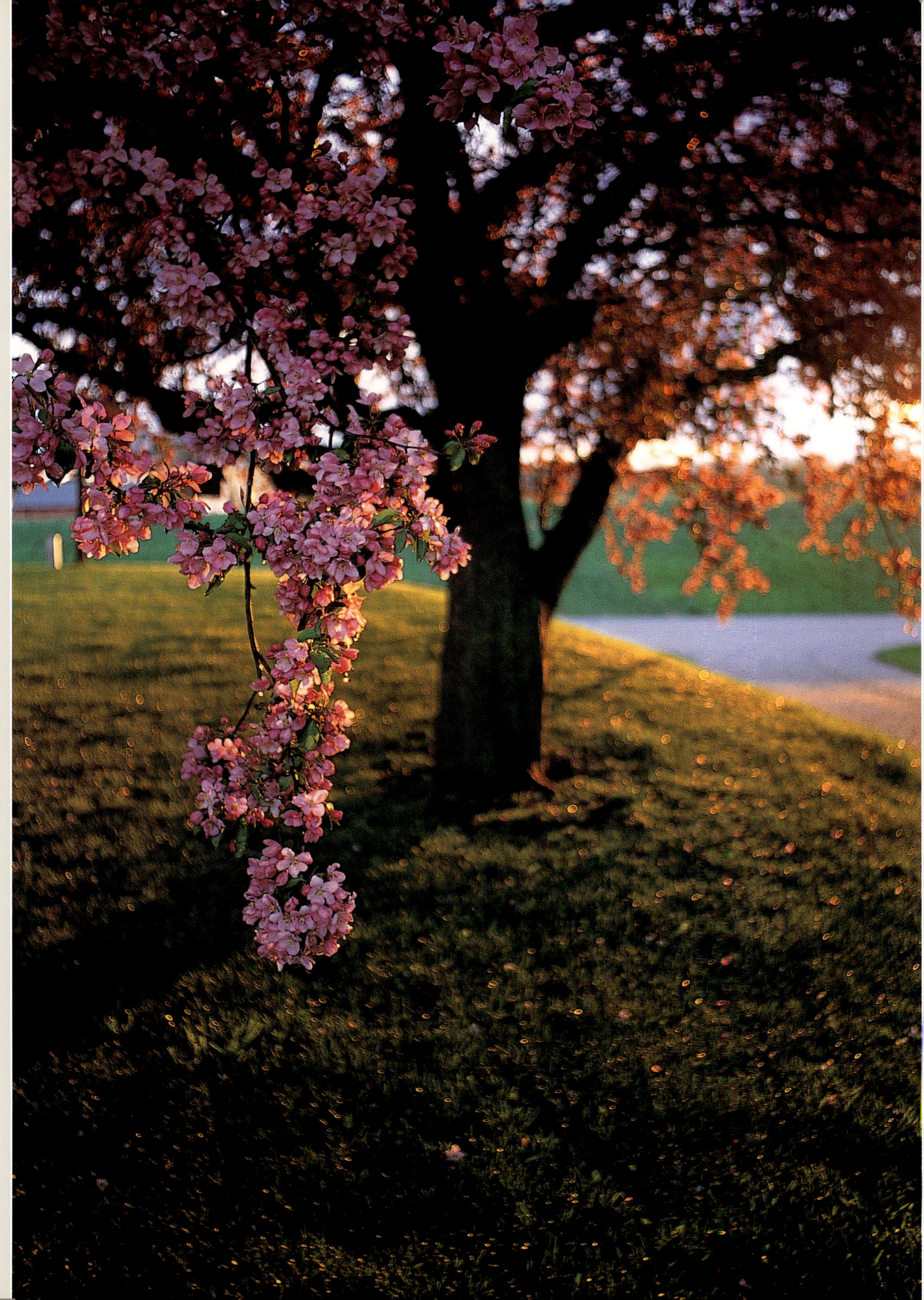

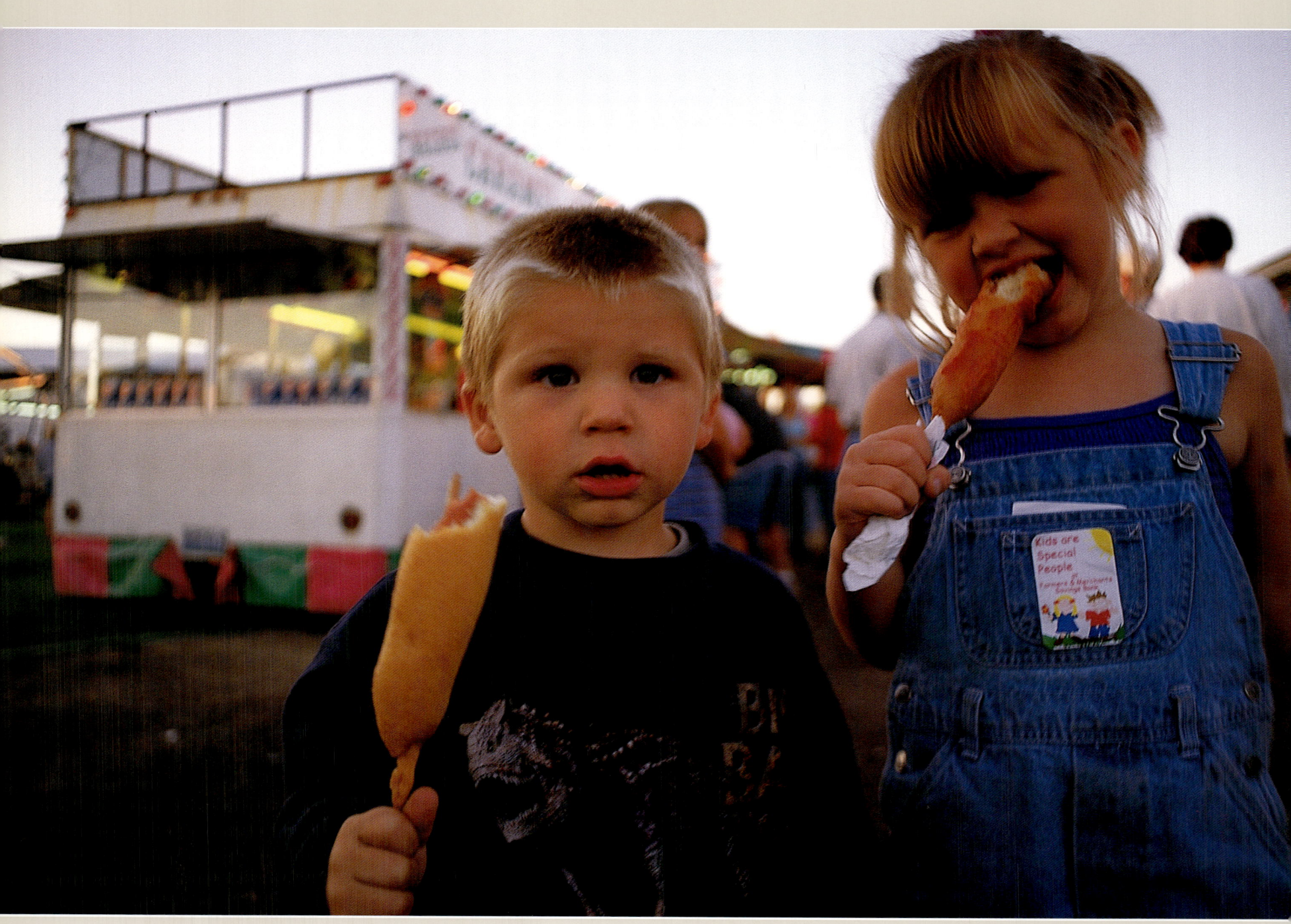

Above: Kids enjoy a summertime favorite: corn dogs at the Allamakee County Fair. LARSH K. BRISTOL

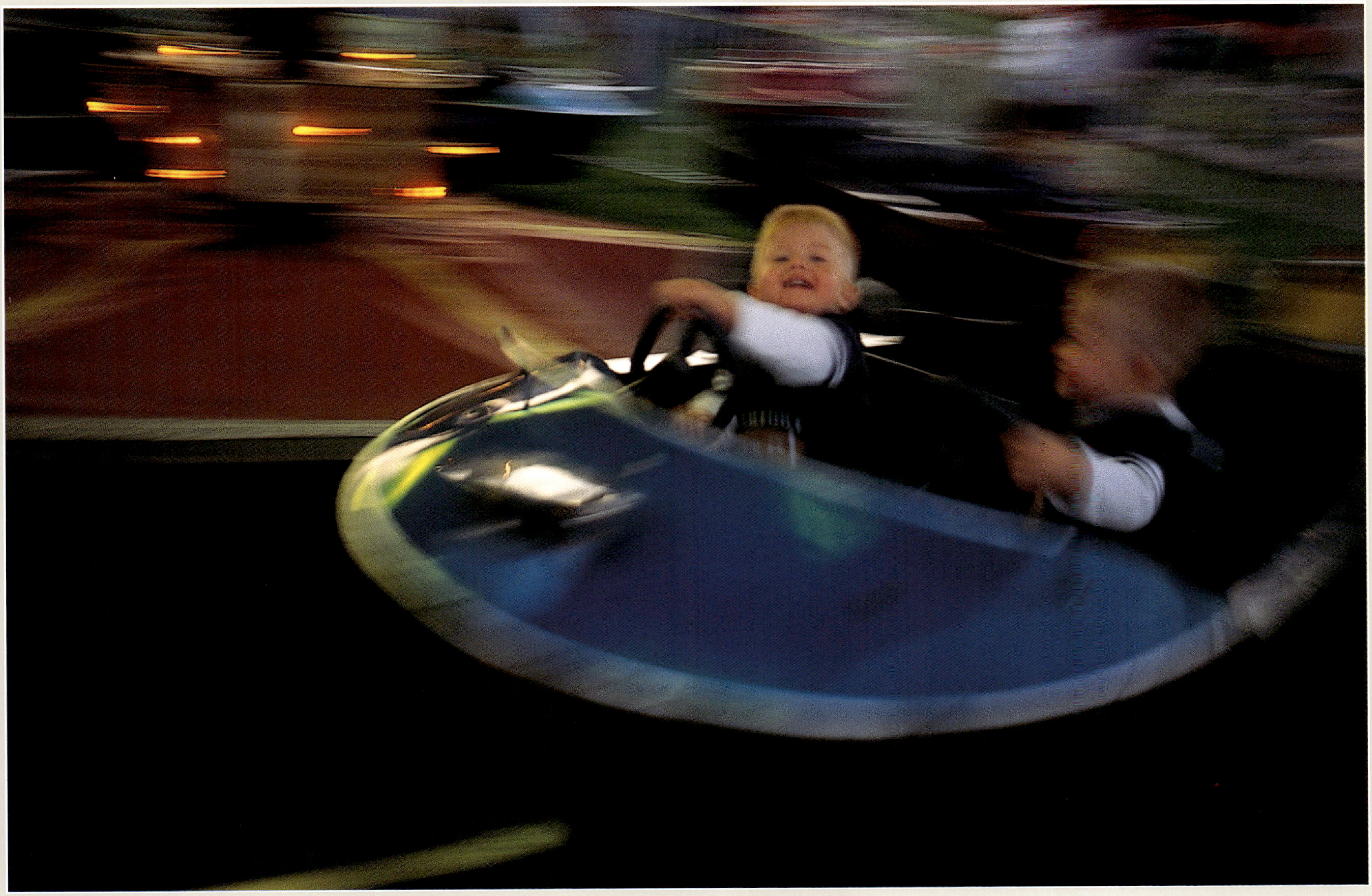

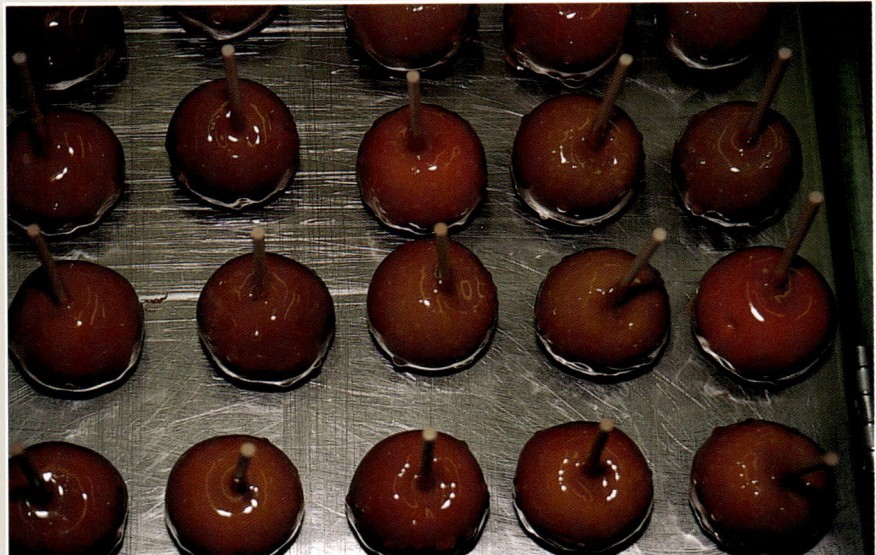

Above: Good times at a county fair in northeast Iowa.
LARSH K. BRISTOL

Left: Caramel apples are the perfect treat. LARSH K. BRISTOL

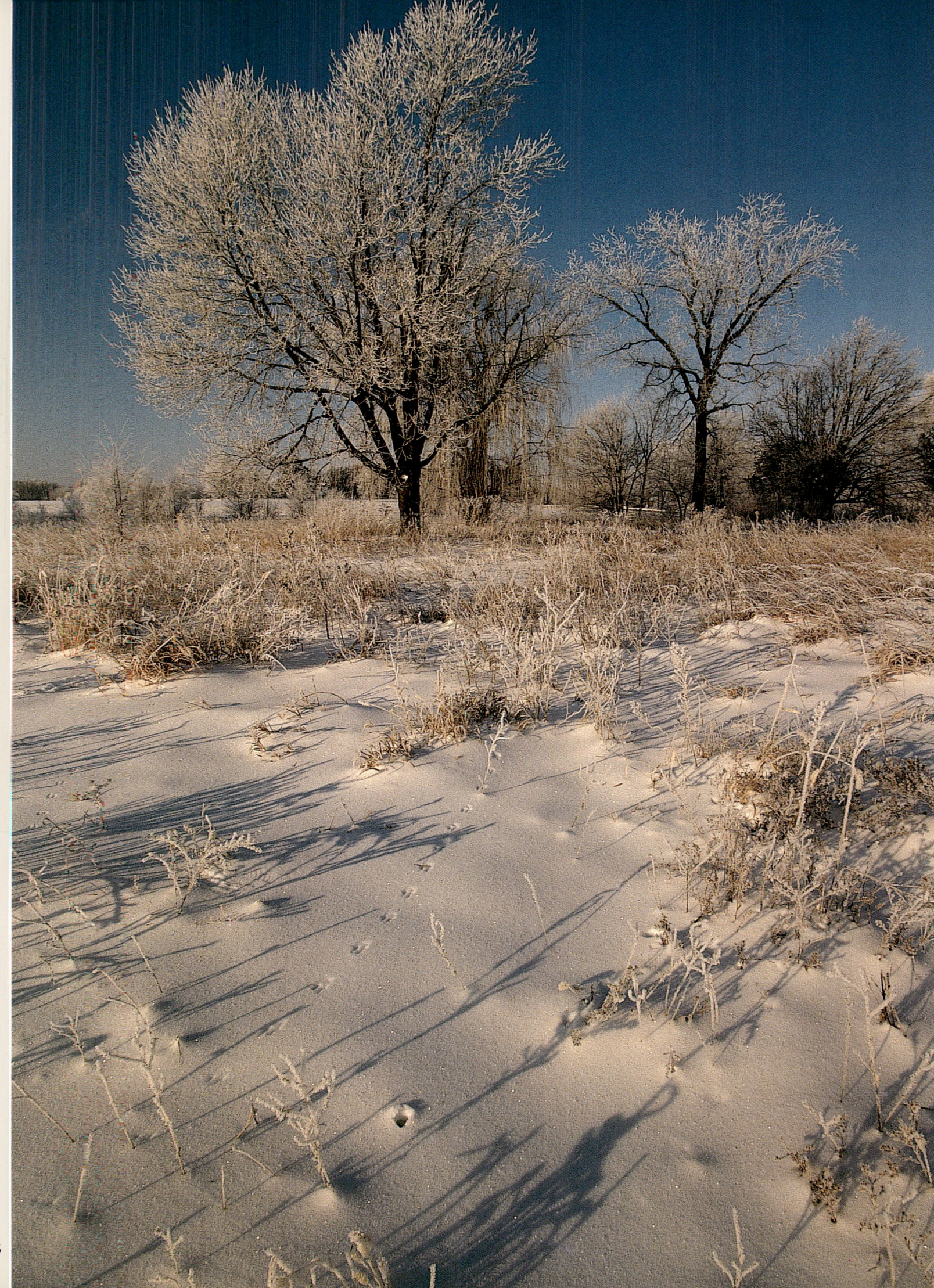

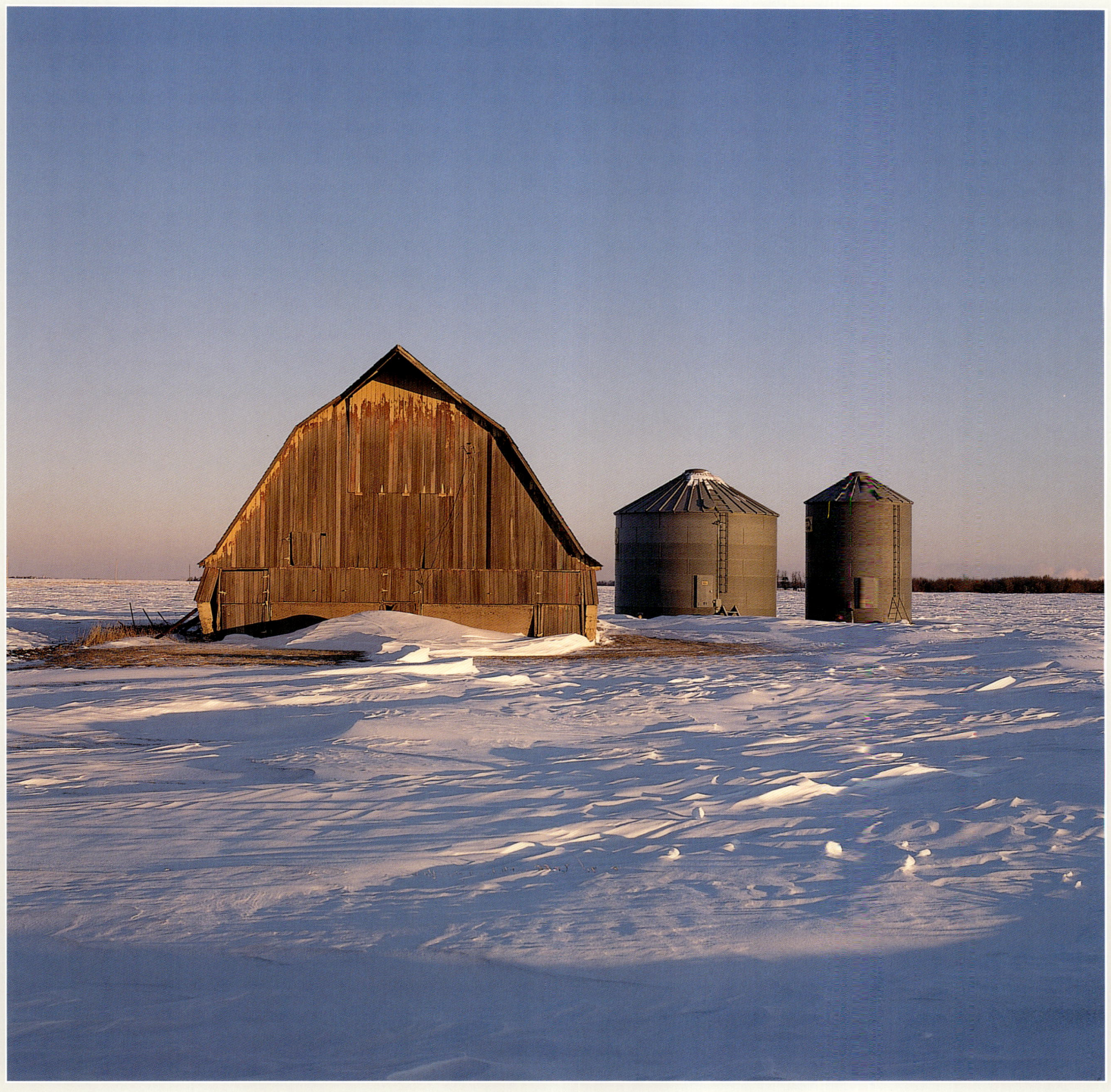

Above: An old barn and grain bins weather another winter near Fort Dodge. CURT MAAS

Facing page: A fresh blanket of snow paired with morning frost make for a lovely winter scene. CURT MAAS

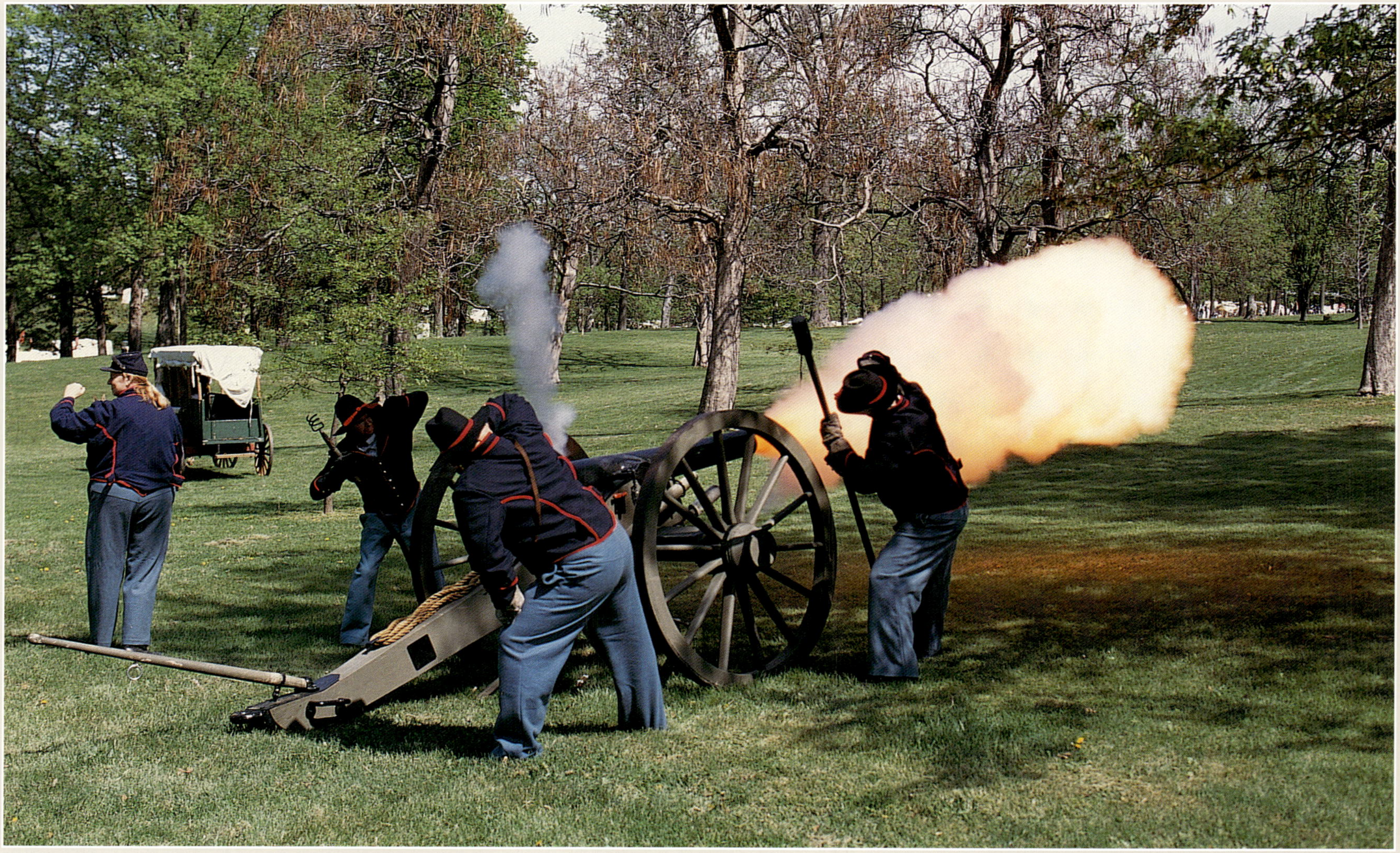

Above: A Civil War battle reenactment in Keokuk of the Battle of Pea Ridge. KENT FOSTER

Right: Union soldiers march in loose formation. KENT FOSTER

Facing page: A young boy carries Old Glory into battle. KENT FOSTER

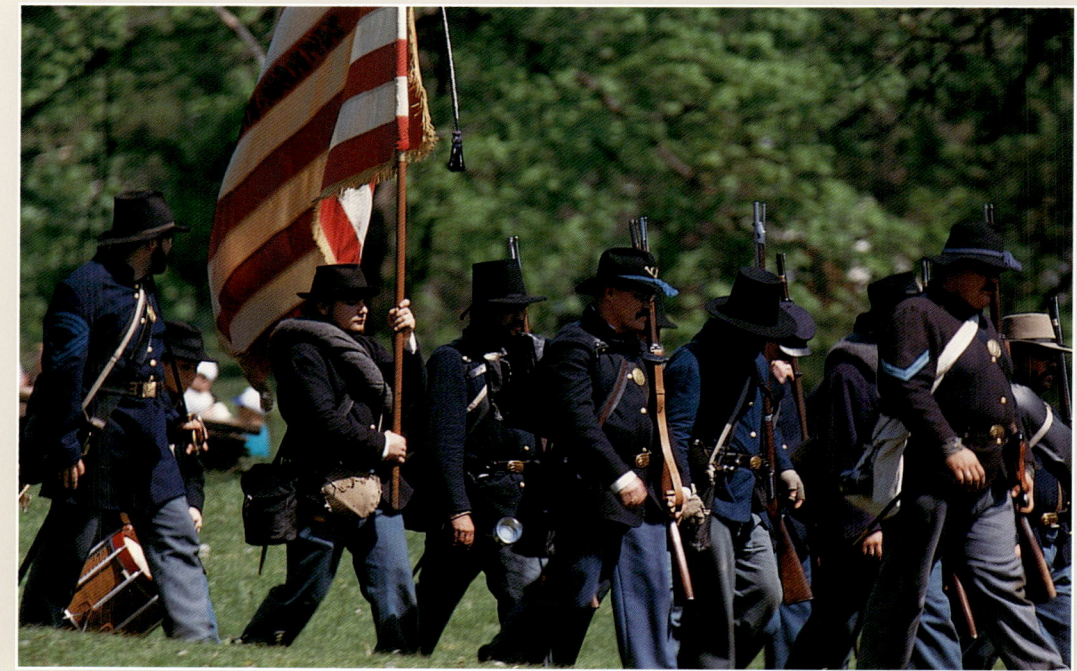

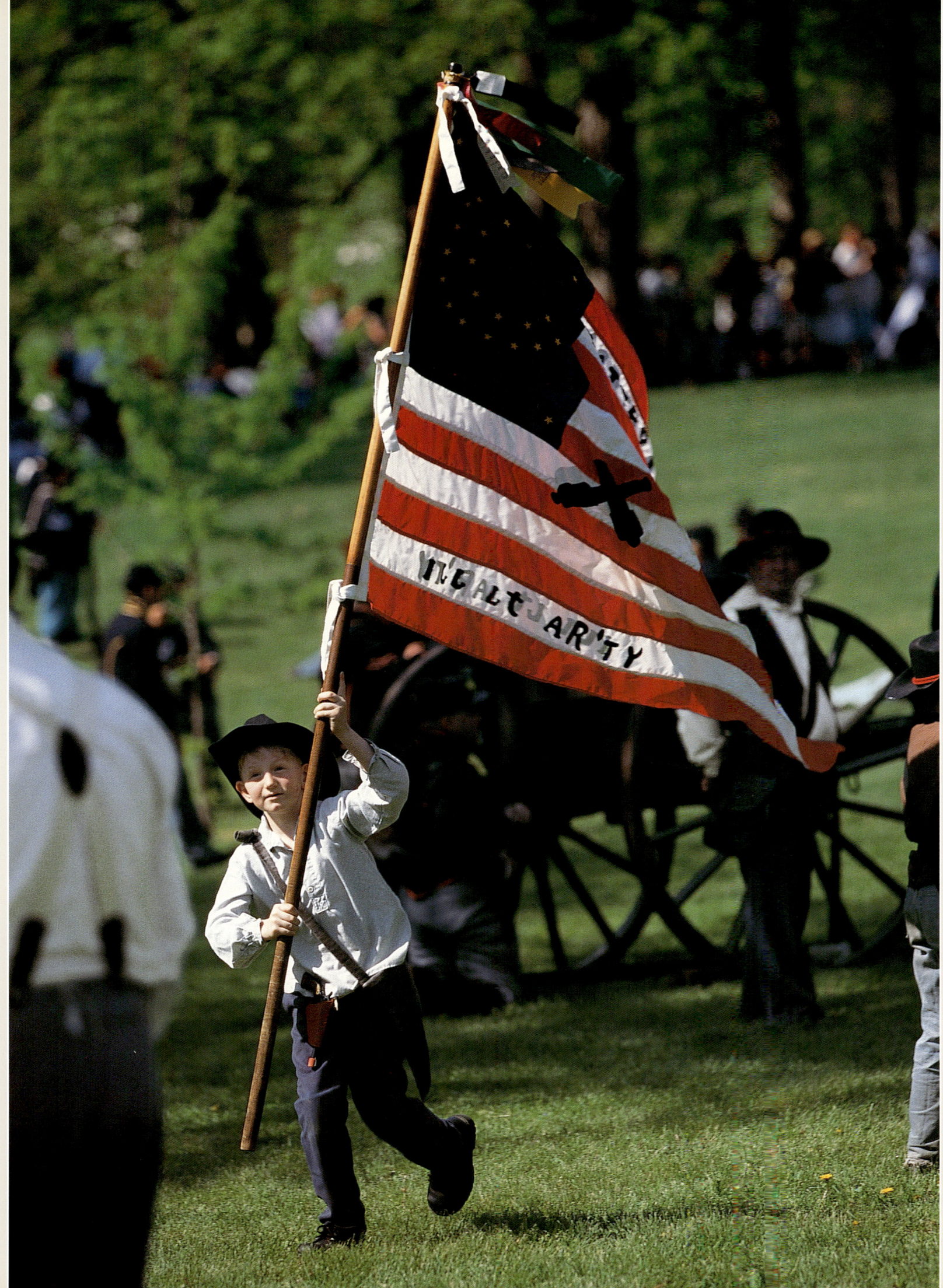

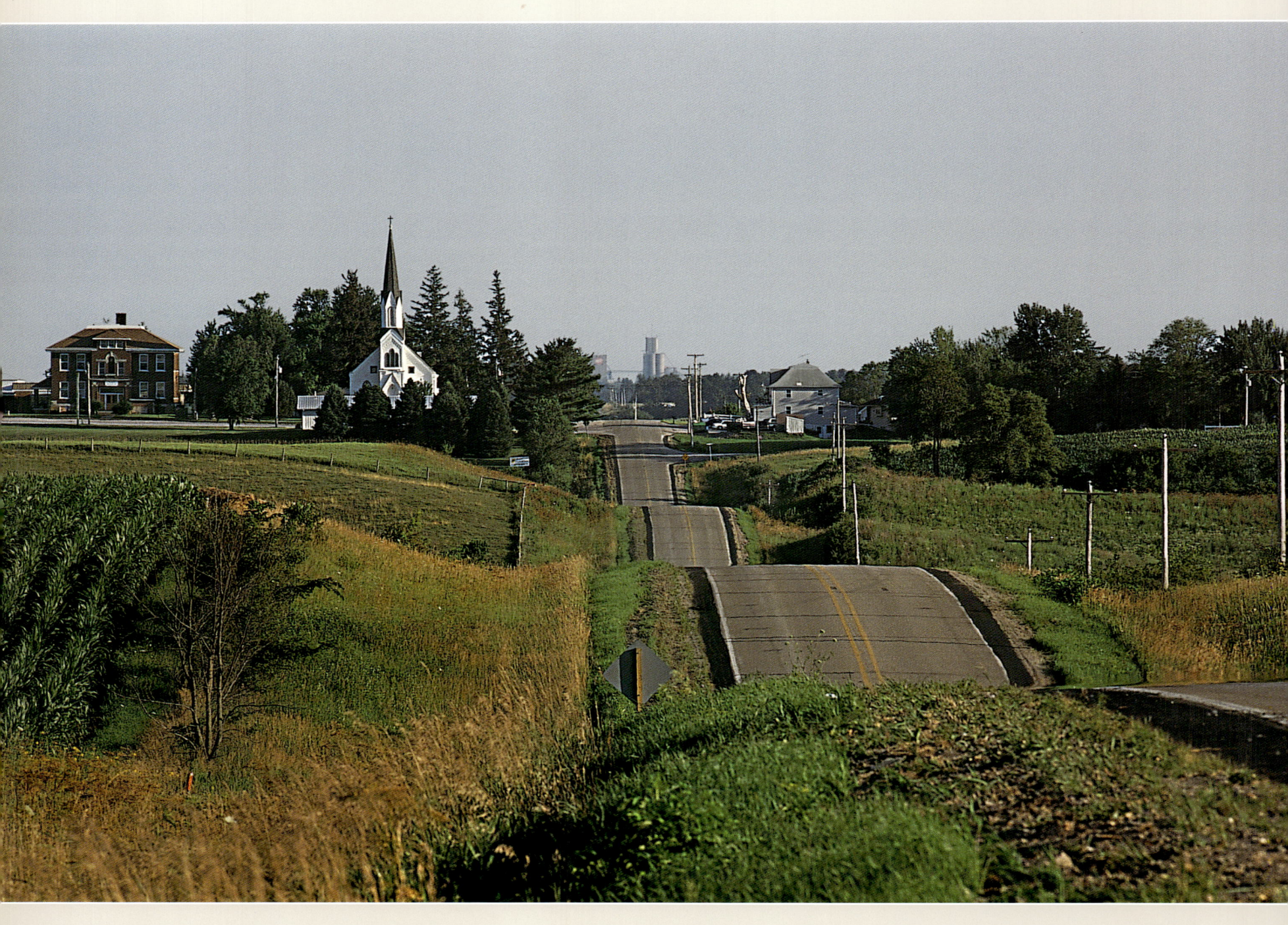

Above: Constructed in 1890, St. Peter's Church in Cosgrove is named after its founder, Father Peter Sullivan. CURT MAAS

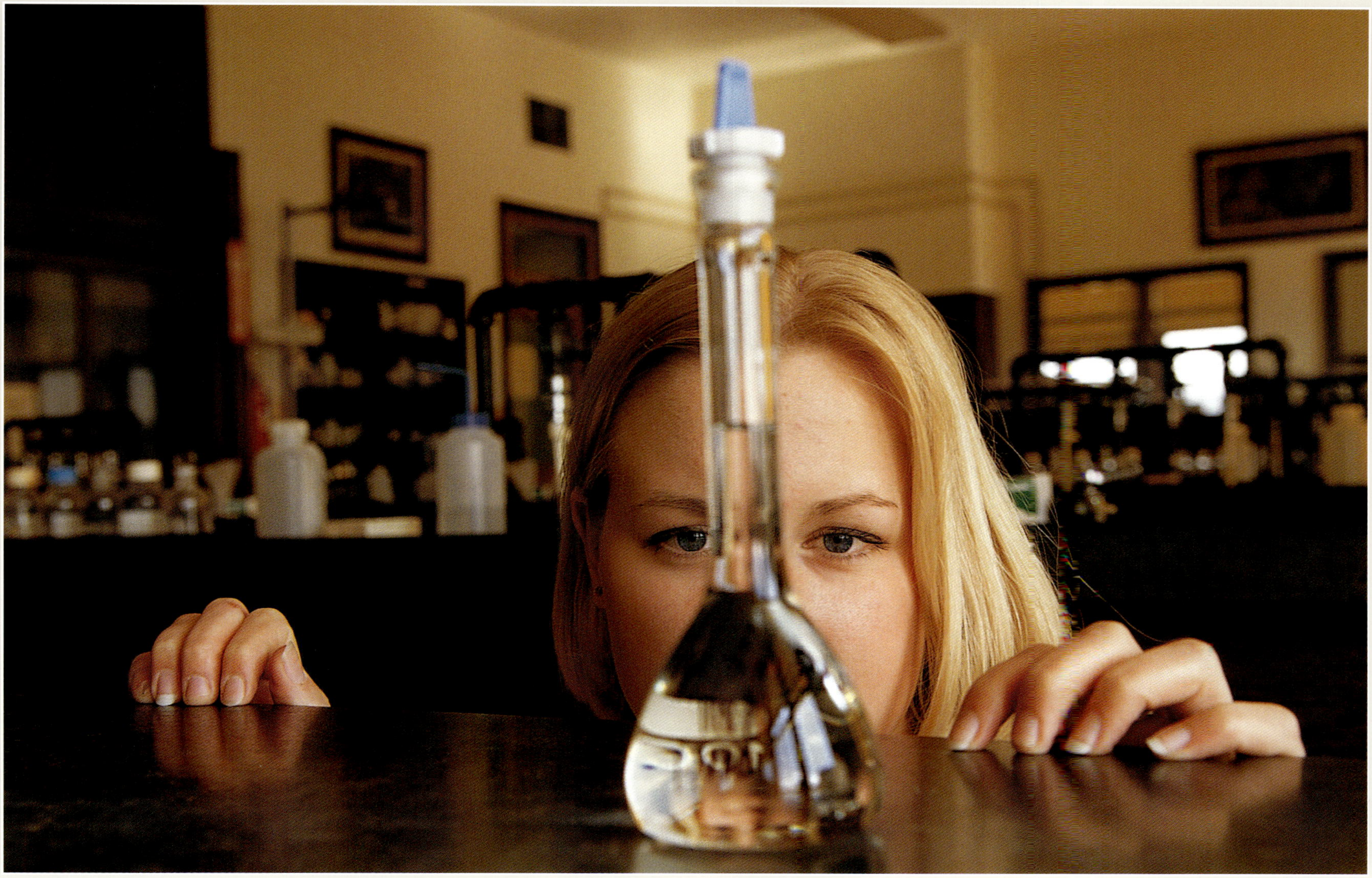

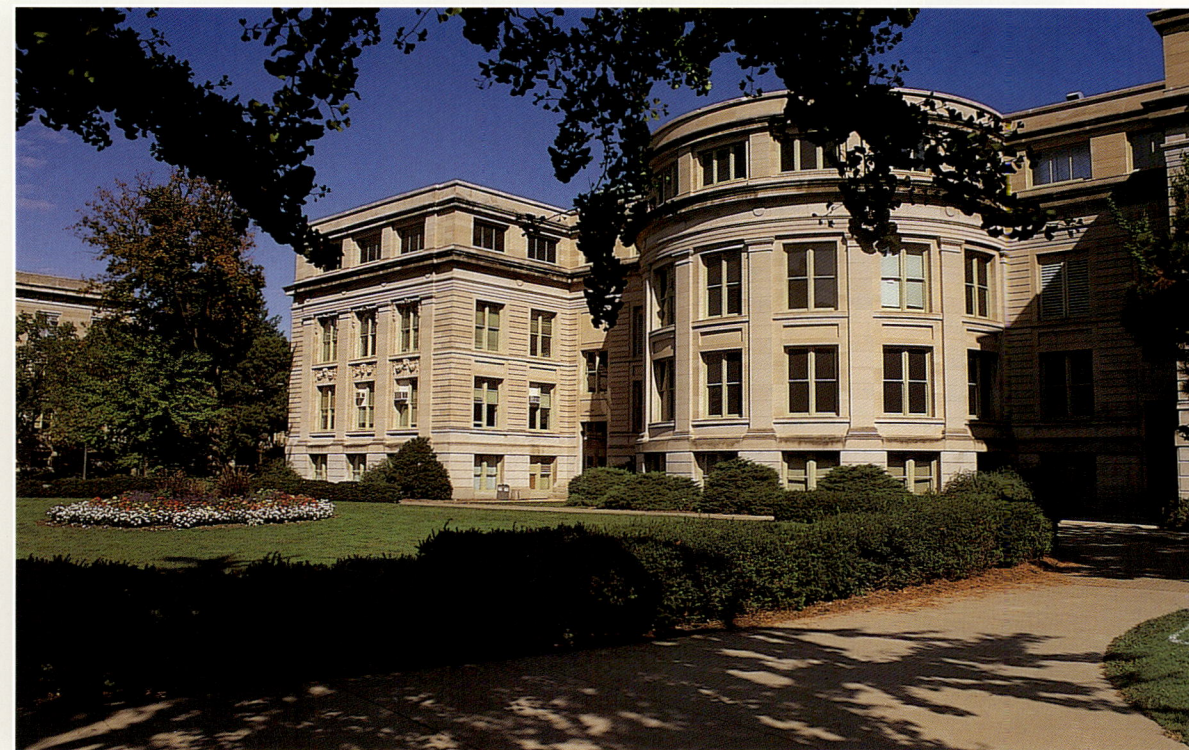

Above: Conducting experiments in the chemistry lab at the University of Northern Iowa in Cedar Falls. LARSH K. BRISTOL

Left: University of Iowa campus in Iowa City. LARSH K. BRISTOL

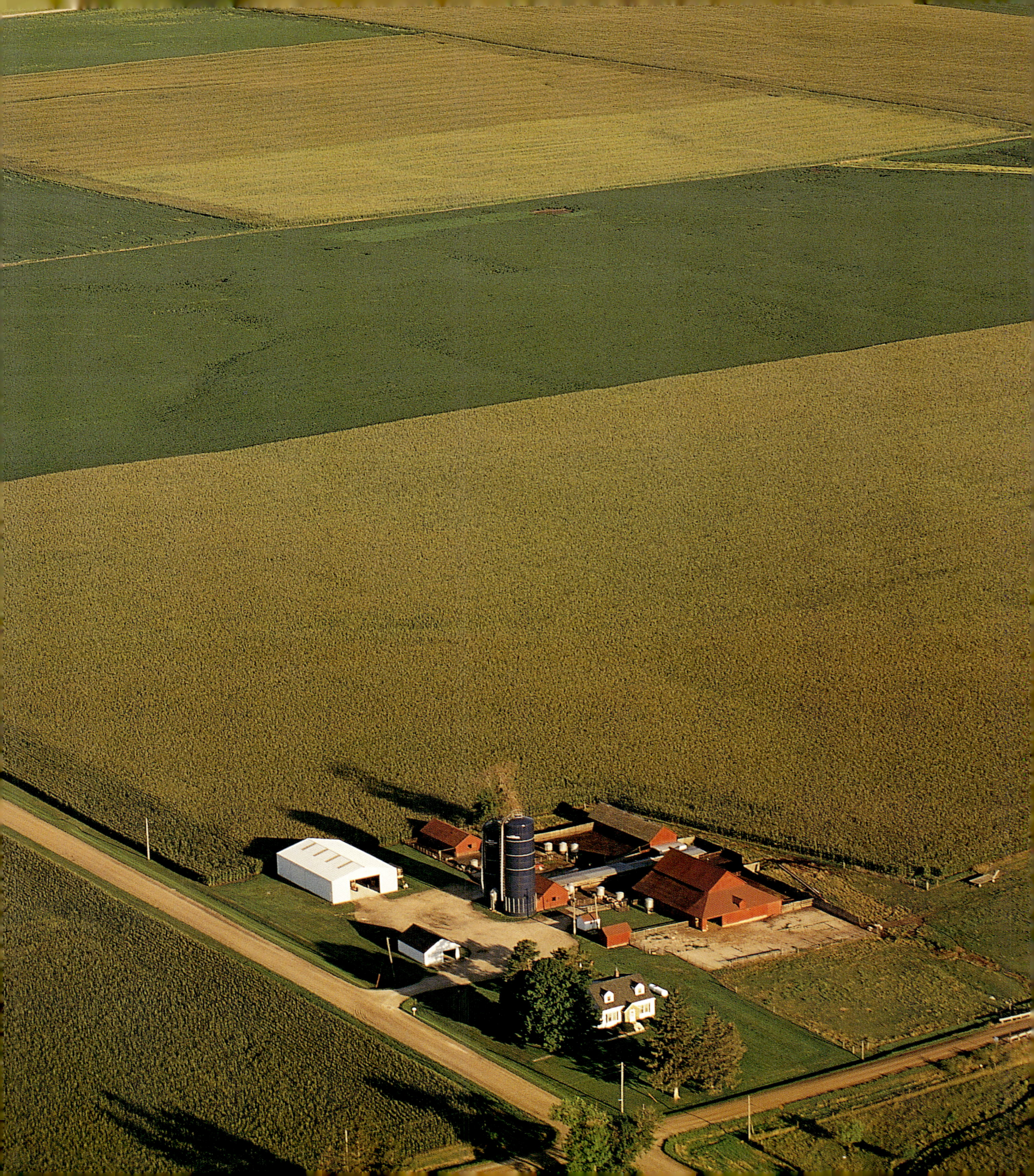

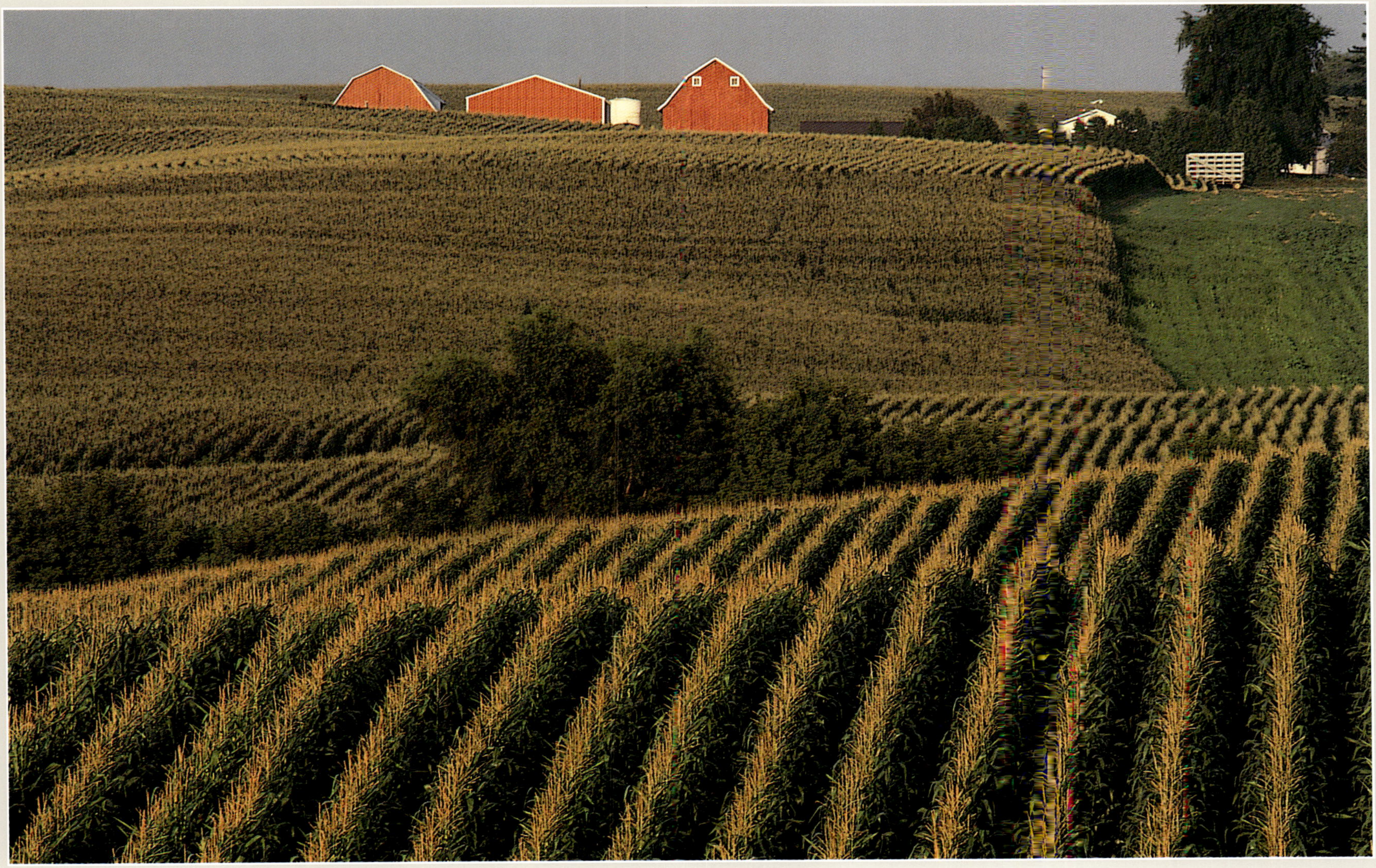

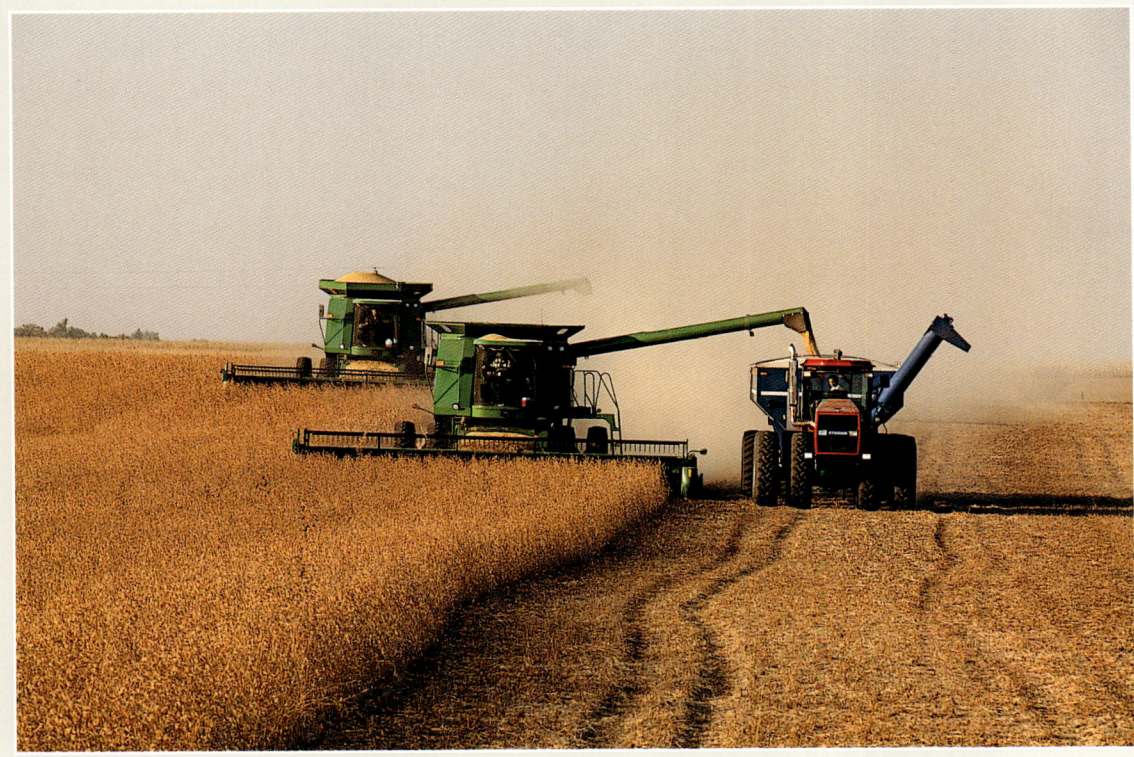

Above: Rows of corn rise and fall with the rolling hills in northeastern Iowa. CURT MAAS

Left: Combines harvest soy beans near Bouton. CURT MAAS

Facing page: An aerial view of farmsteads and the central Iowa countryside during late summer. CURT MAAS

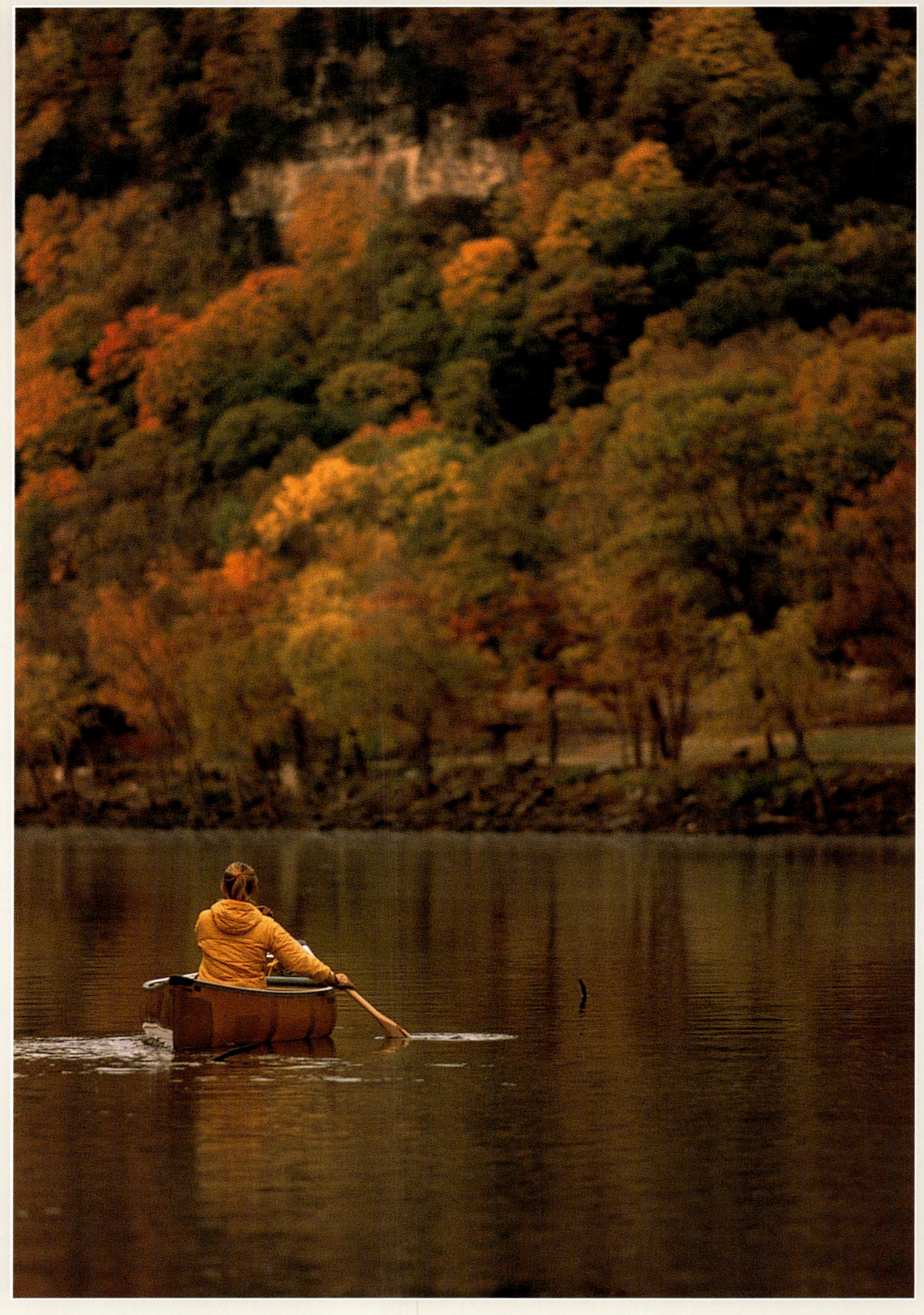

Above: An Iowa woman enjoys a serene canoe ride in fall. LARSH K. BRISTOL

Facing page: Marsh cattails begin to break open and disperse their seeds. LARSH K. BRISTOL

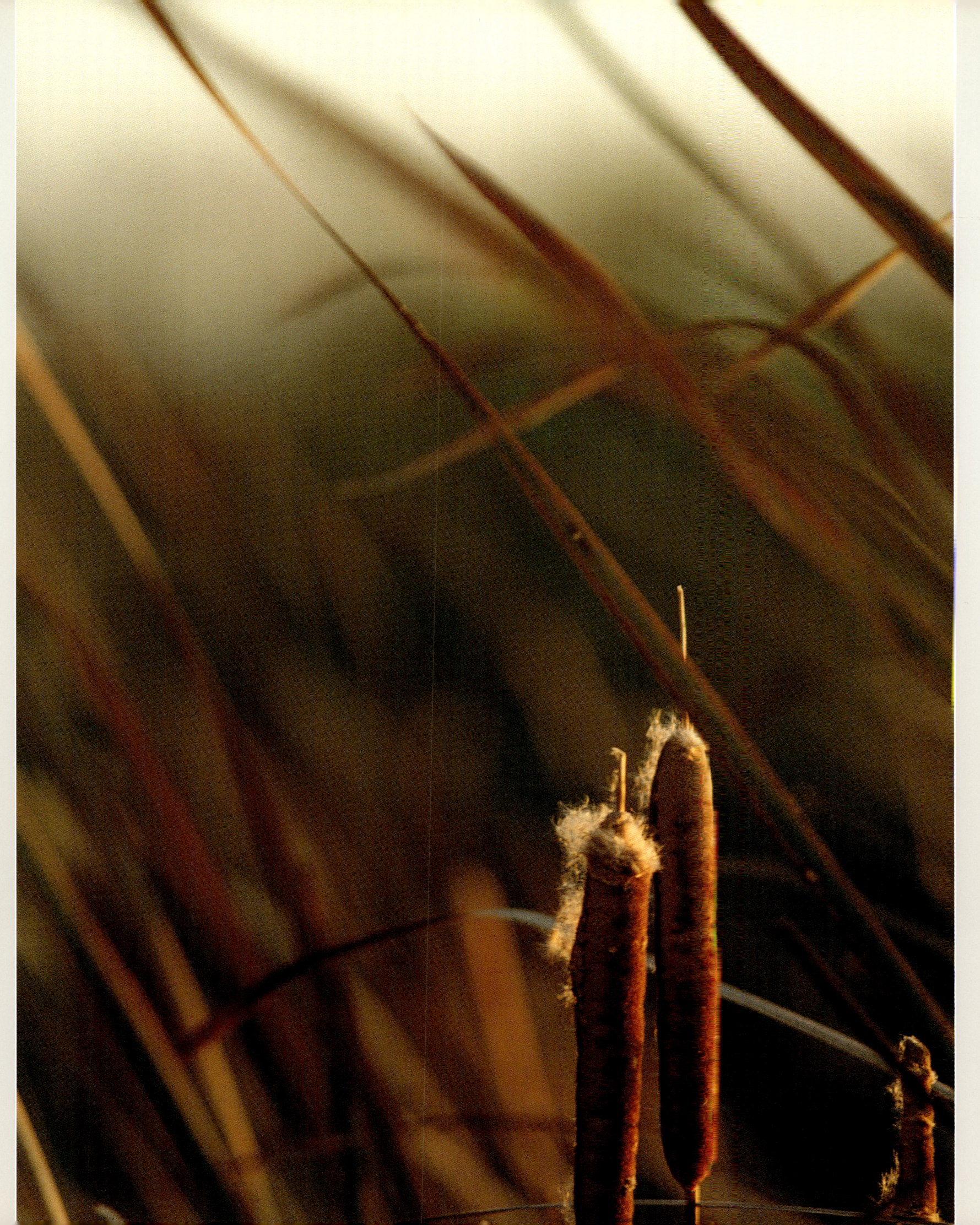

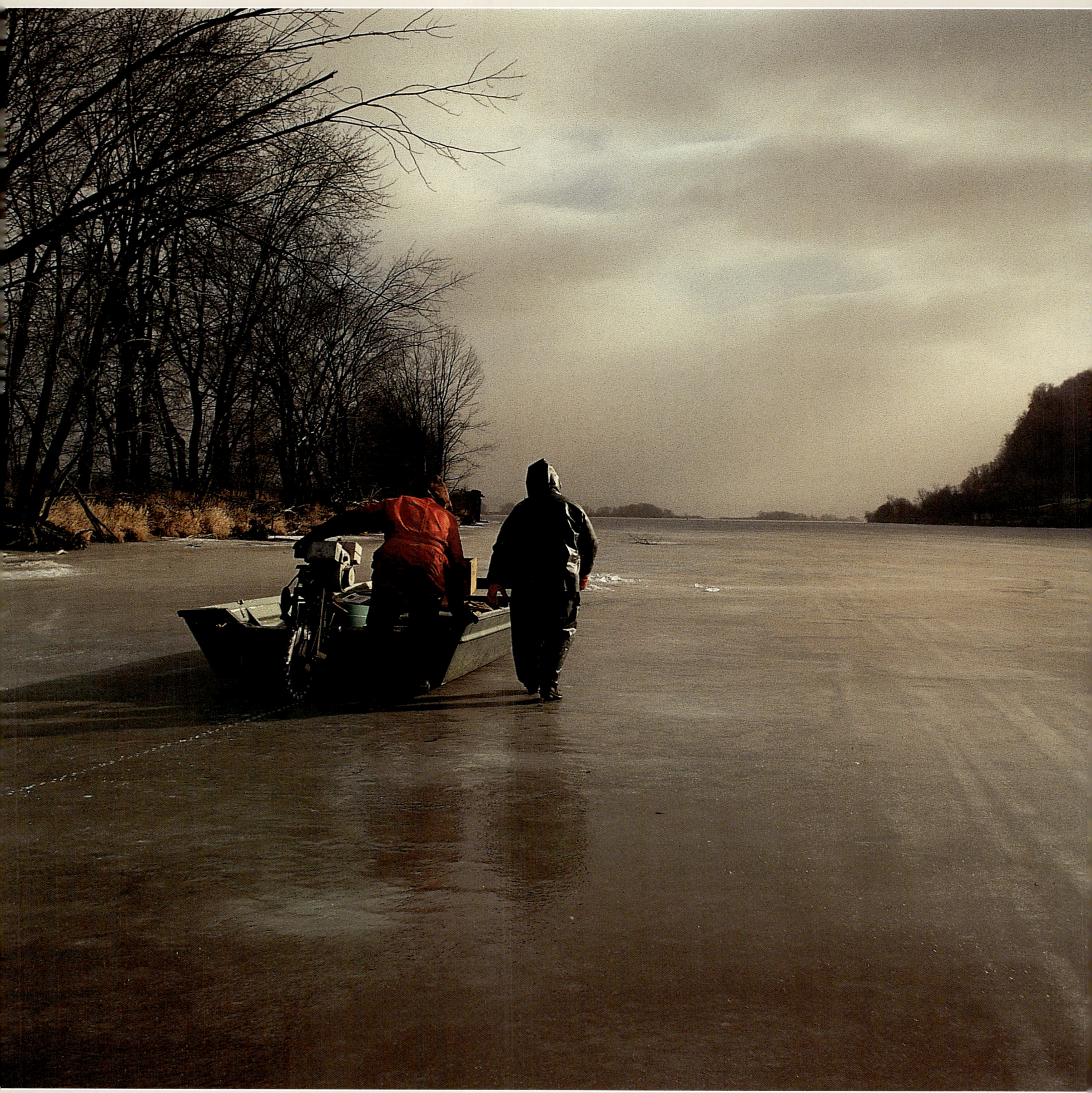

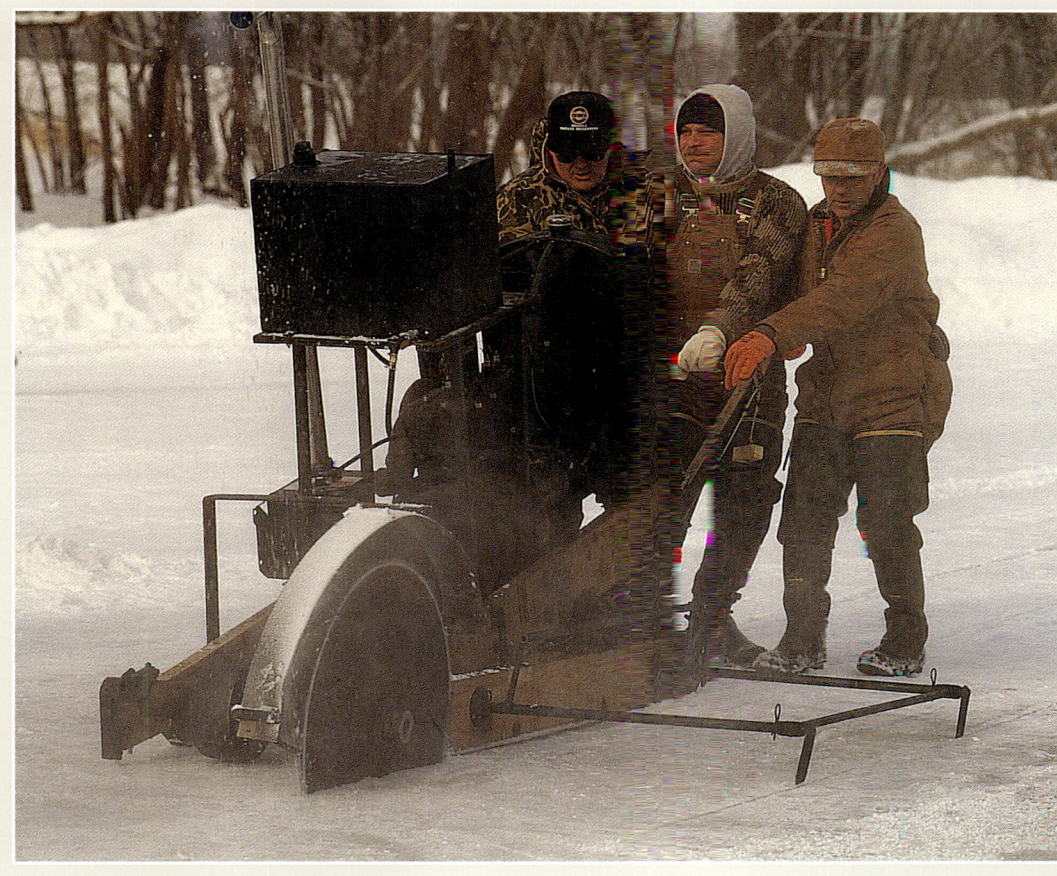

Above: "High-tech" ice cutting. LARSH K. BRISTOL

Left: Commercial fisherman head out onto the ice for another day of work near Lansing. LARSH K. BRISTOL

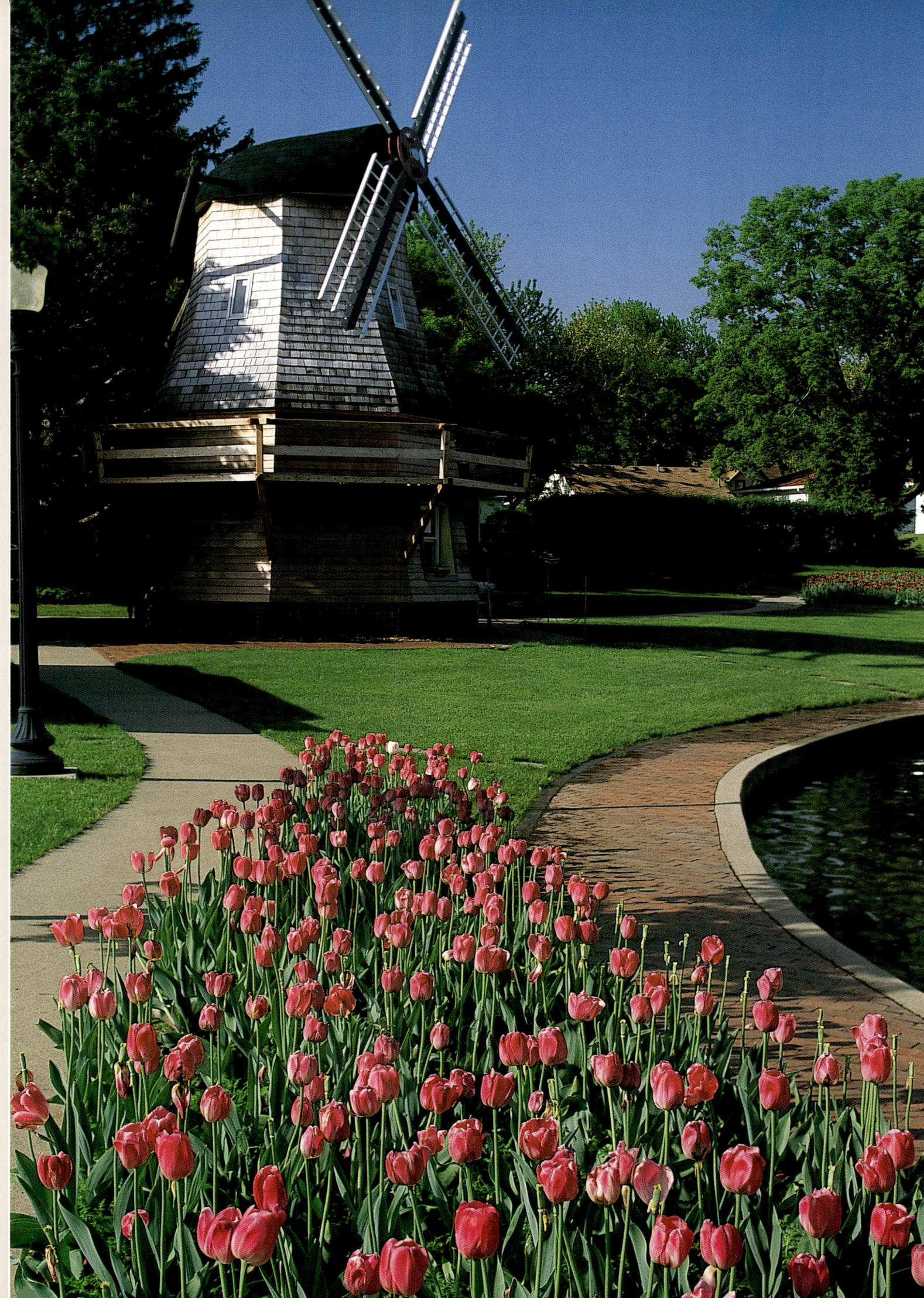

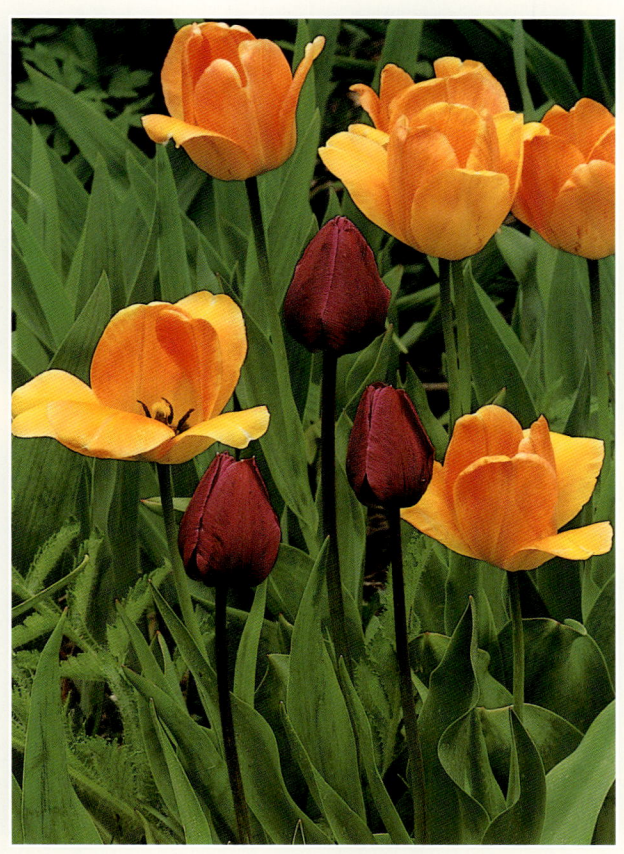

Left: Tulips, harbingers of spring. KENT FOSTER

Below: Dutch cheese-market races at the Pella Tulip Festival. KENT FOSTER

Facing page: Sunken Gardens Park, with its Dutch windmill, tulips, and pond in the shape of a wooden shoe, comes alive in spring with the vibrant blooms of more than 15,000 tulips. KENT FOSTER

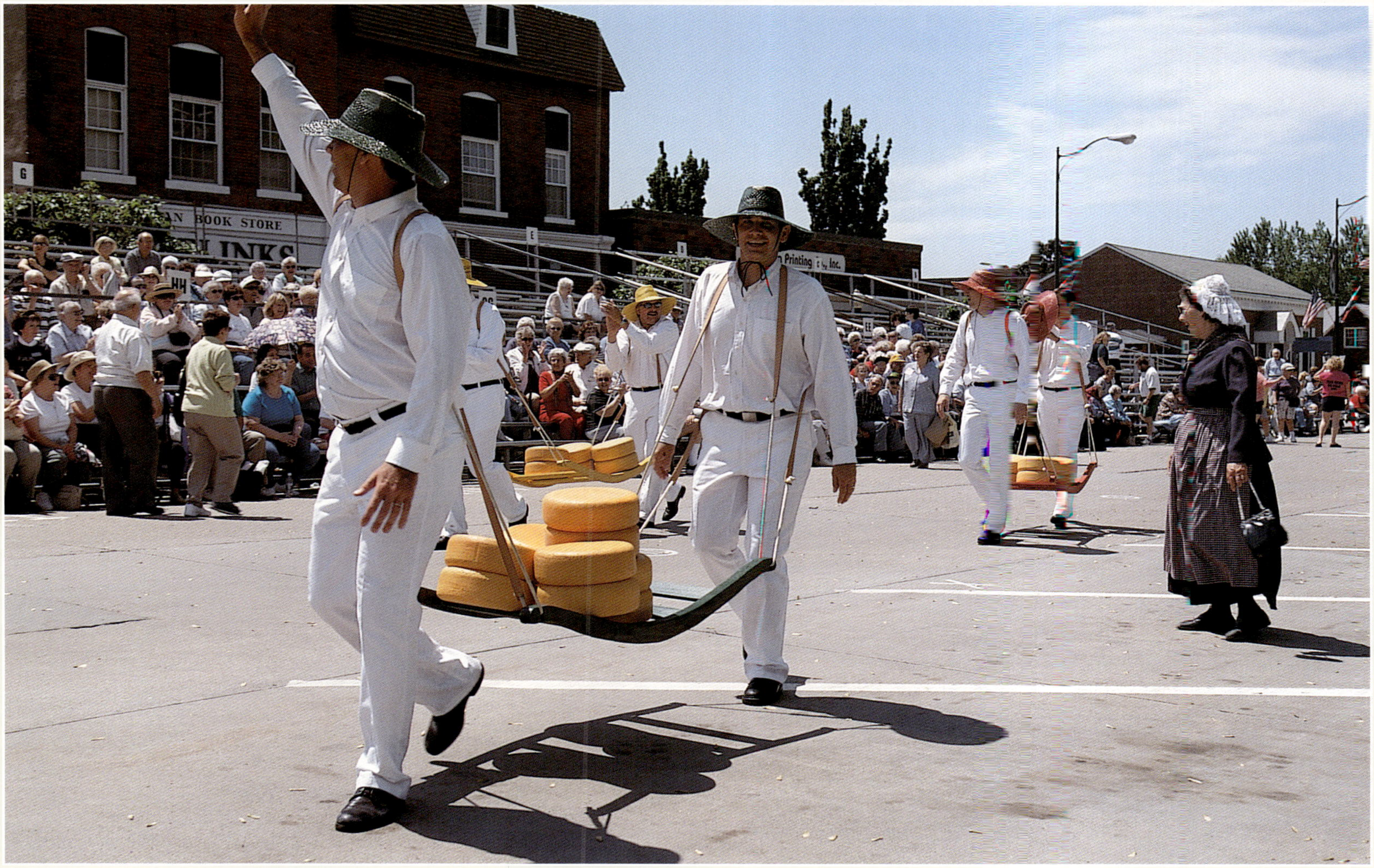

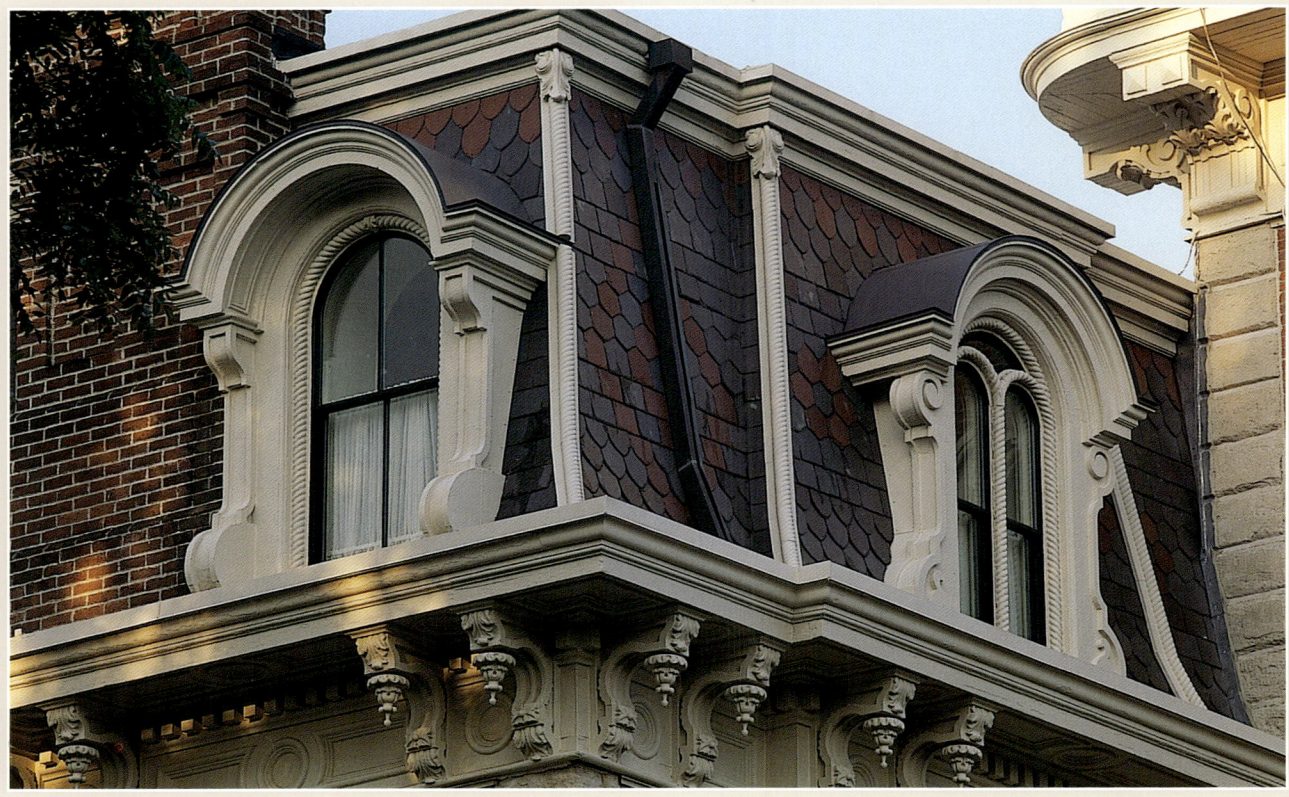

Above: Elegant dormers and subtley patterned slate roof of Terrace Hill Governor's Mansion in Des Moines. KENT FOSTER

Right: Benjamin Franklin Allen, a wealthy Iowan, built Terrace Hill between 1866 and 1869 as his personal residence. The stunning mansion was given to the state of Iowa by the F. M. Hubbell family in 1971. KENT FOSTER

Facing page: Since Terrace Hill was opened to the public in 1978, guests from around the world have visited this beautiful Victorian-era mansion. KENT FOSTER

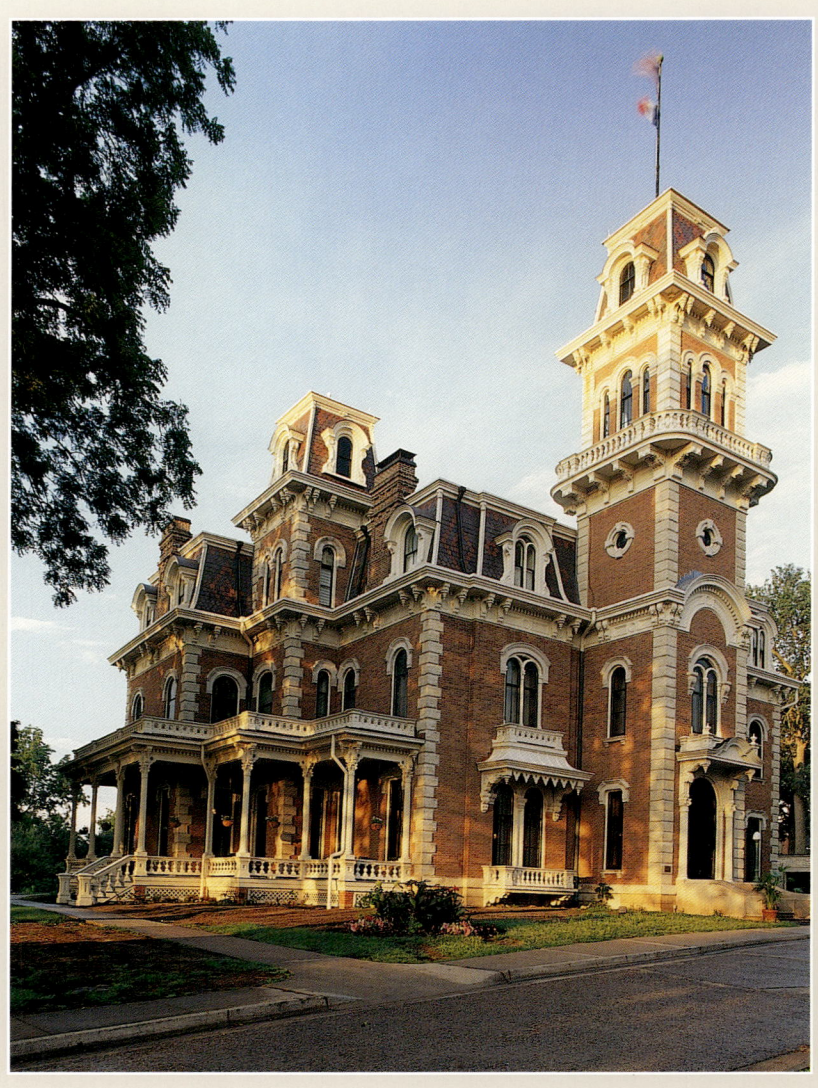

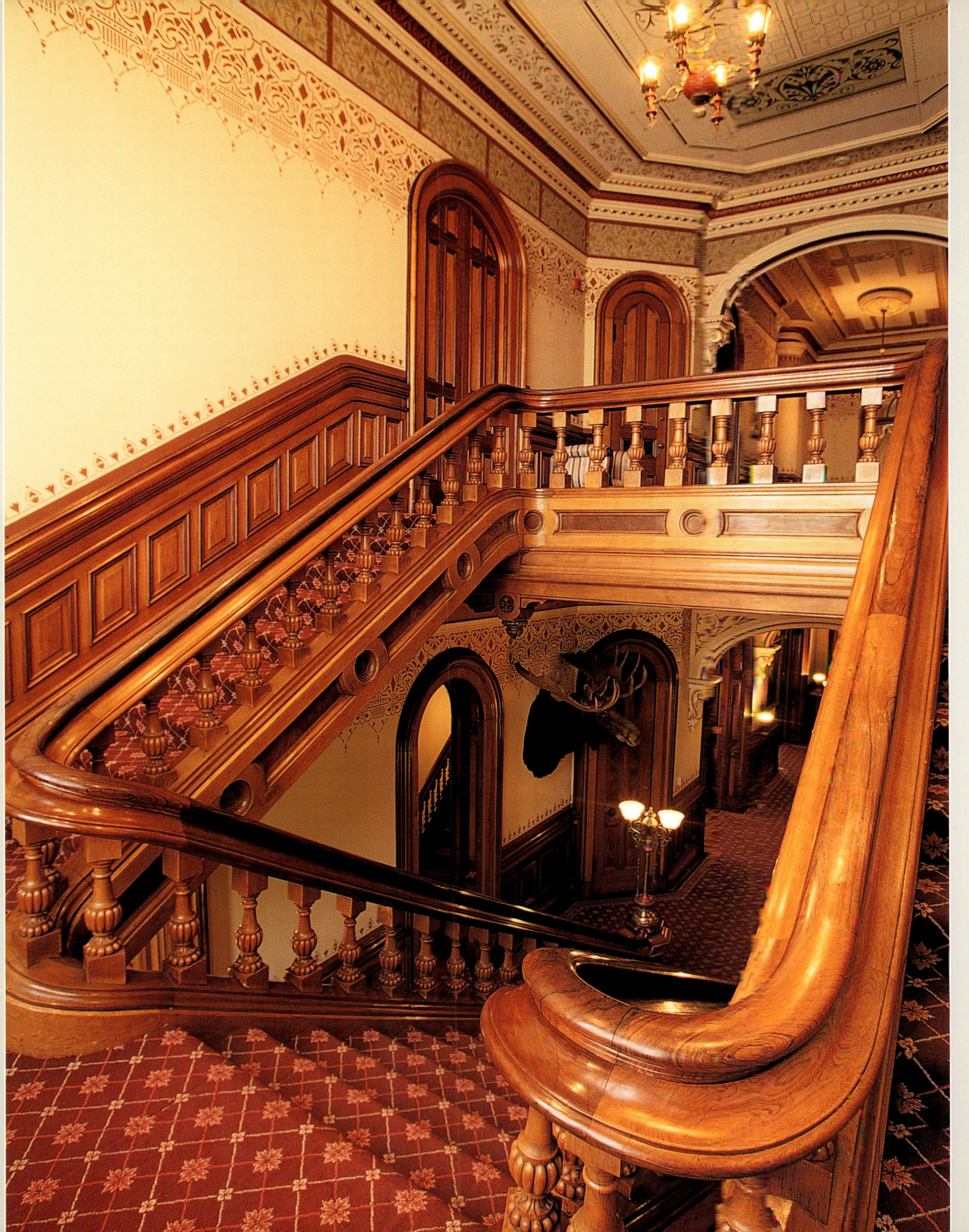

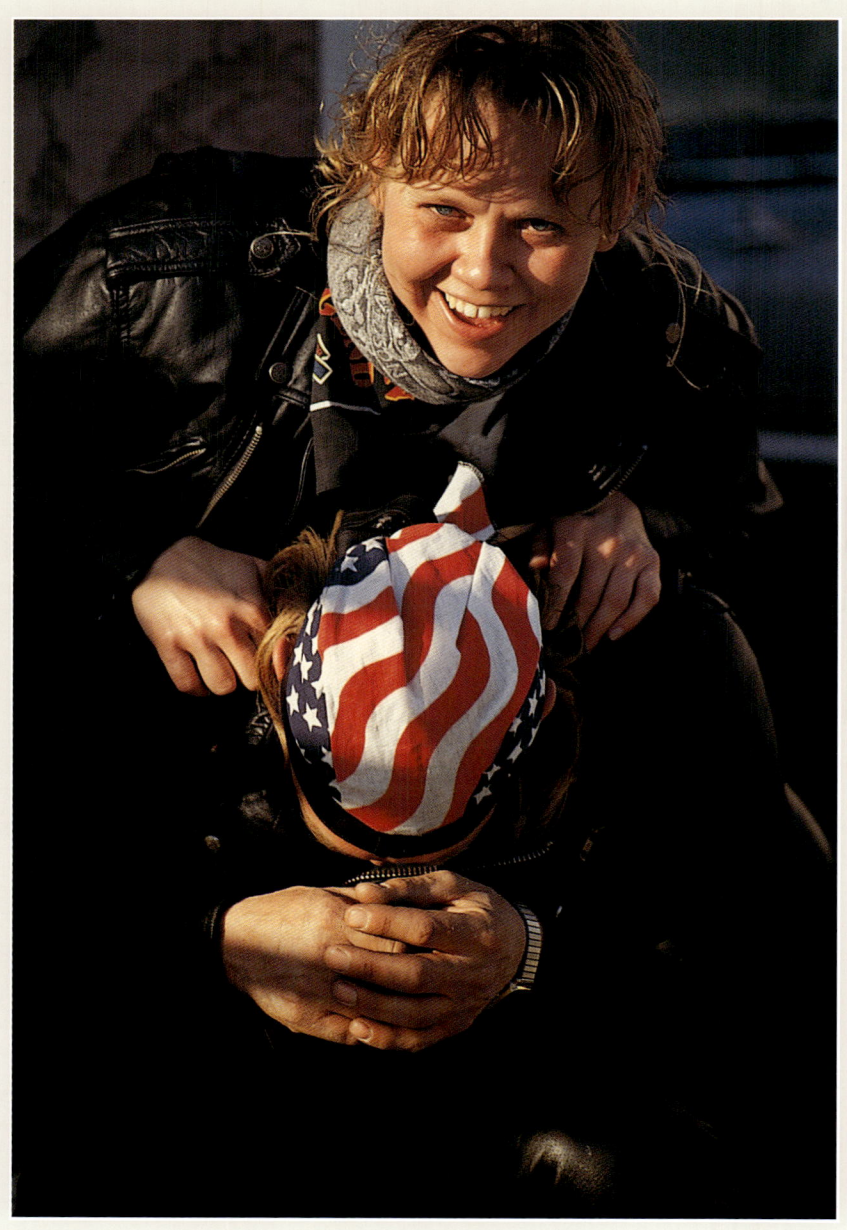
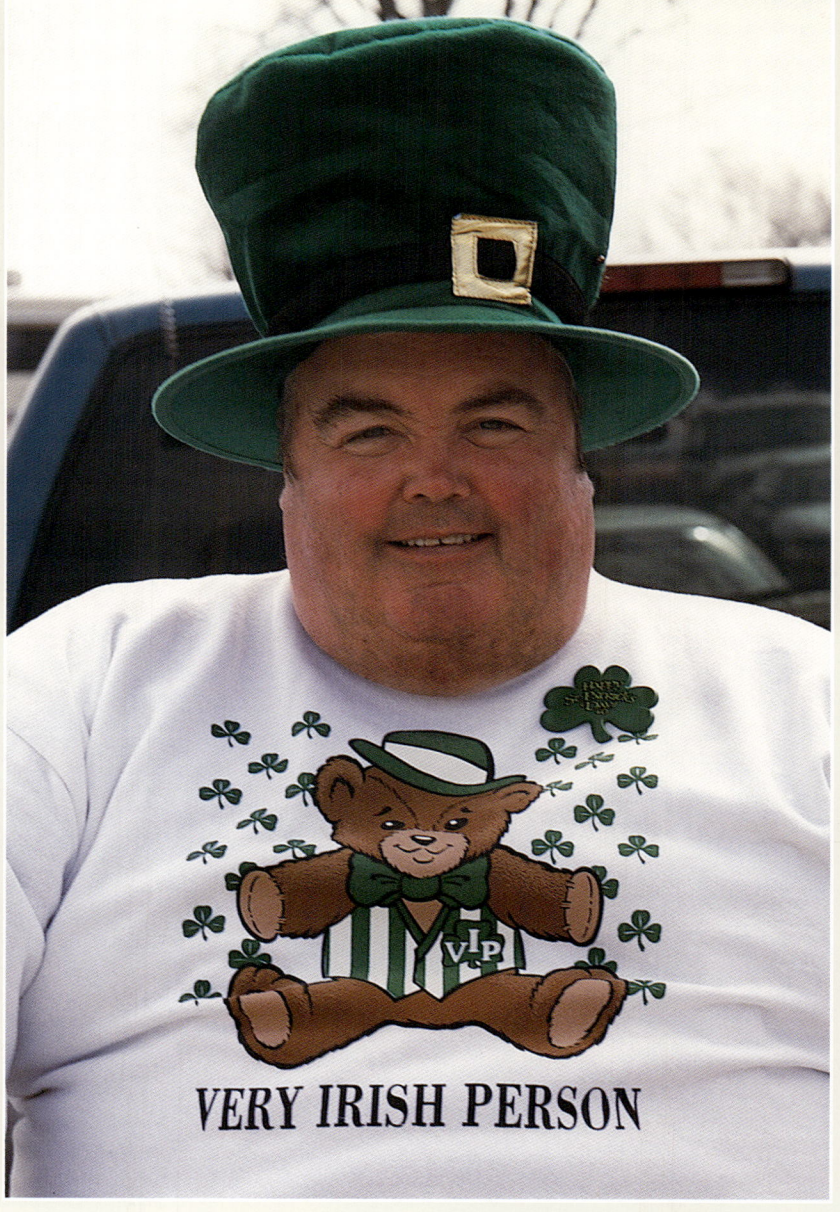

Above left: Motorcyclists mug for (and hide from) the camera. LARSH K. BRISTOL

Above right: Ottie Baxter, Waukon's resident Irishman. LARSH K. BRISTOL

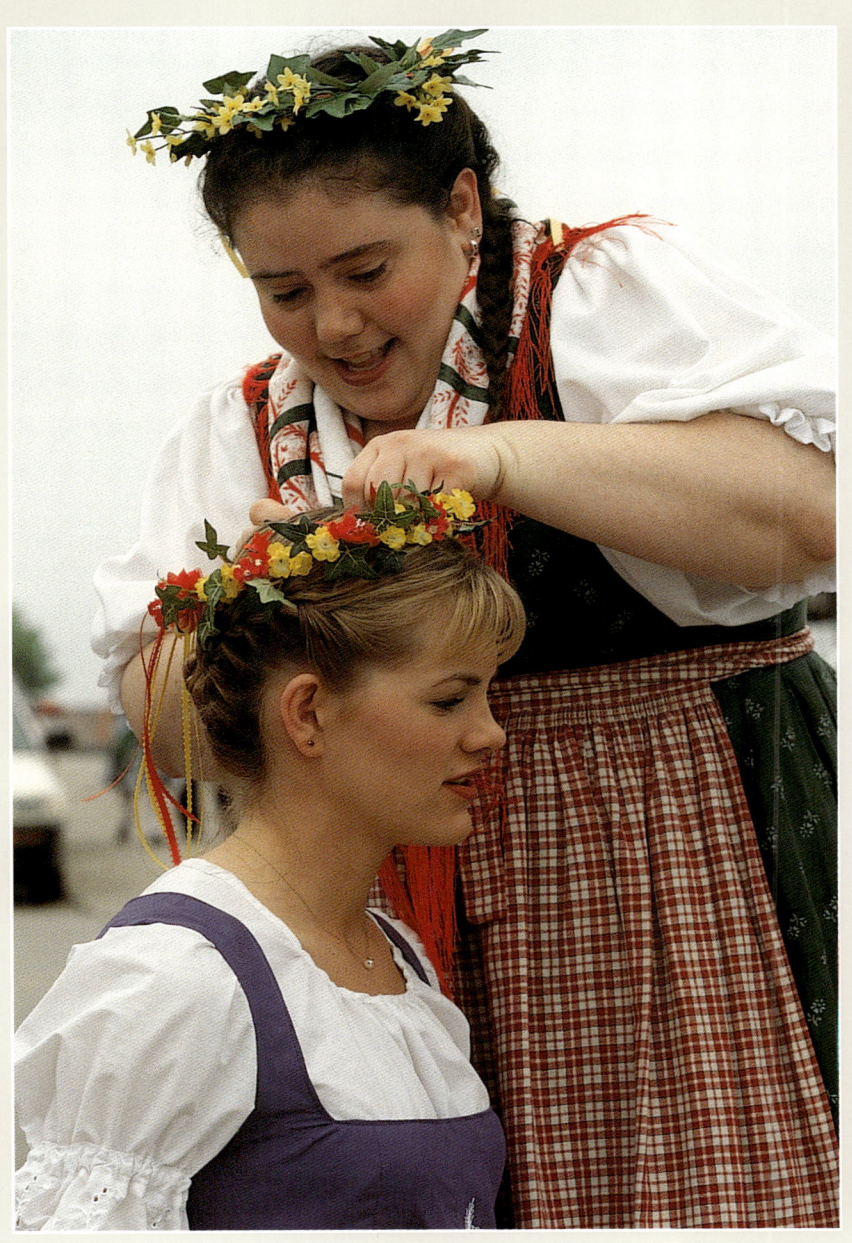
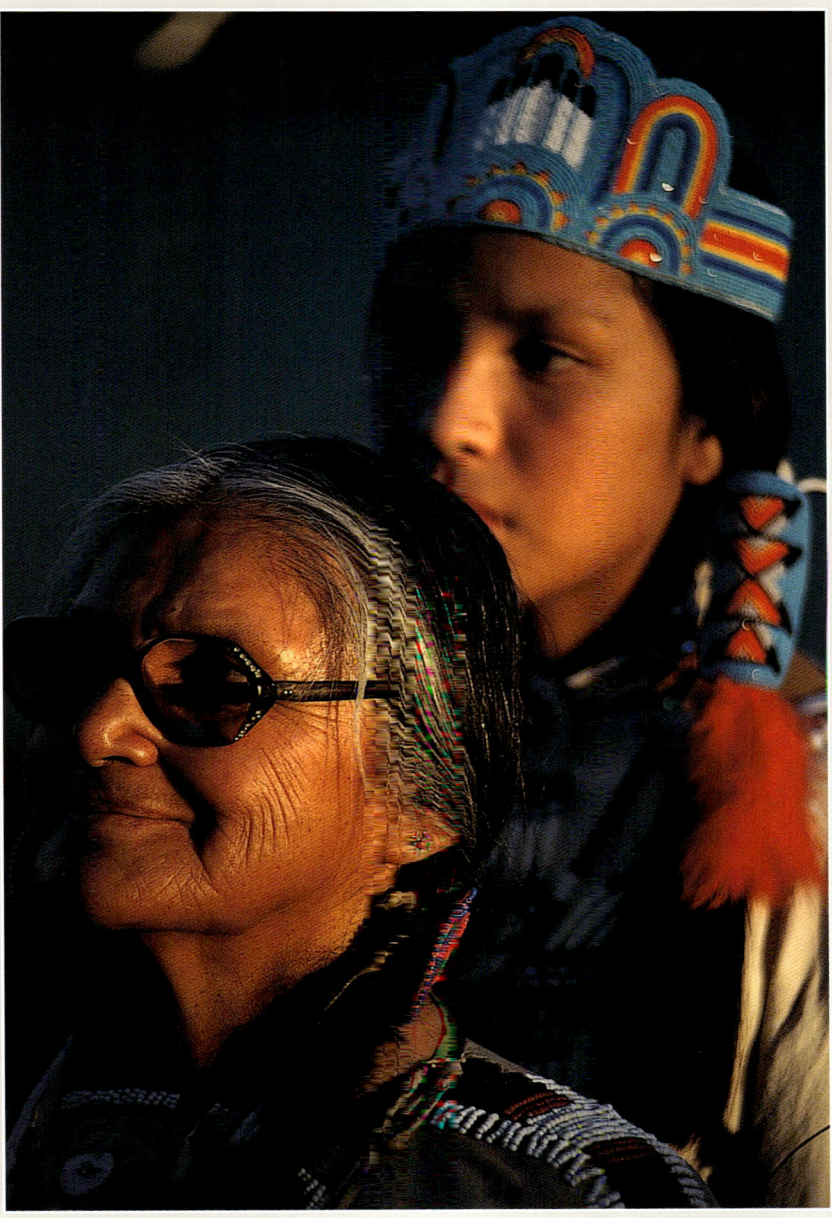

Above left: Maifest dancers prepare for a celebration at the Amana Colonies. KENT FOSTER

Above right: Native Americans at an Effigy National Monument celebration. LARSH K. BRISTOL

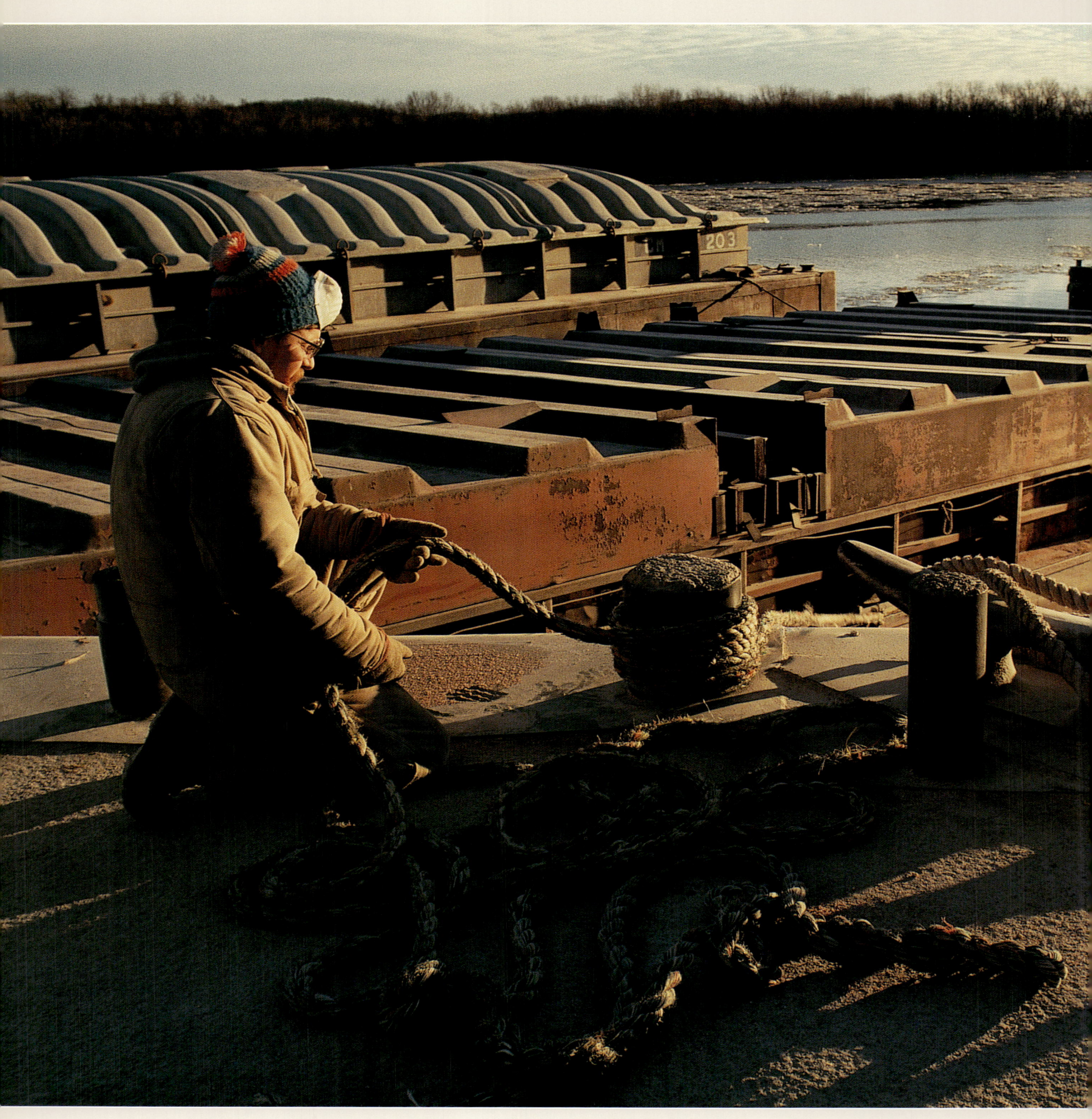

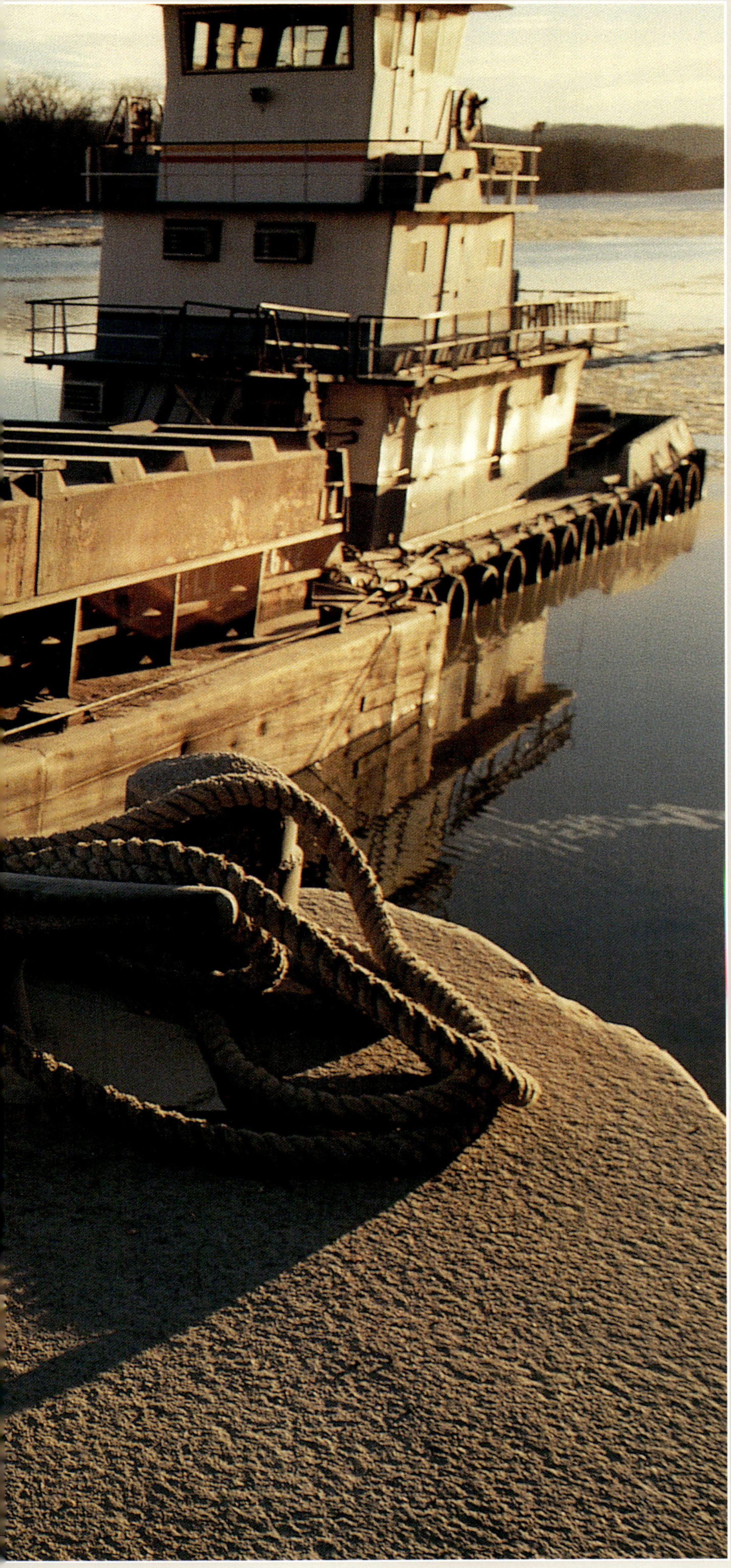

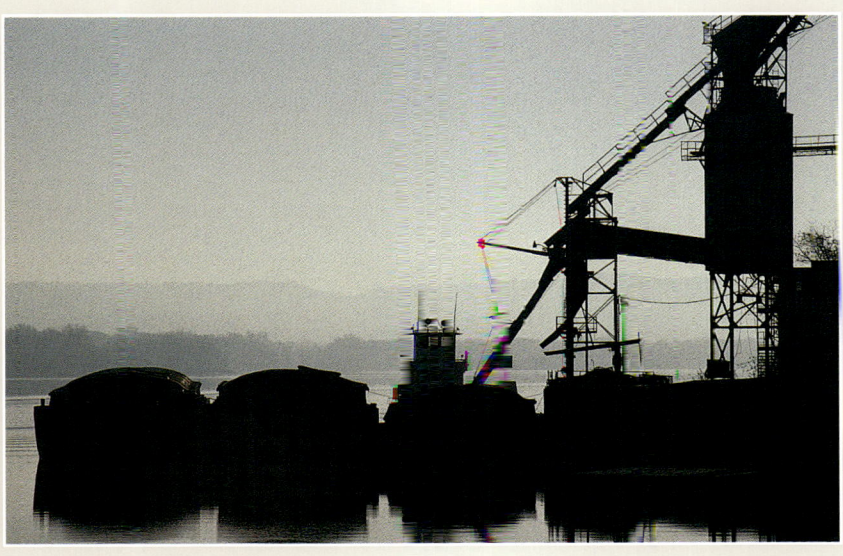

Above: Grain barges line up at the Clayton grain elevator on the Mississippi River. LARSH K. BRISTOL

Left: Securing a barge to a dock on the Mississippi.
LARSH K. BRISTOL

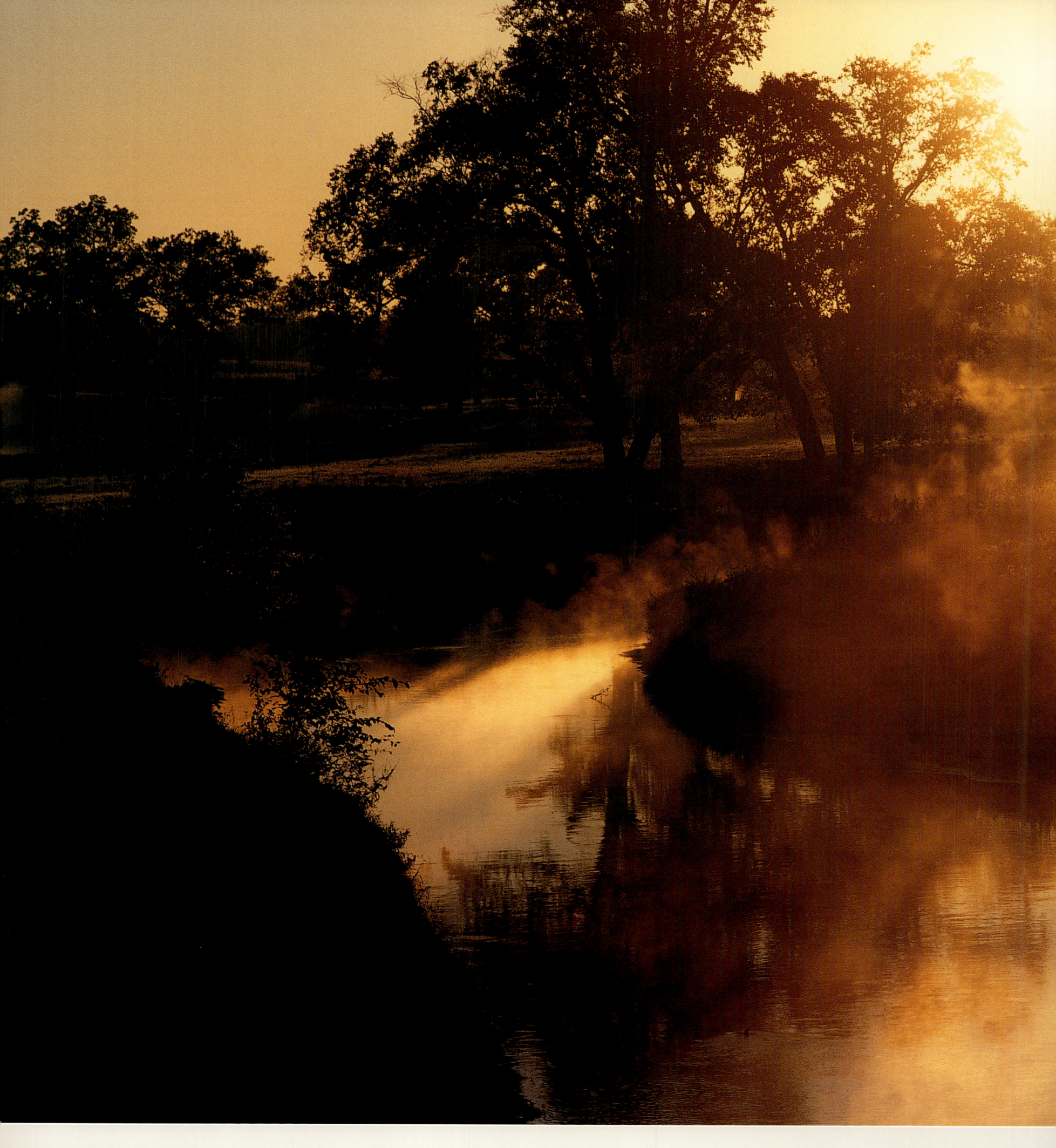

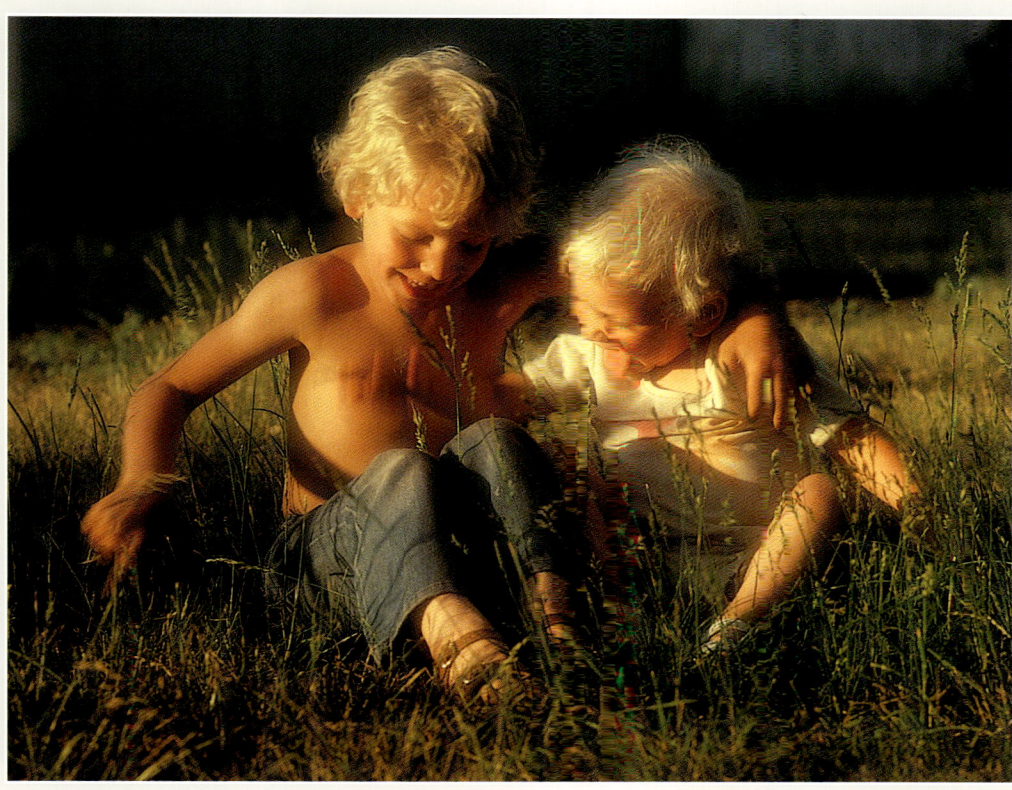

Above: Children enjoy a comfortable bed of grass and the warm summer sun. CURT MAAS

Left: Another beautiful sunset over Iowa waters. CURT MAAS

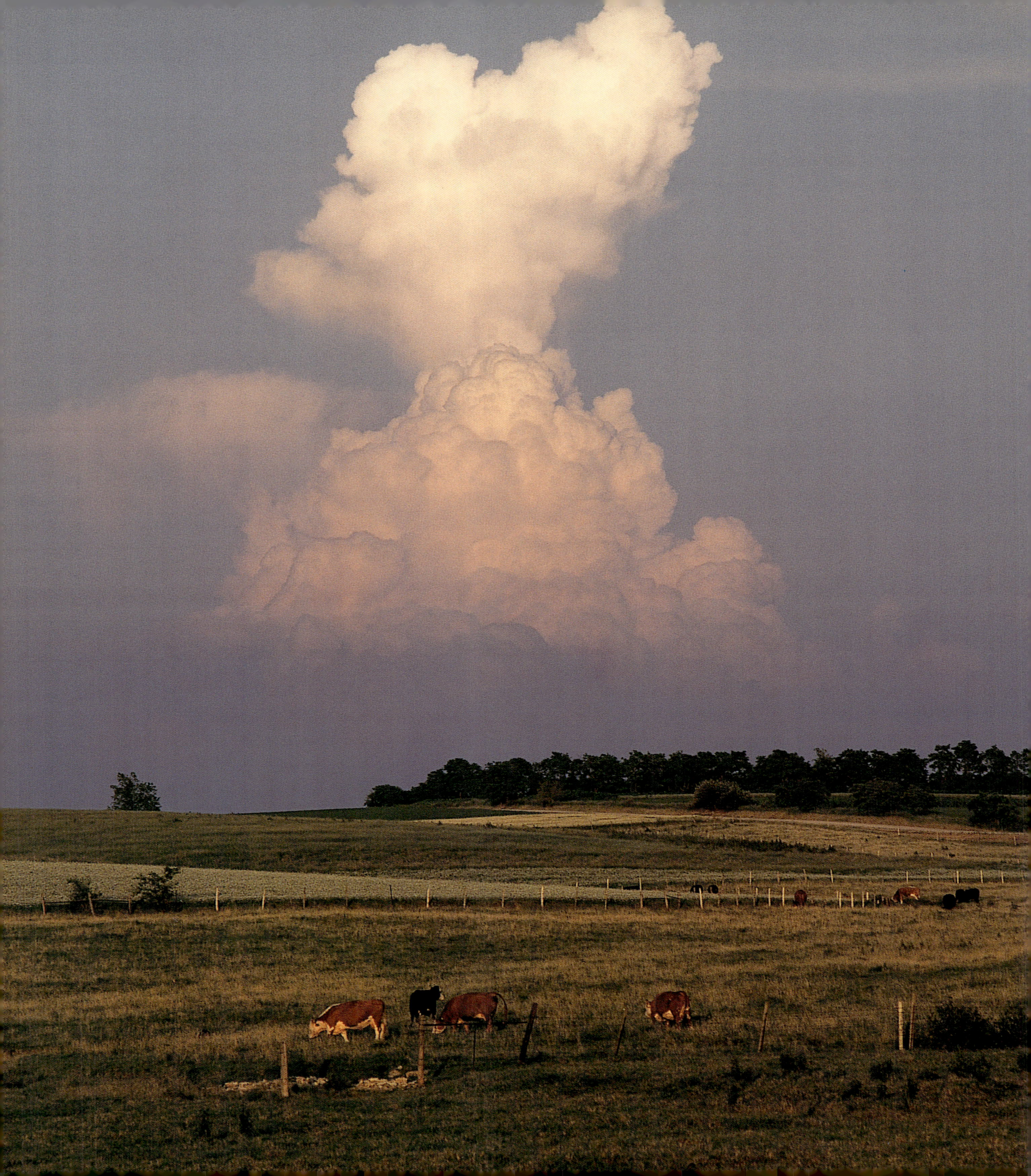

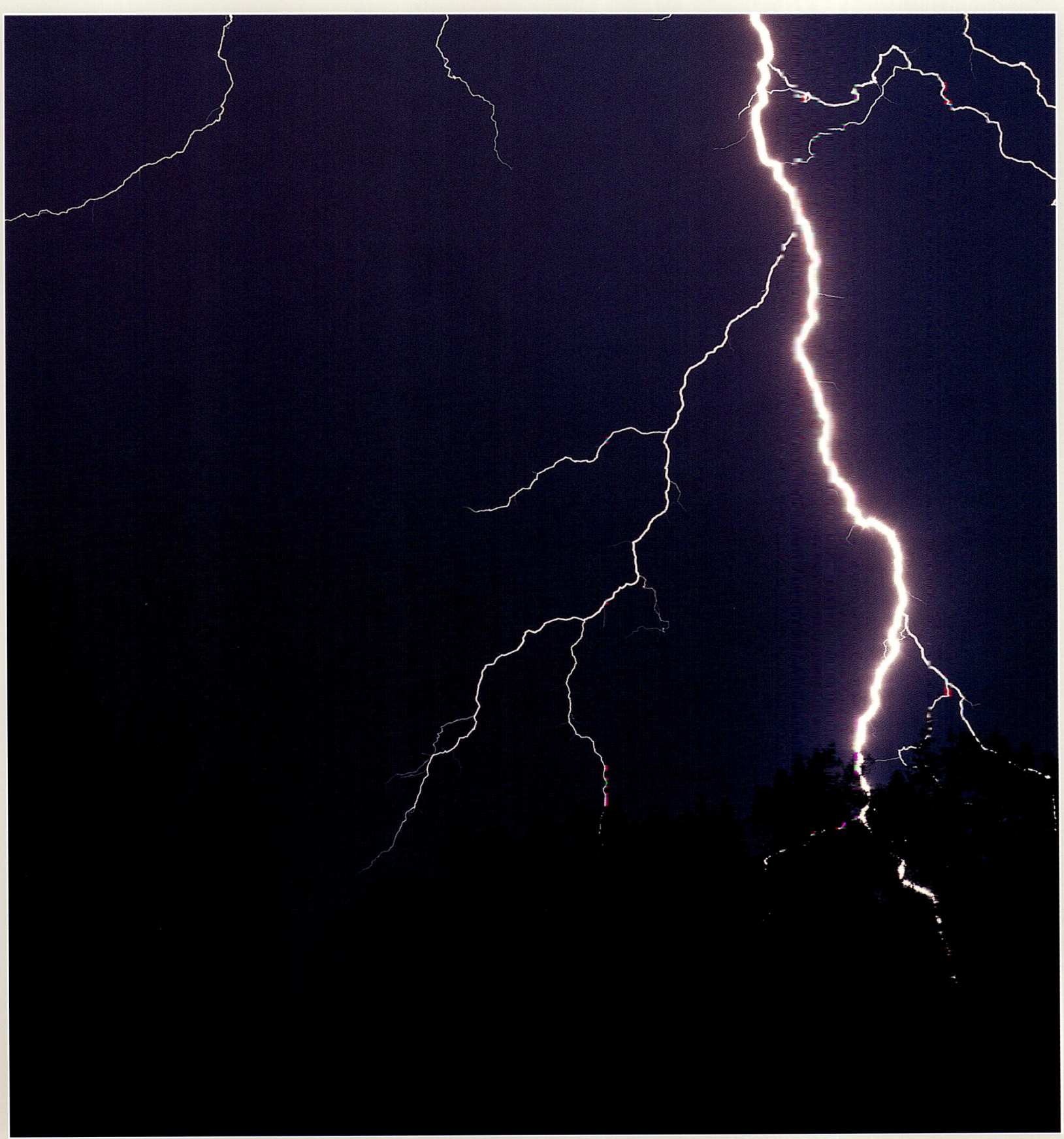

Above: Lightning from a dramatic summer storm. CURT MAAS

Facing page: A plains thunderhead looms over the countryside near Audubon. CURT MAAS

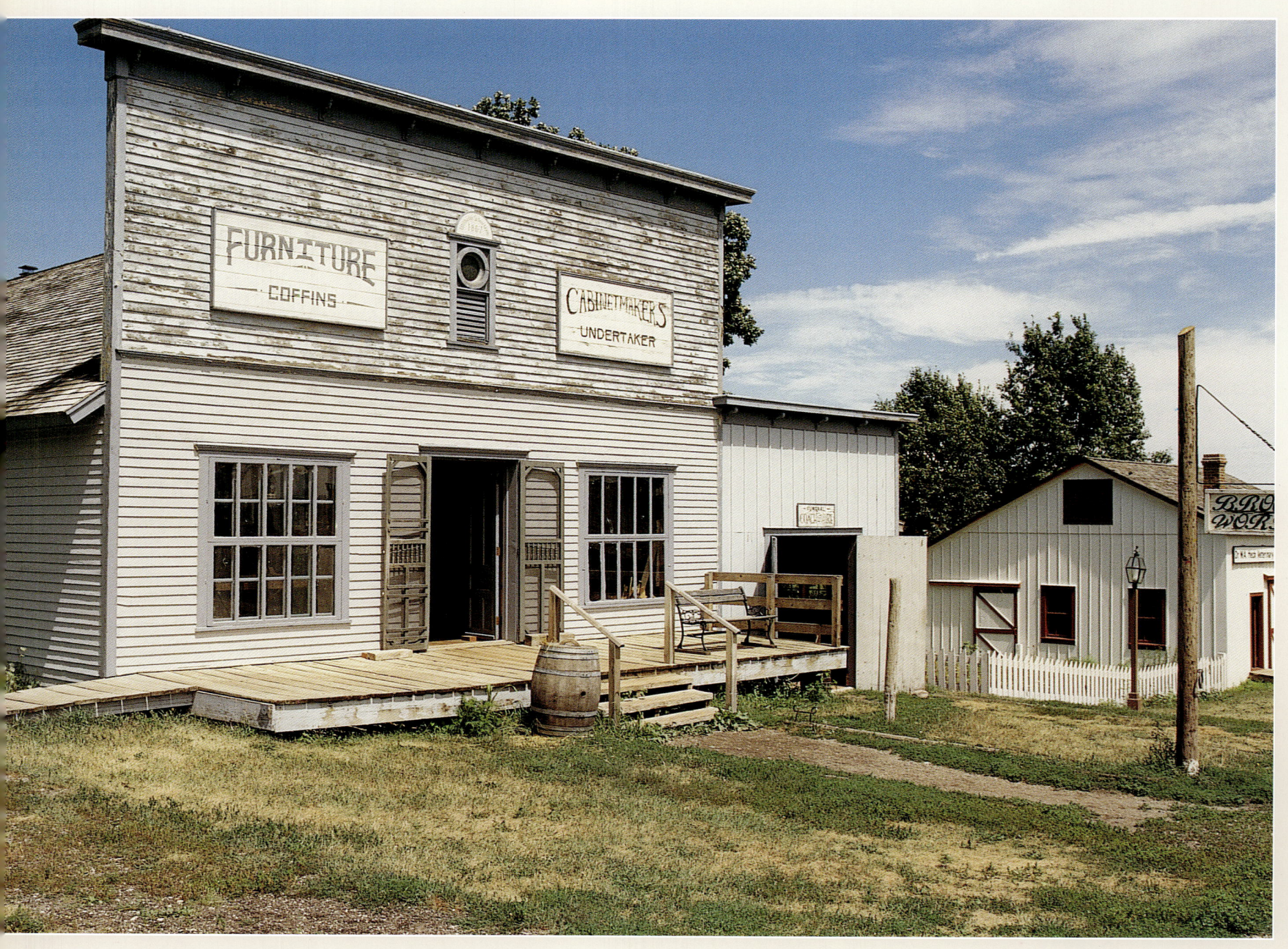

Above: A cabinetmaker's store, circa 1875, part of the Living History Farms in Urbandale. KENT FOSTER

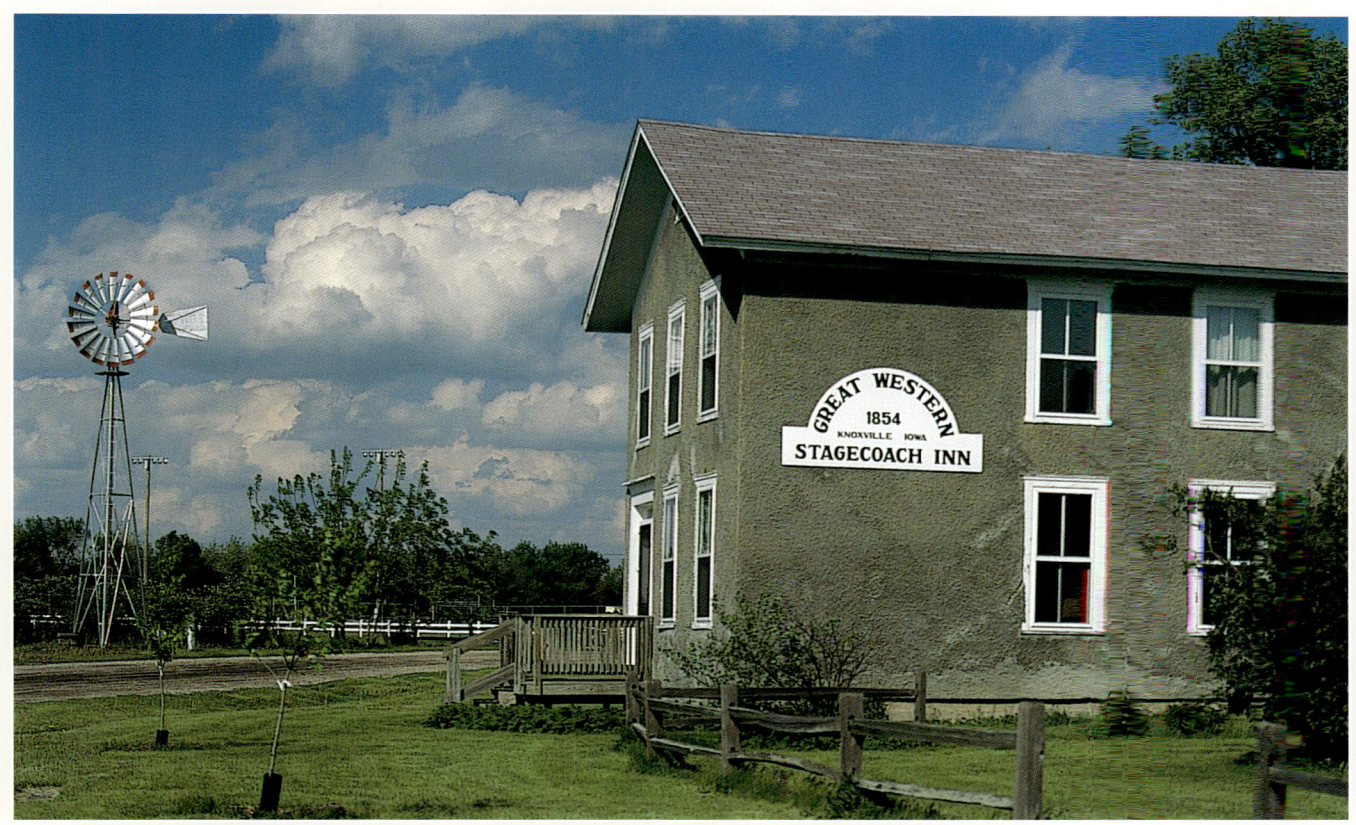

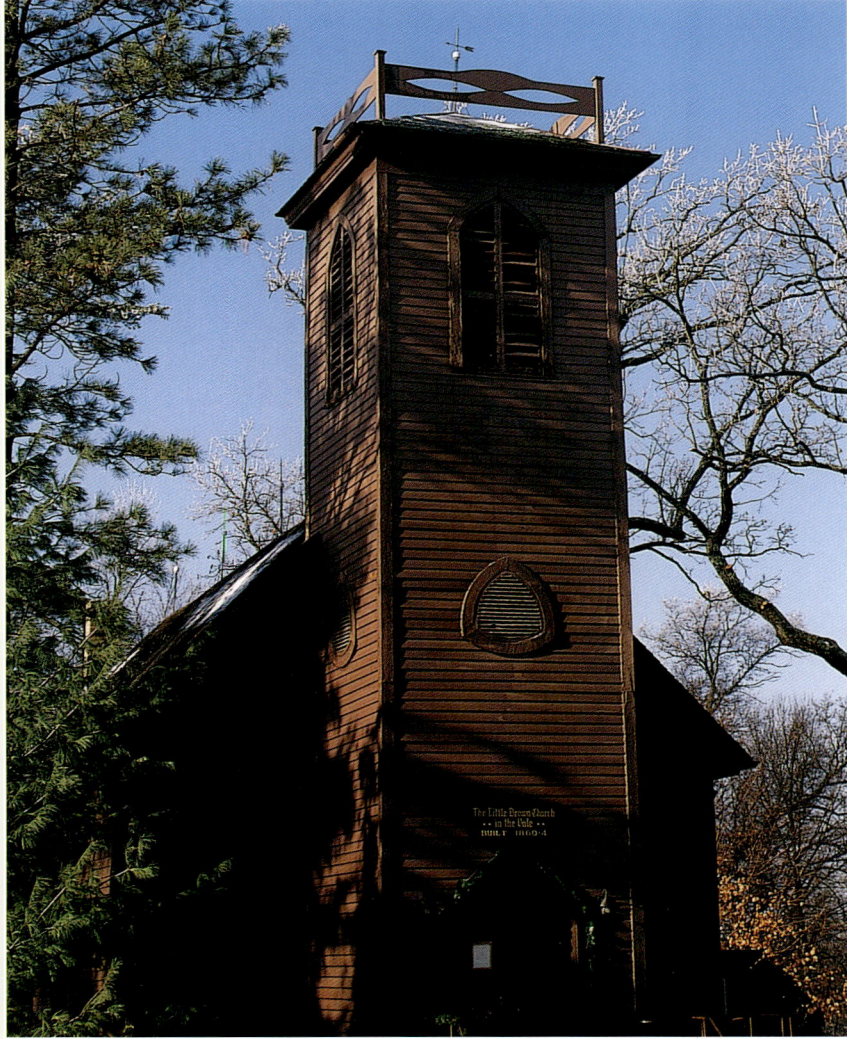

Above: The Great Western Stage Coach Inn, in addition to a schoolhouse, general store, cabin, church, railroad station, and museum, is located at the Marion County Historical Village in Knoxville. KENT FOSTER

Left: The Little Brown Church in Vale was constructed from 1860 to 1862 almost entirely through donated time and material; the least-expensive paint at the time was a brown mineral paint, and the parishioners have insisted on keeping the traditional color. LARSH K. BRISTOL

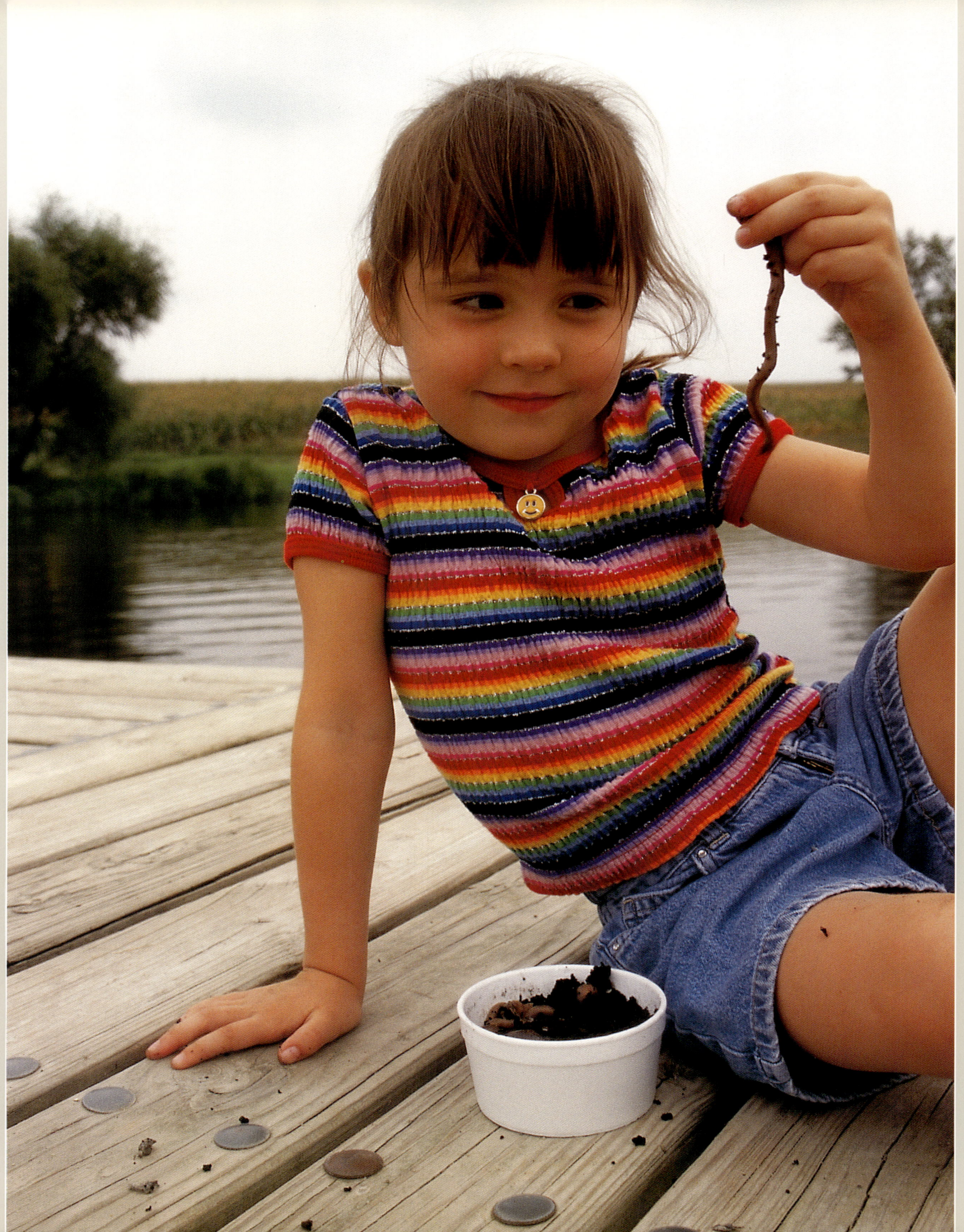

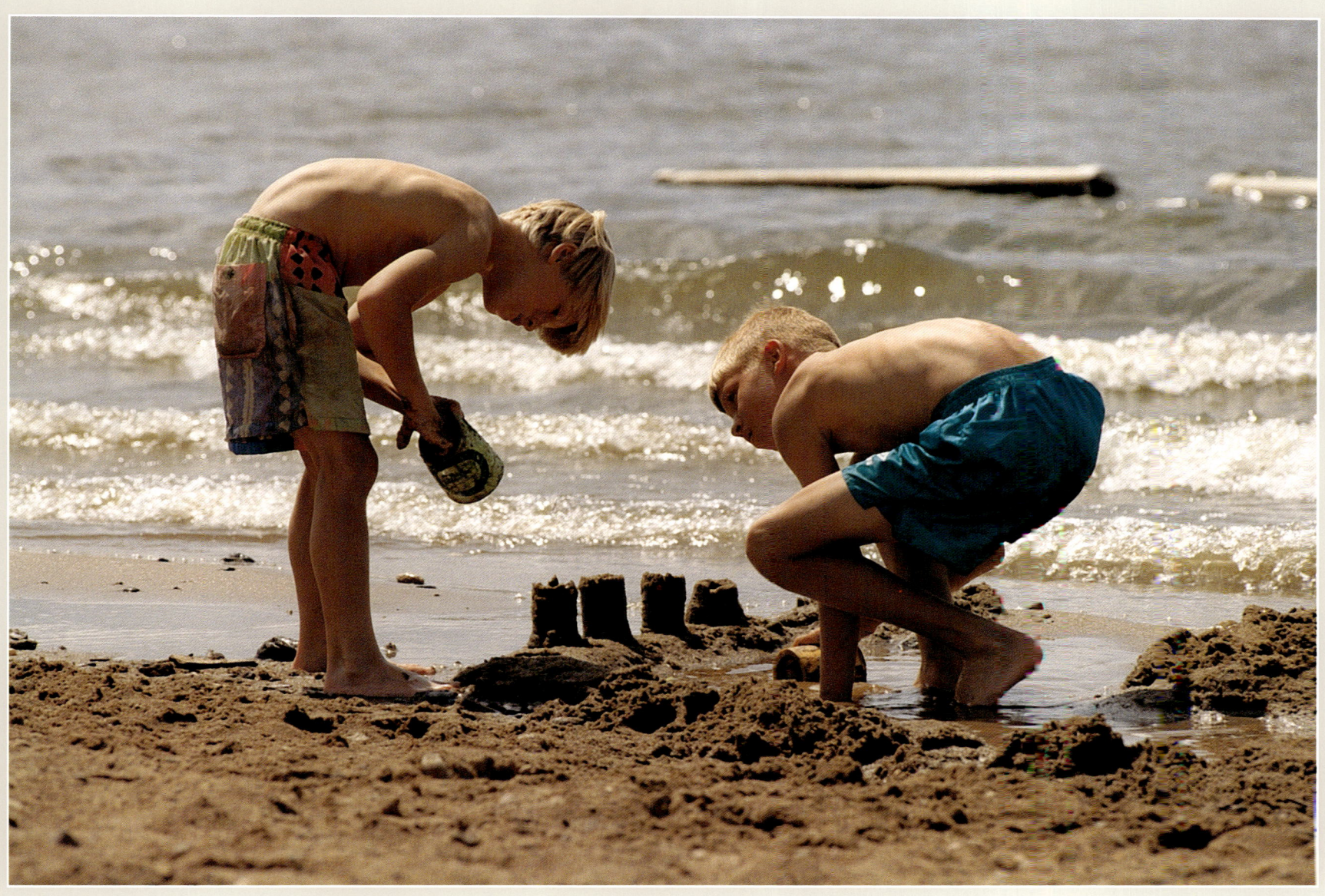

Above: Building a sand castle on the shores of Saylorville Lake, between Polk City and Johnston. CURT MAAS

Facing page: She's not squirmy when it comes to worms. CURT MAAS

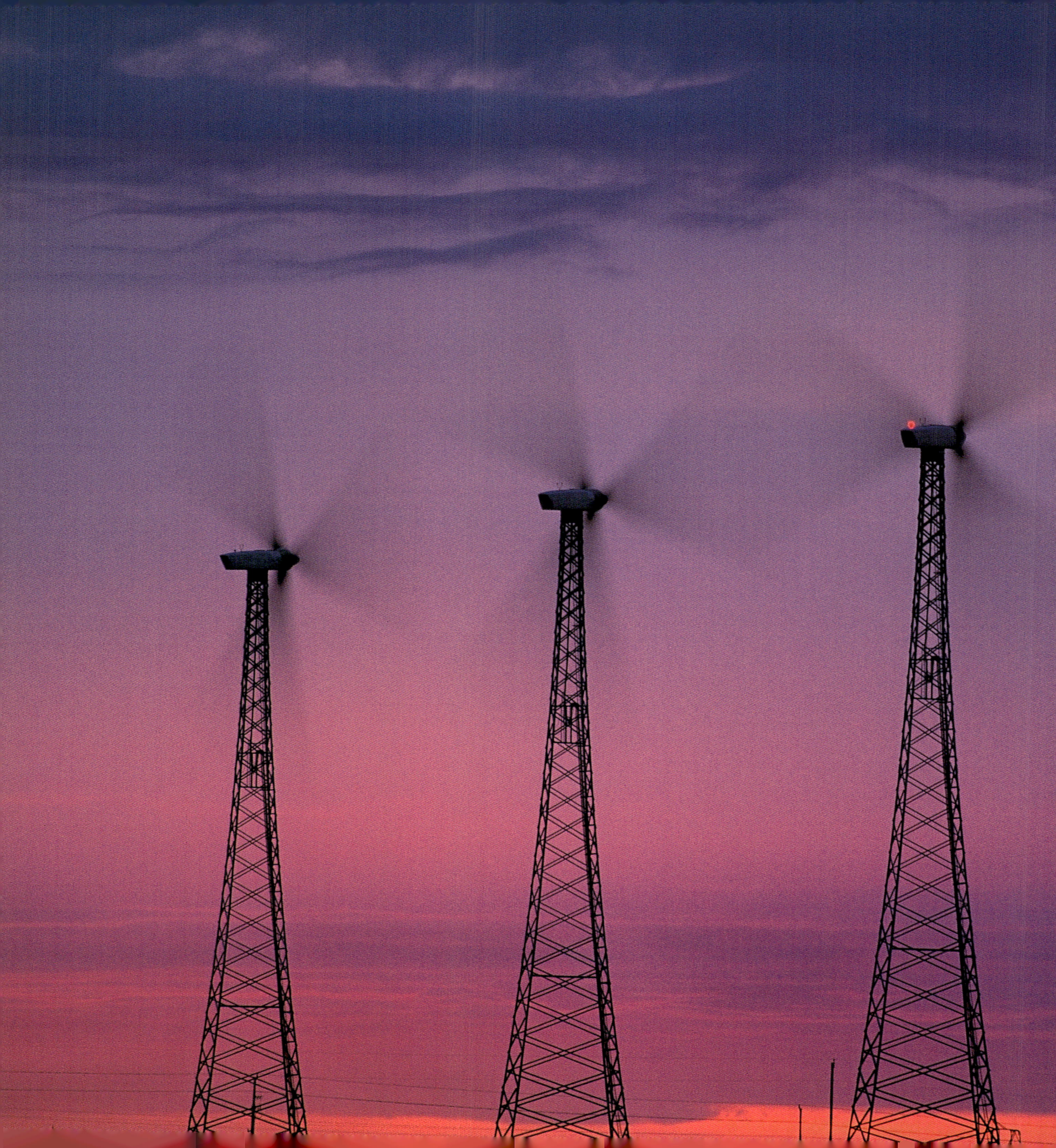

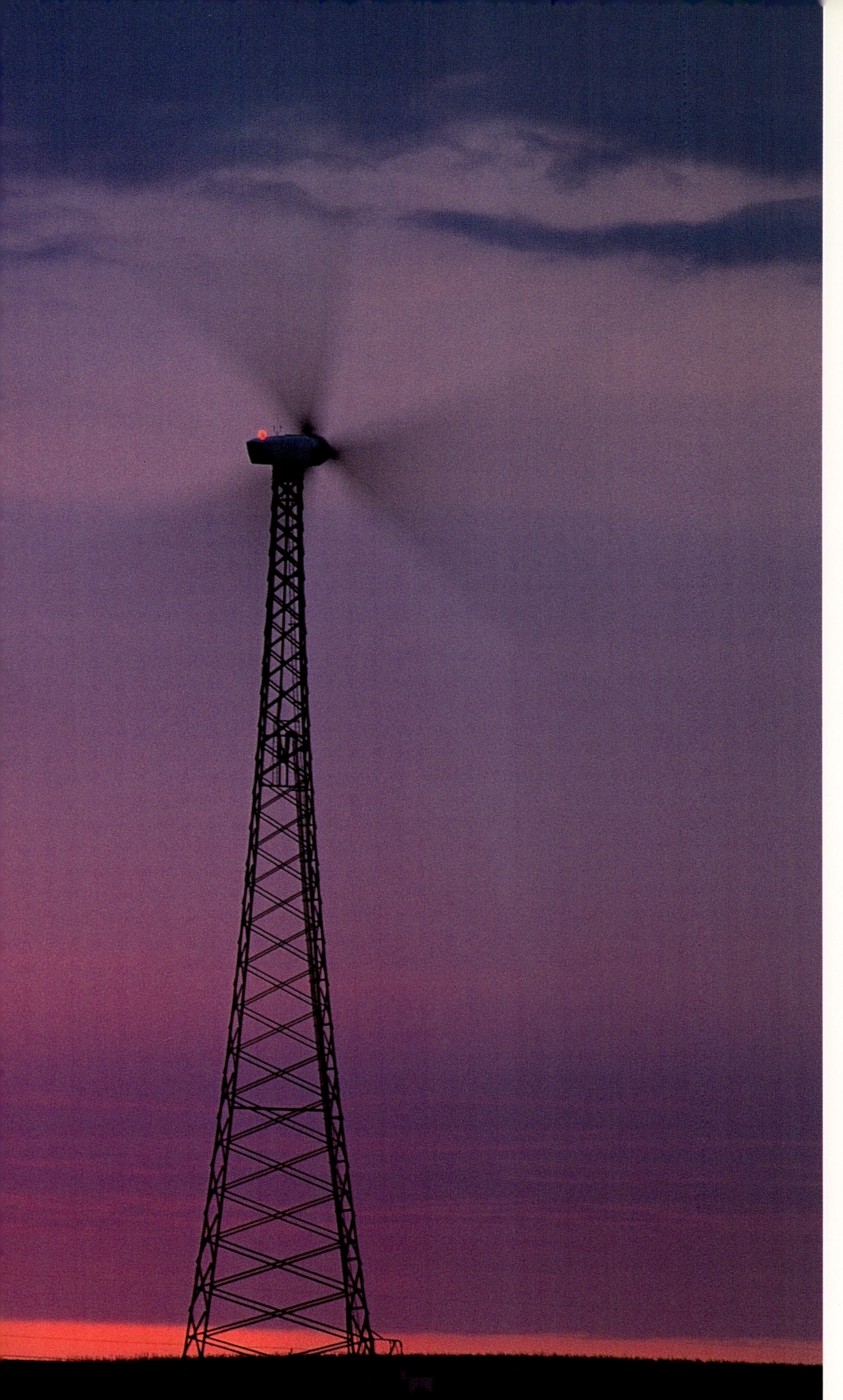

With hundreds of wind turbines, Iowa is one of the leading states in wind power production. KENT FOSTER

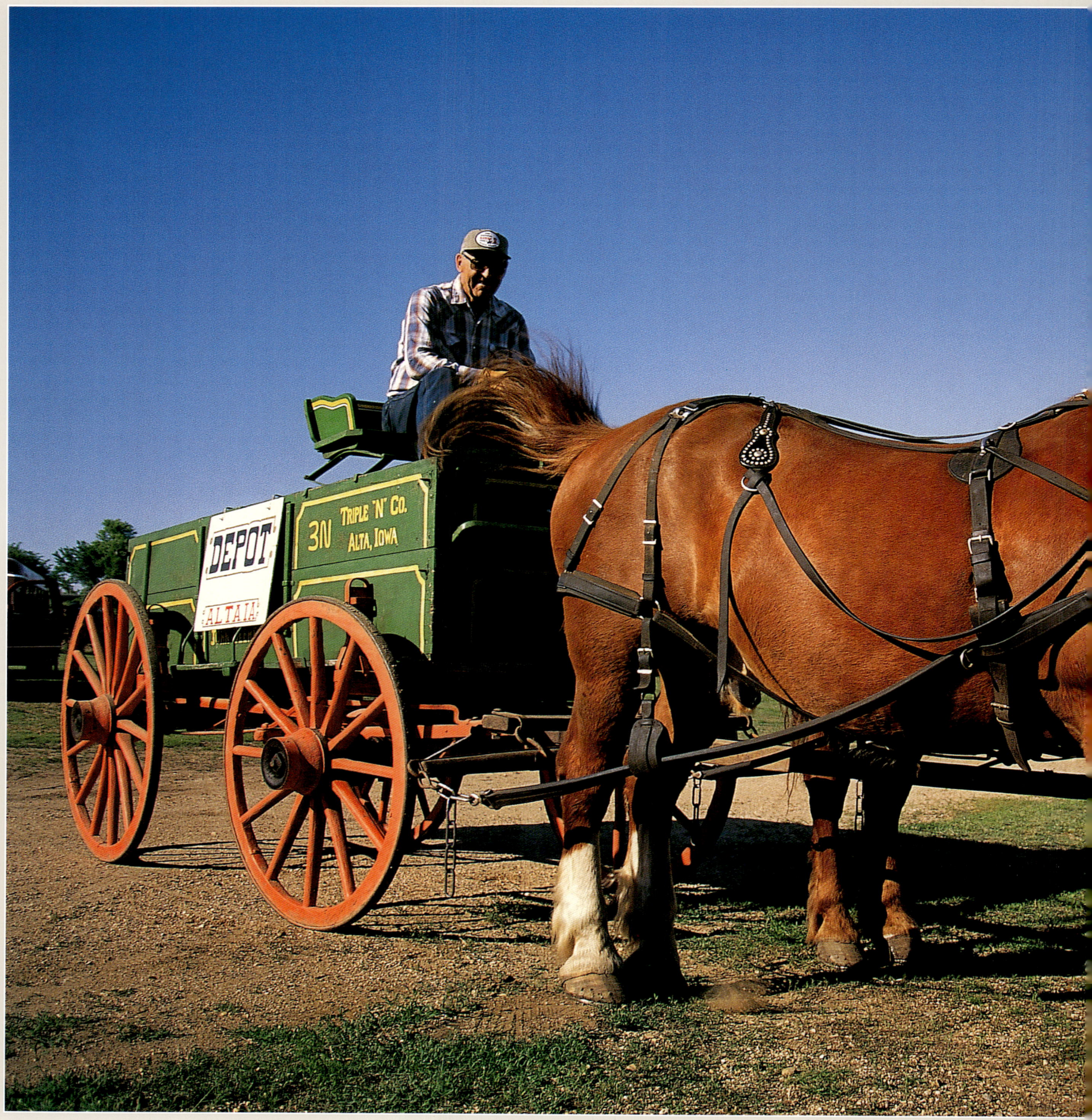

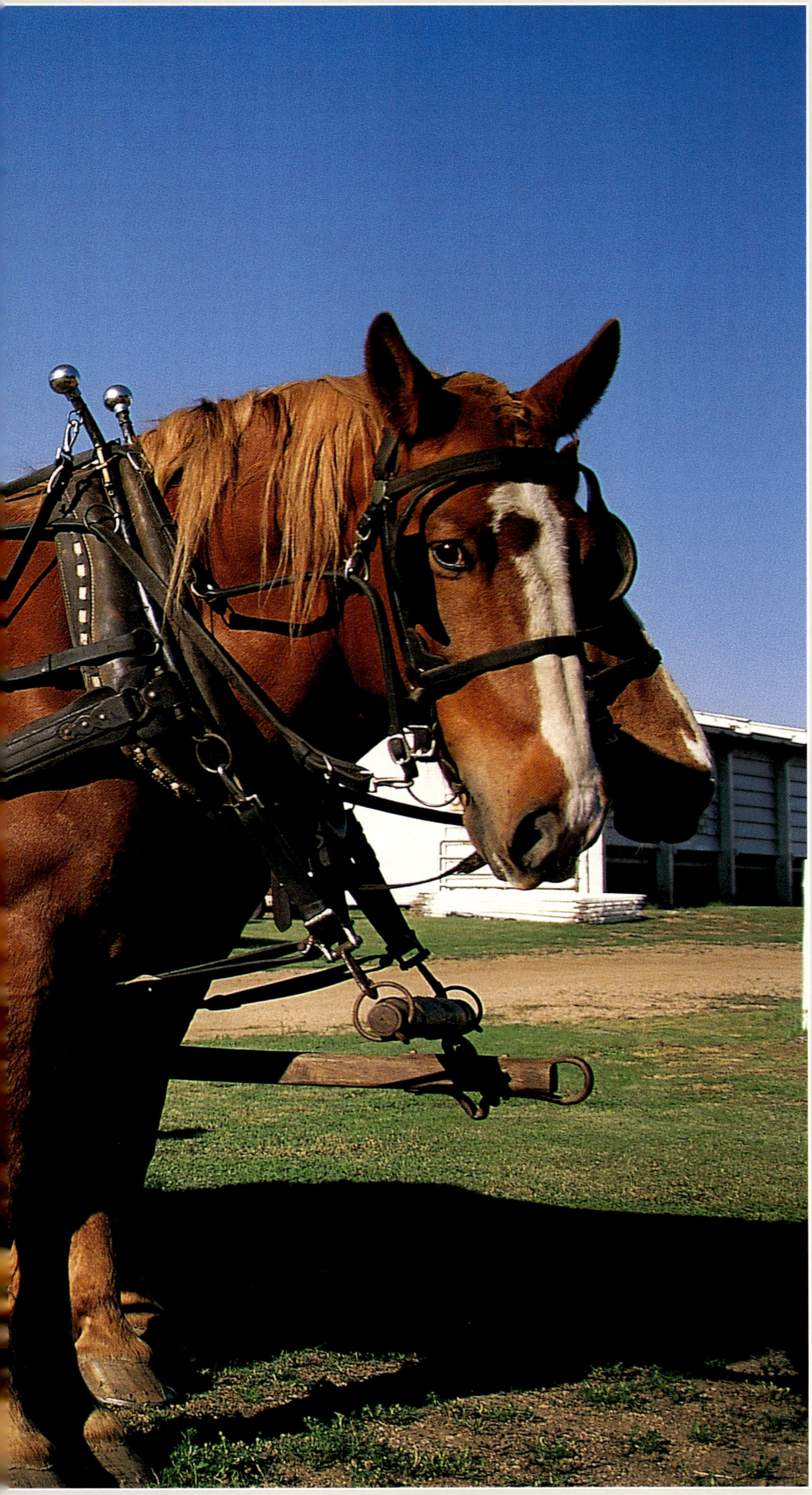

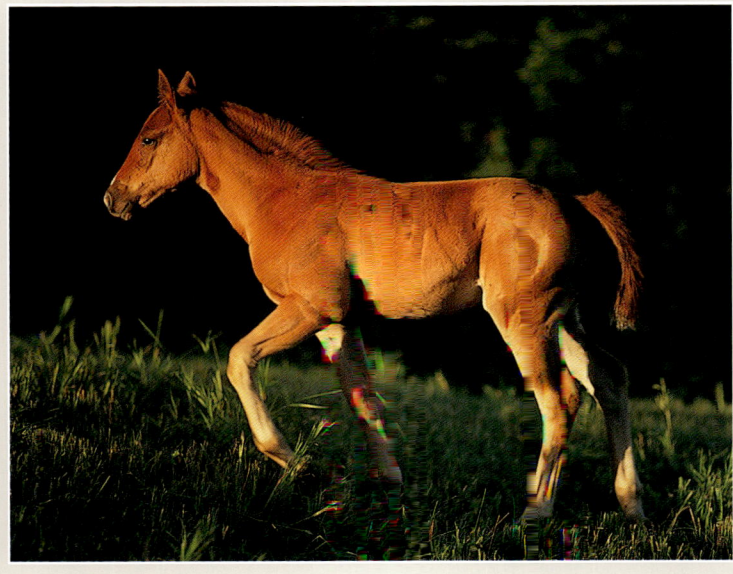

Above: A registered quarter-horse foal in evening light. KENT FOSTER

Left: A draft-horse hitch team shows its stuff at a rodeo in Cherokee. KENT FOSTER

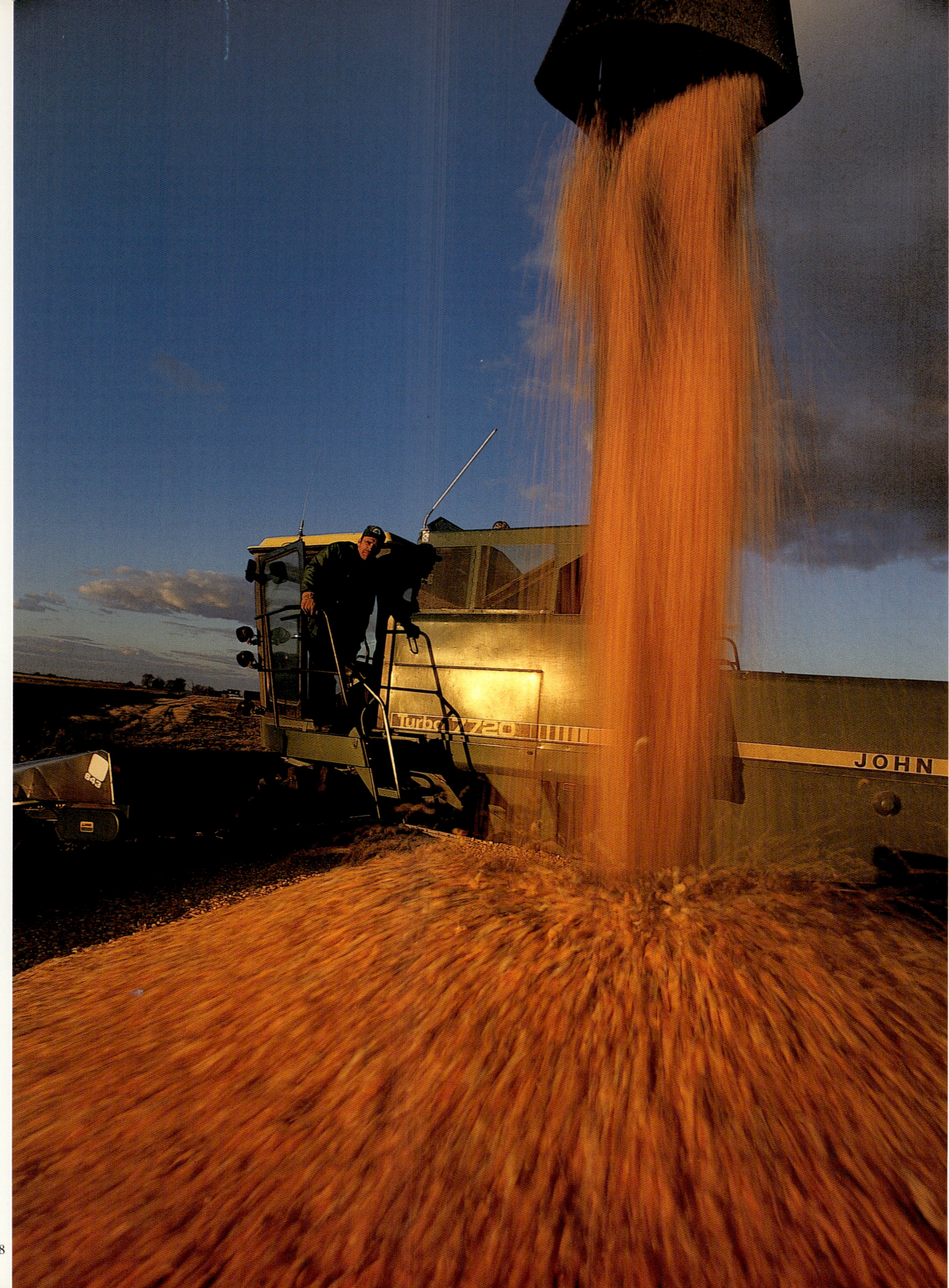

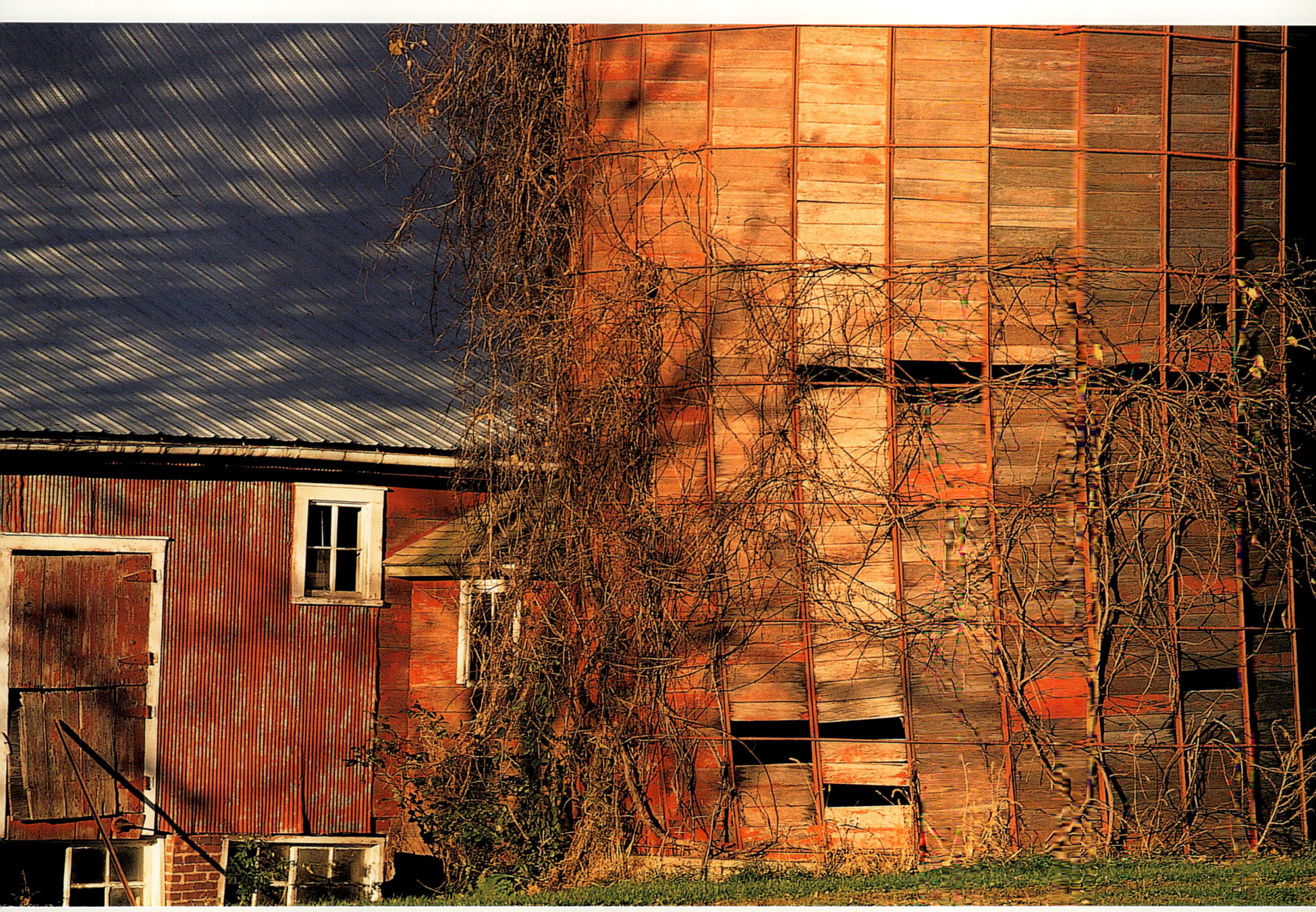

Above: An old barn and silo succumb to time and weather in rural Iowa. LARSH K. BRISTOL

Facing page: Farmer augering corn into a grain wagon near Humeston. CURT MAAS

Above: A Hereford cow moves through the early morning fog near Monona. LARSH K. BRISTOL

Facing page: The oldest church west of the Mississippi, Wexford Church provides a moonlit backdrop to headstones in Harpers Ferry. LARSH K. BRISTOL

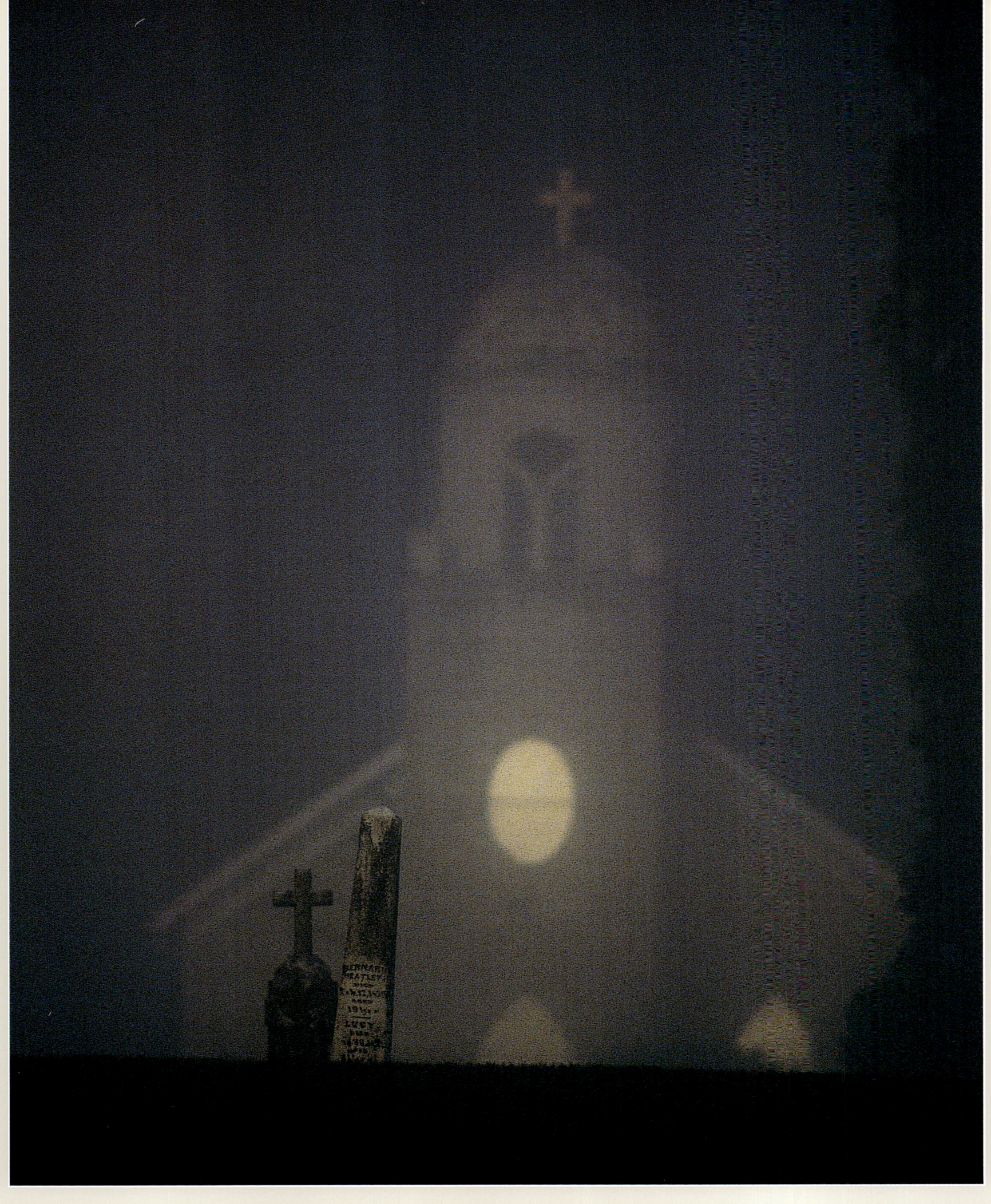

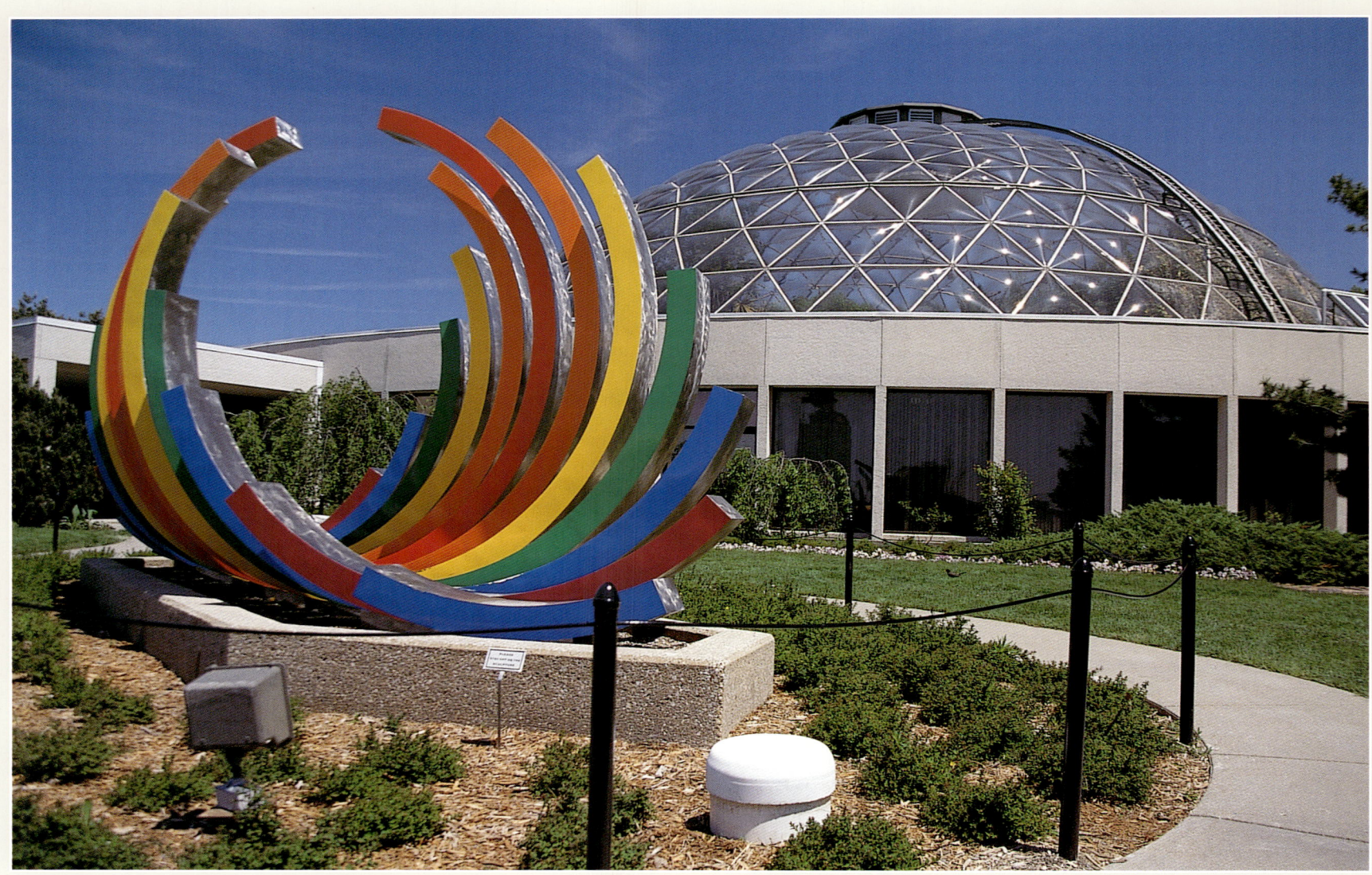

Above: Entrance to the Des Moines Botanical Center, a fourteen-acre facility on the east bank of the Des Moines River. KENT FOSTER

Facing page: The unusual flowers of the lollipop plant, this one at the Des Moines Botanical Center, open in early spring to midsummer. KENT FOSTER

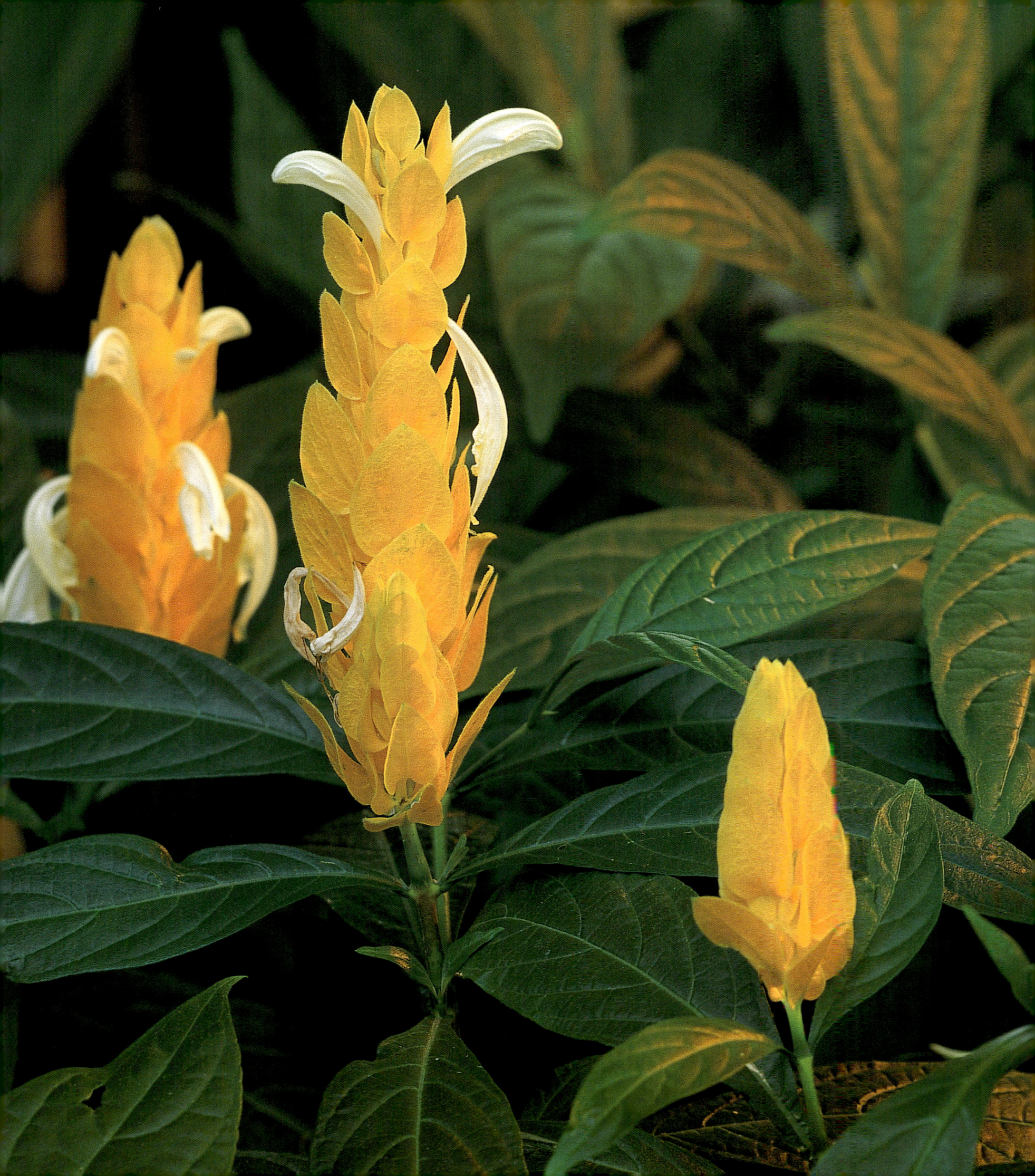

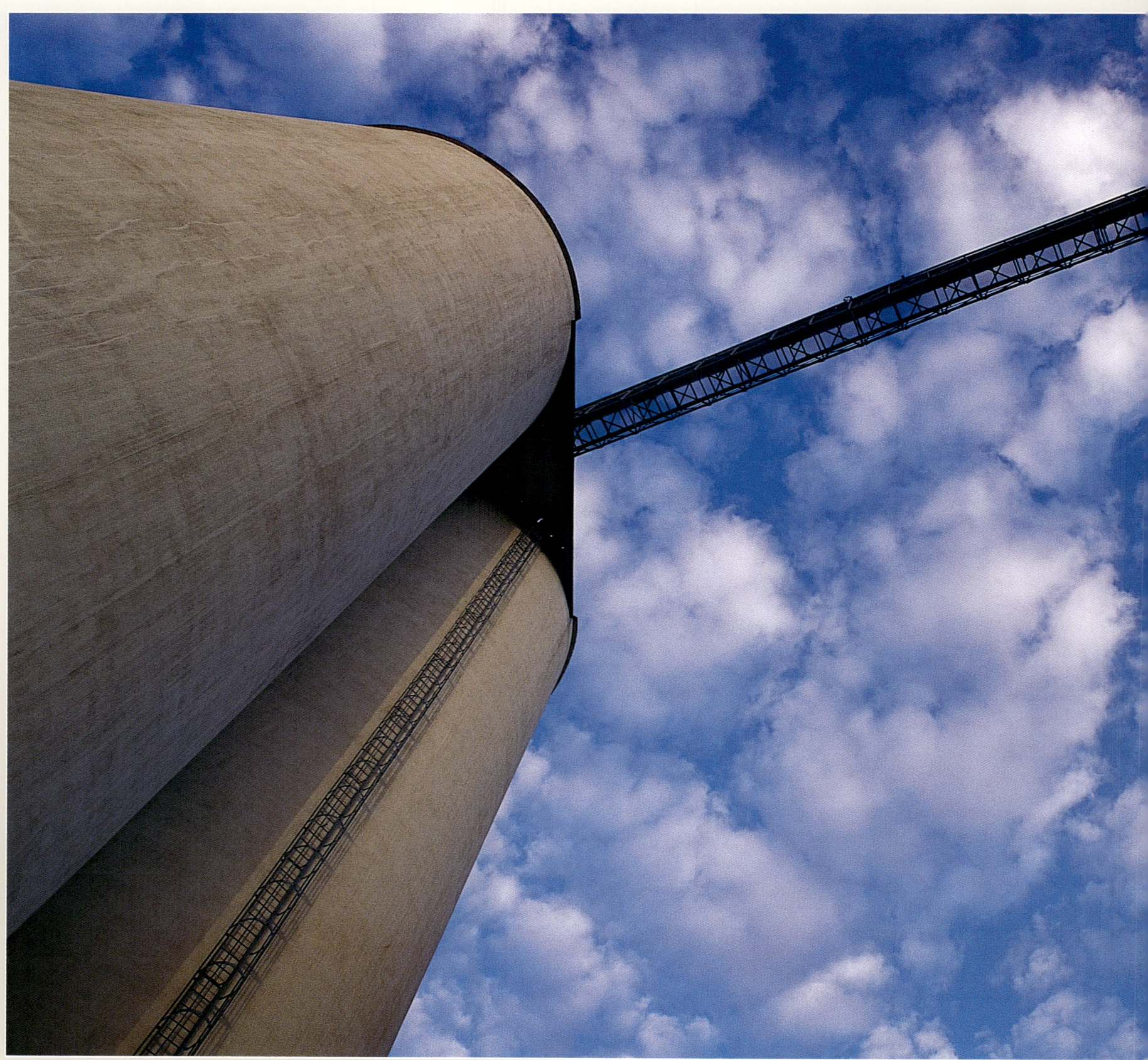

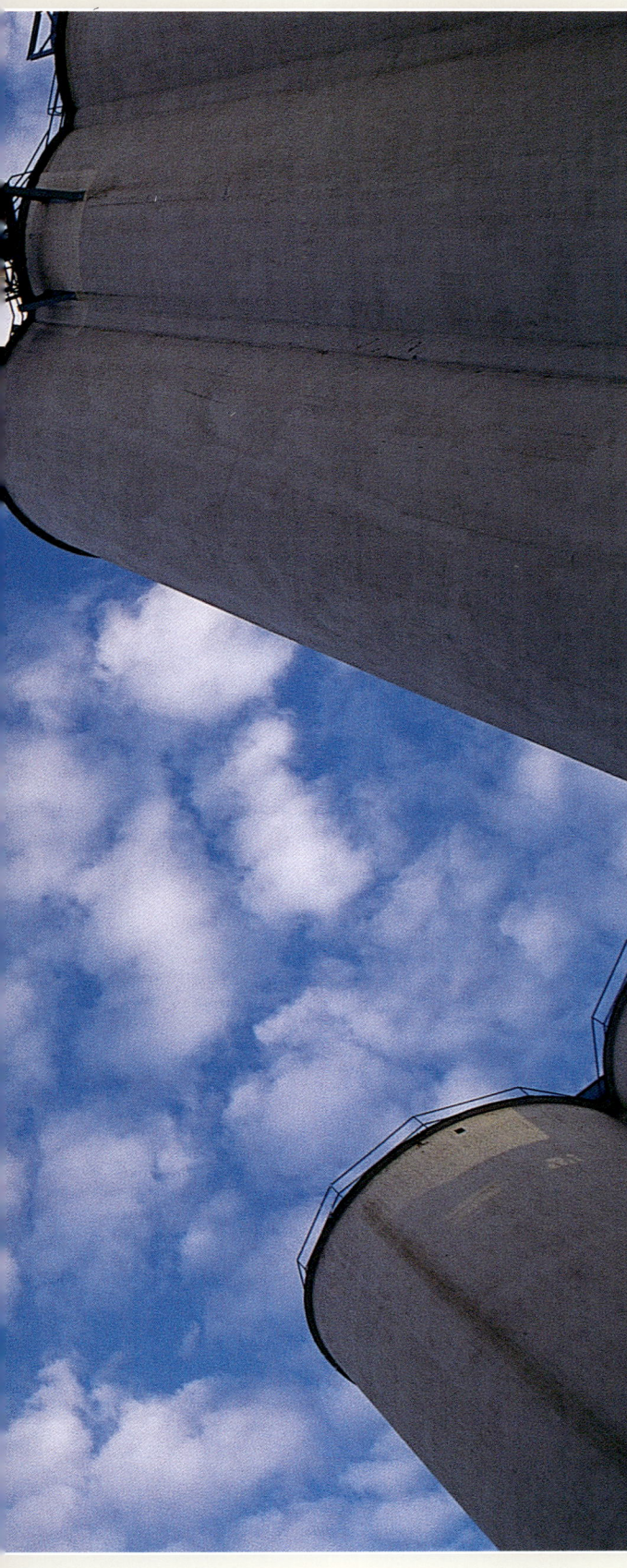

Left: An interesting contrast of soft clouds and linear architecture in Fort Dodge.
LARSH K. BRISTOL

Below: A soy bean seedling emerges from the soil into light. CURT MAAS

Bottom: In Woodward, a farmer sprays herbicide on early corn. CURT MAAS

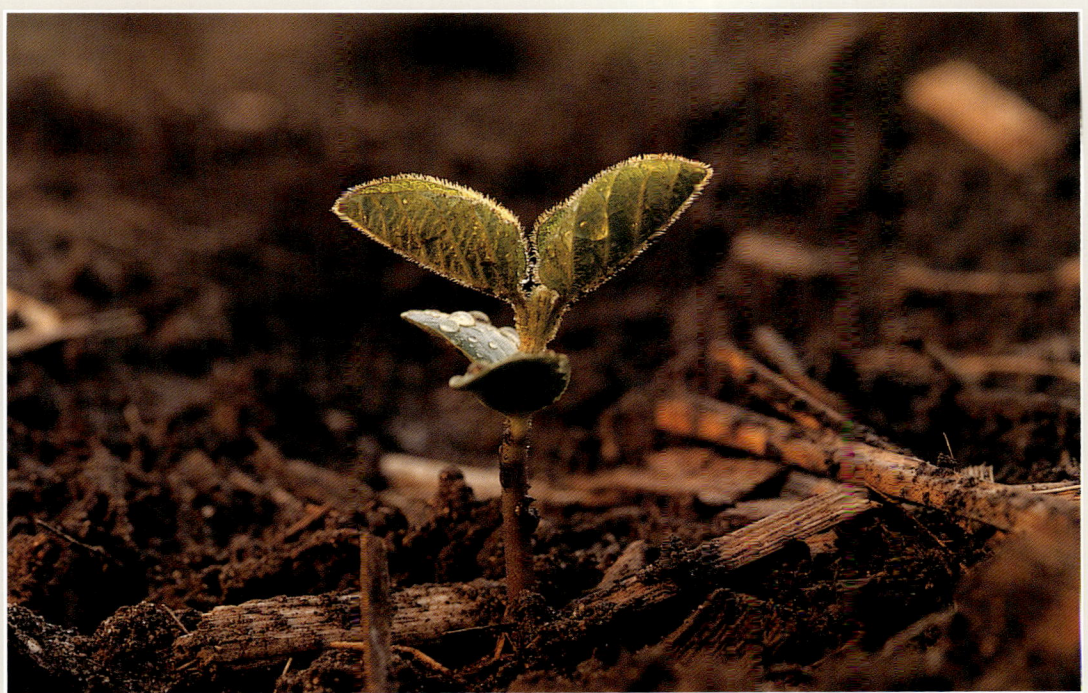

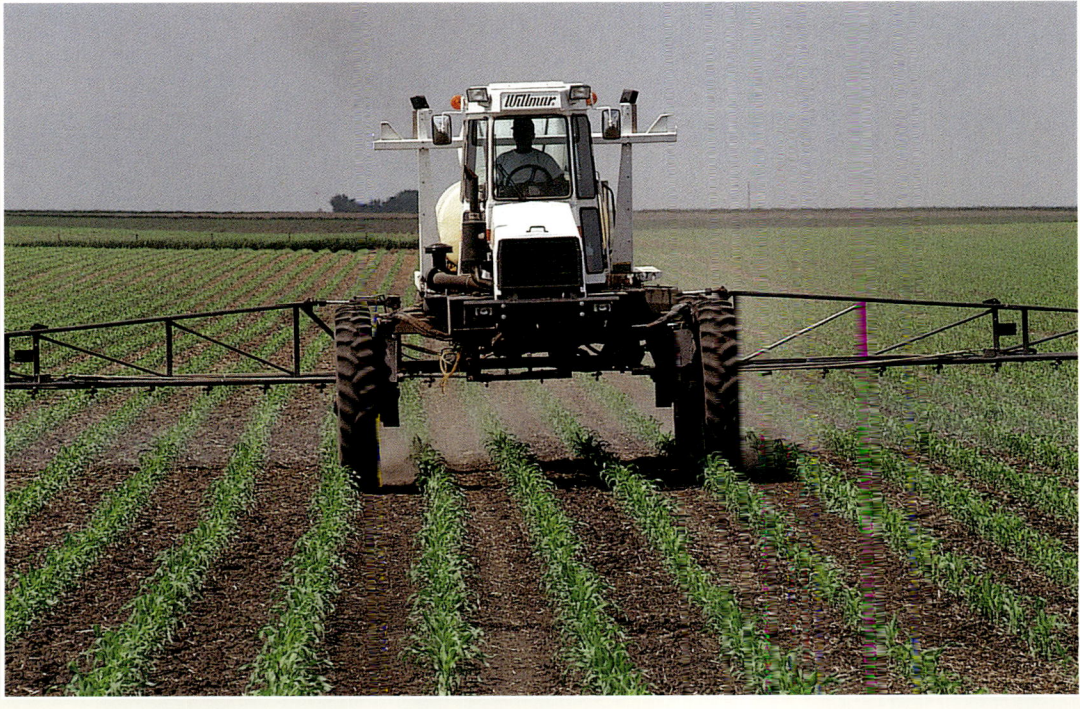

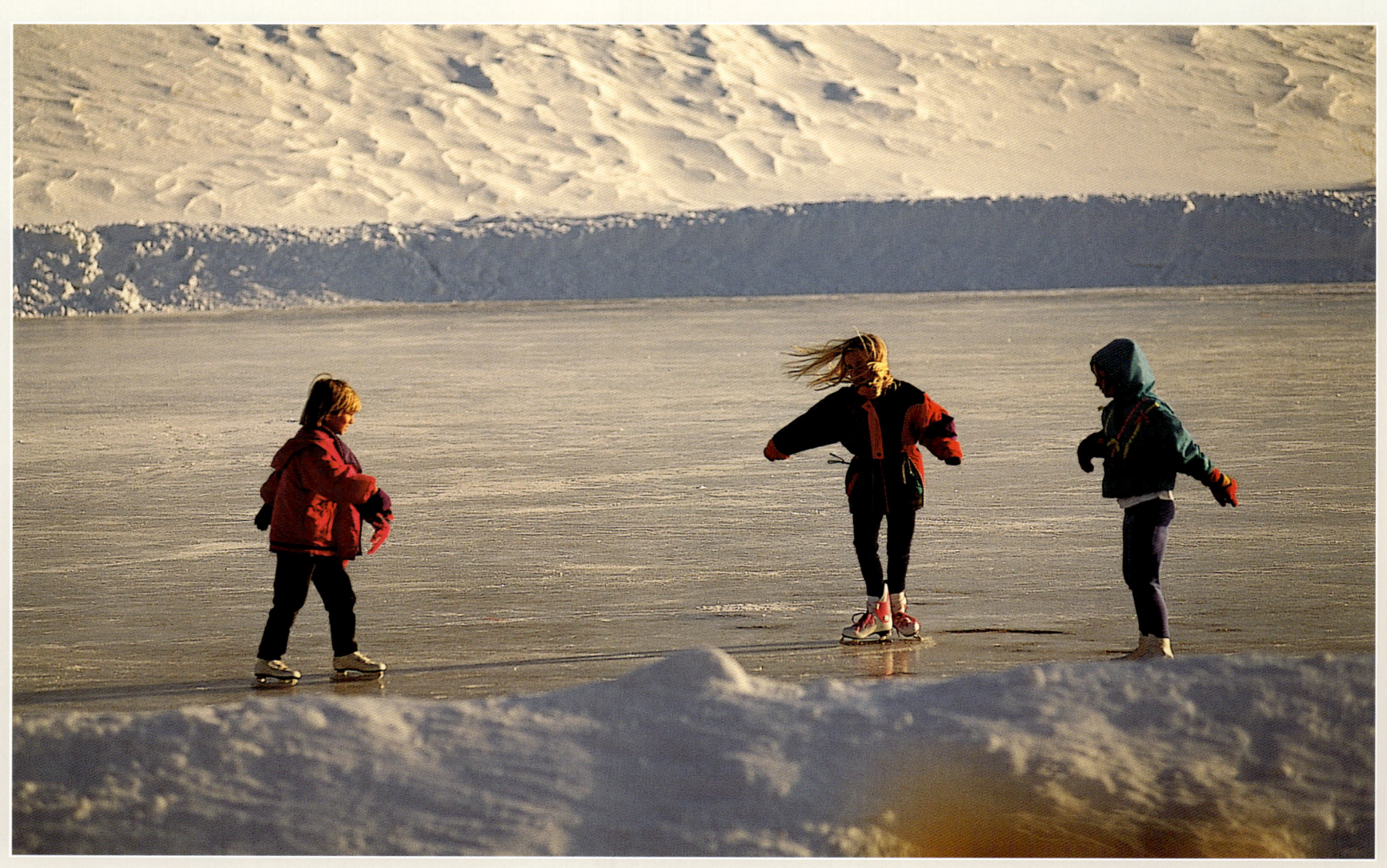
Above: Future champions practice their ice-skating moves in Decorah. LARSH K. BRISTOL

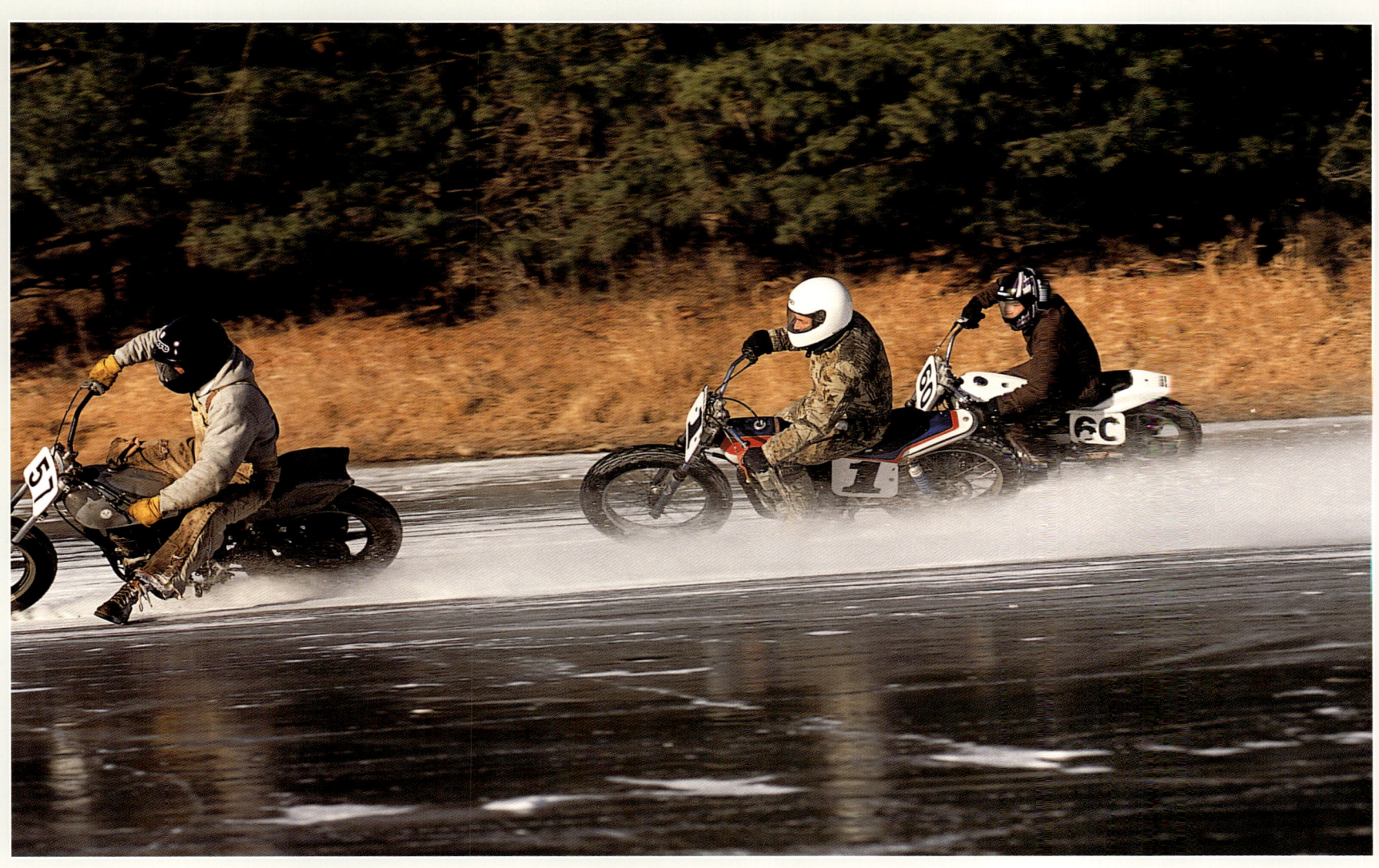
Above: In Castalia, a new winter sport has emerged: motorcycle racing on ice. LARSH K. BRISTOL

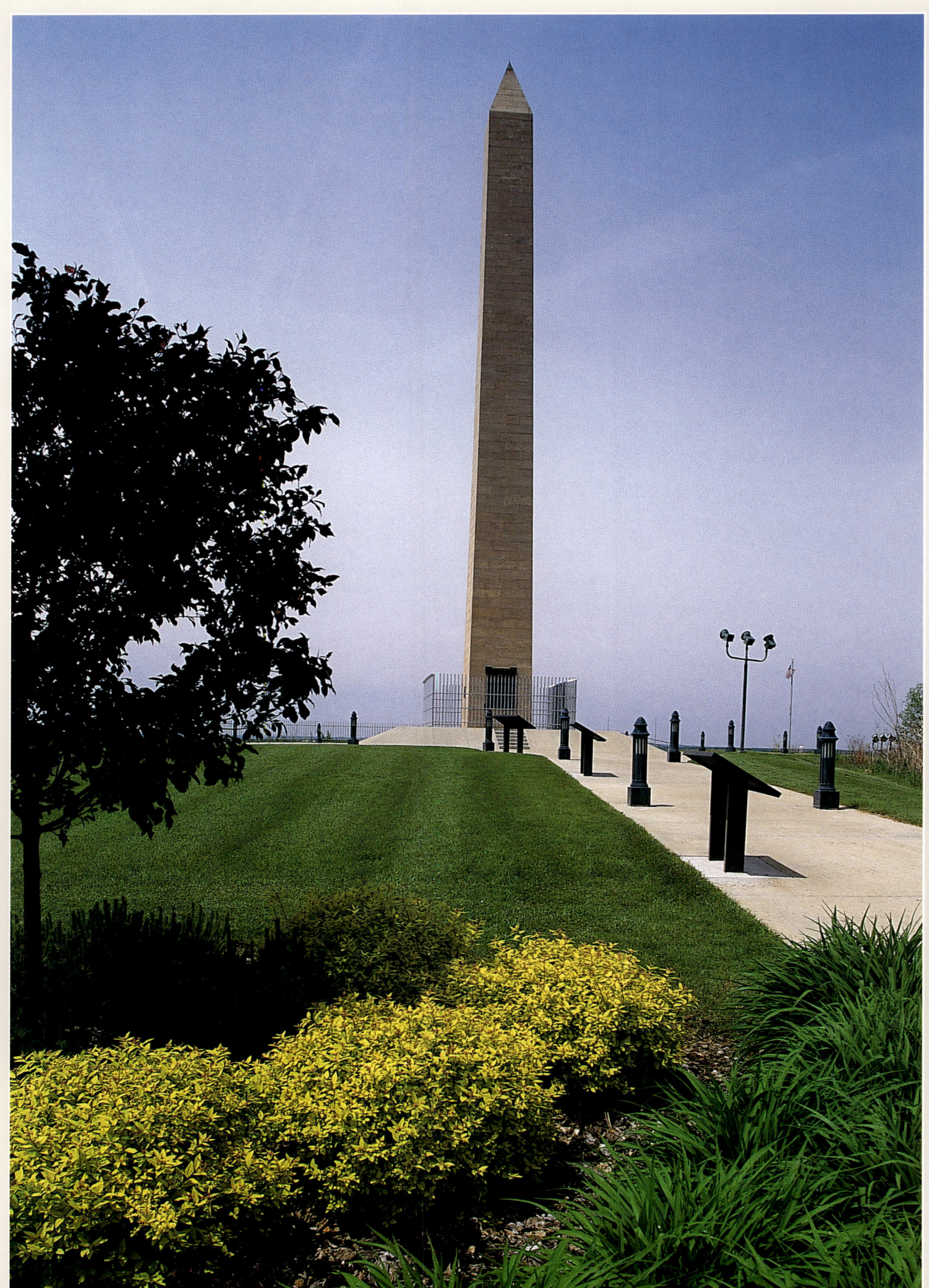

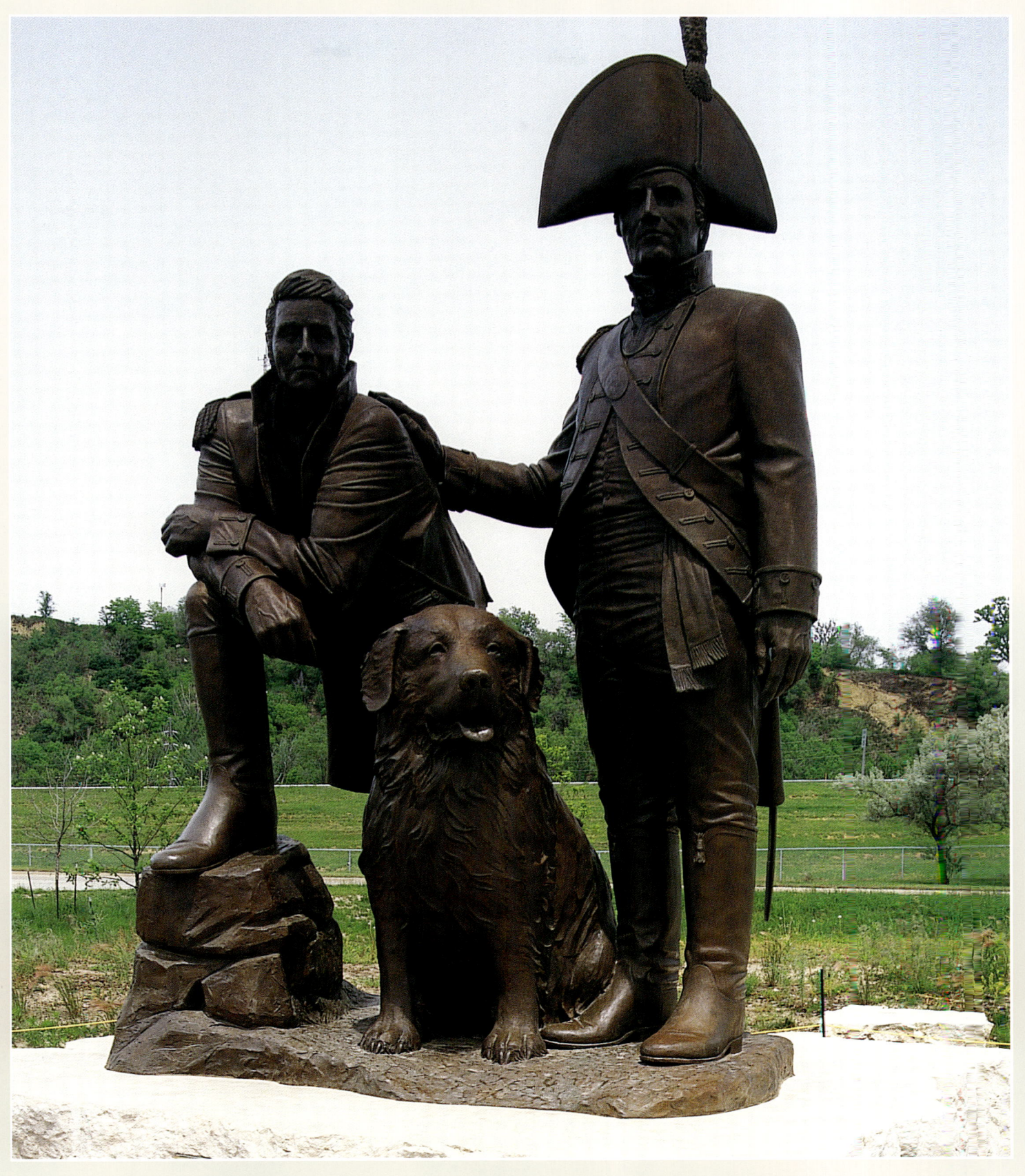

Above: Statue of Captains Meriwether Lewis and William Clark and Seaman, the only canine member of the Corps of Discovery, at the Sioux City Visitor Center. LARSH K. BRISTOL

Facing page: Sergeant Floyd Monument in Sioux City. Floyd was the only member of the Corps of Discovery to die during the journey. LARSH K. BRISTOL

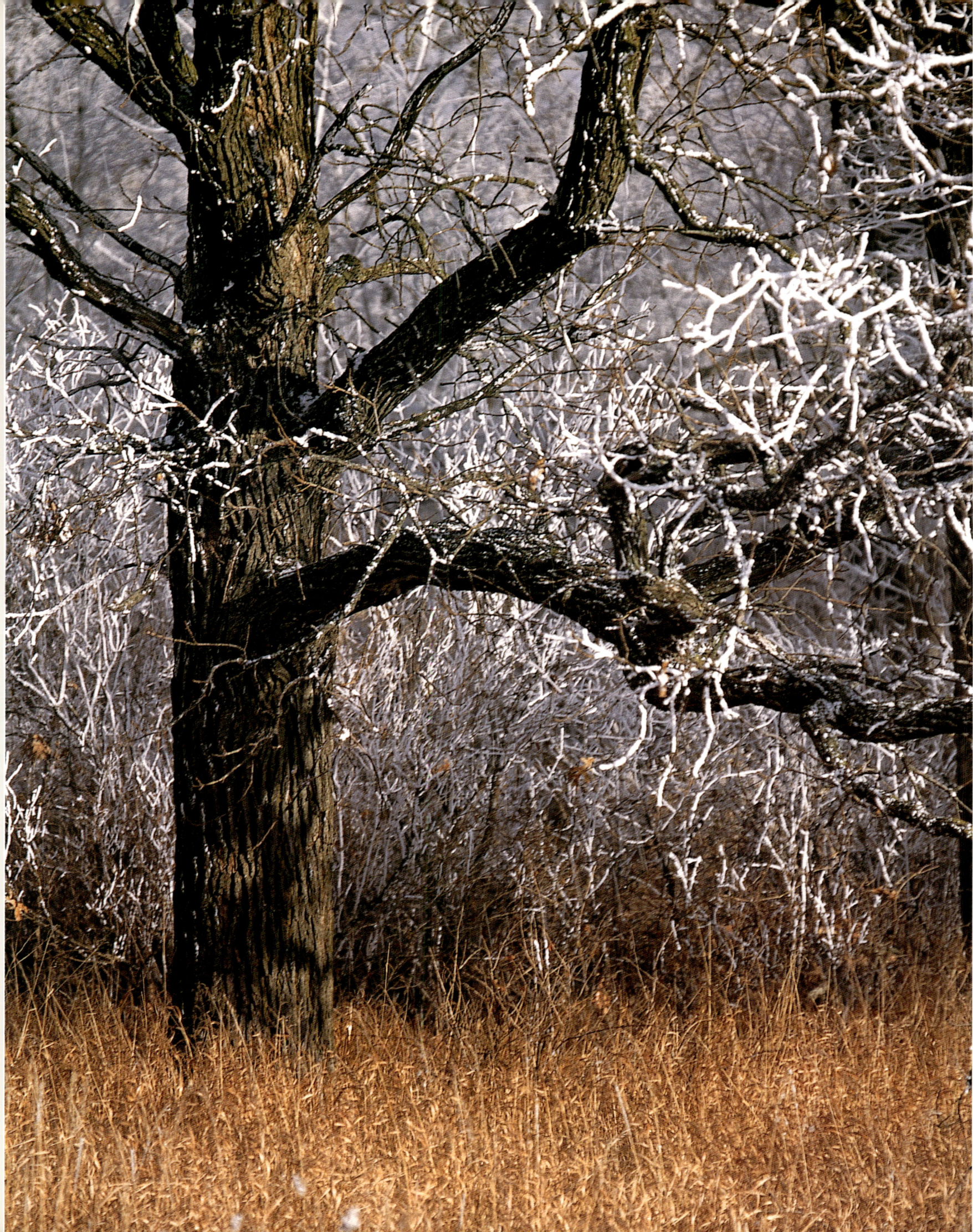

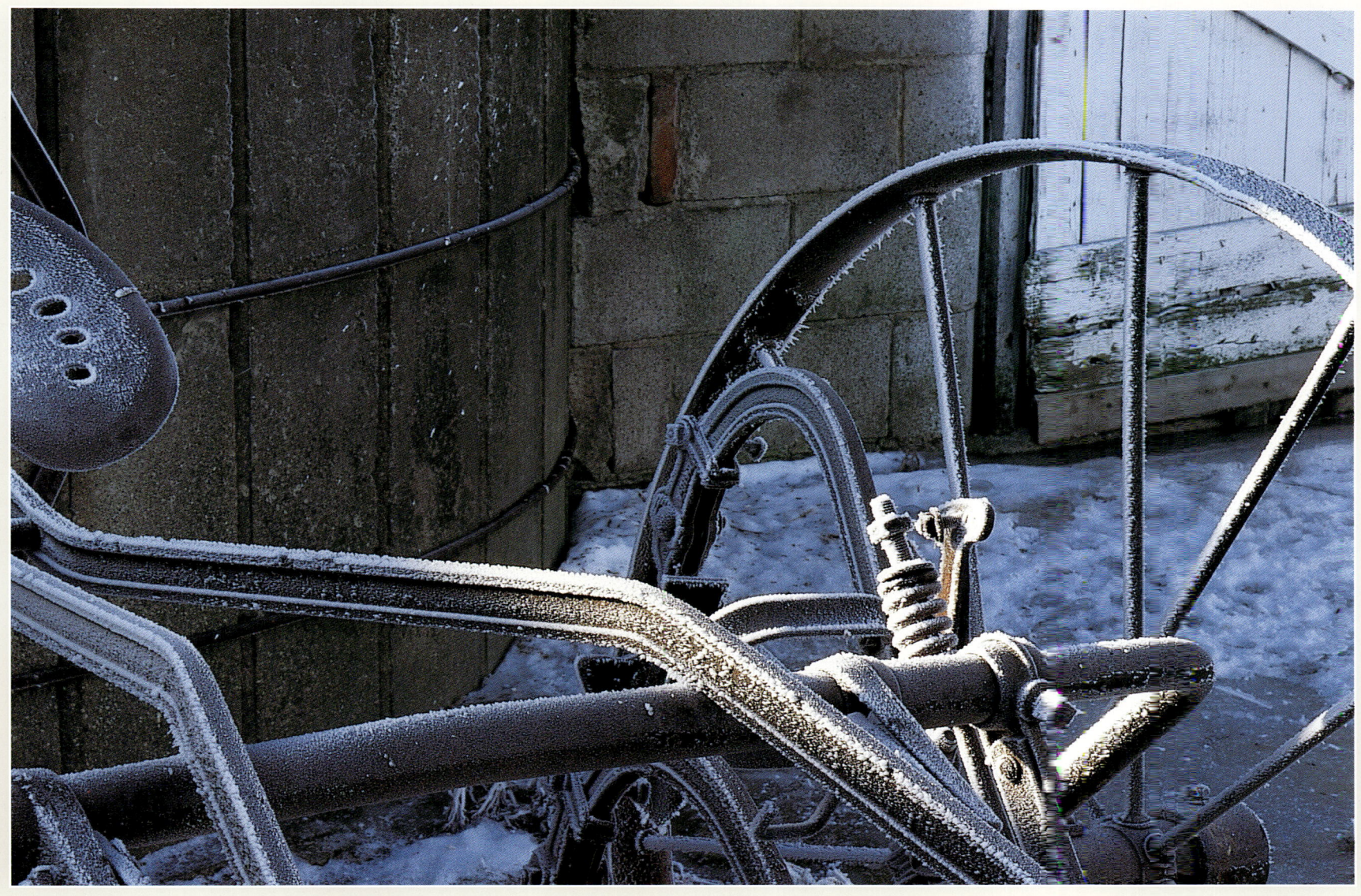

Above: Frost tinges the aged surface of an antique cultivator. KENT FOSTER

Facing page: A sugar maple tree shivers under a coating of hoarfrost. KENT FOSTER

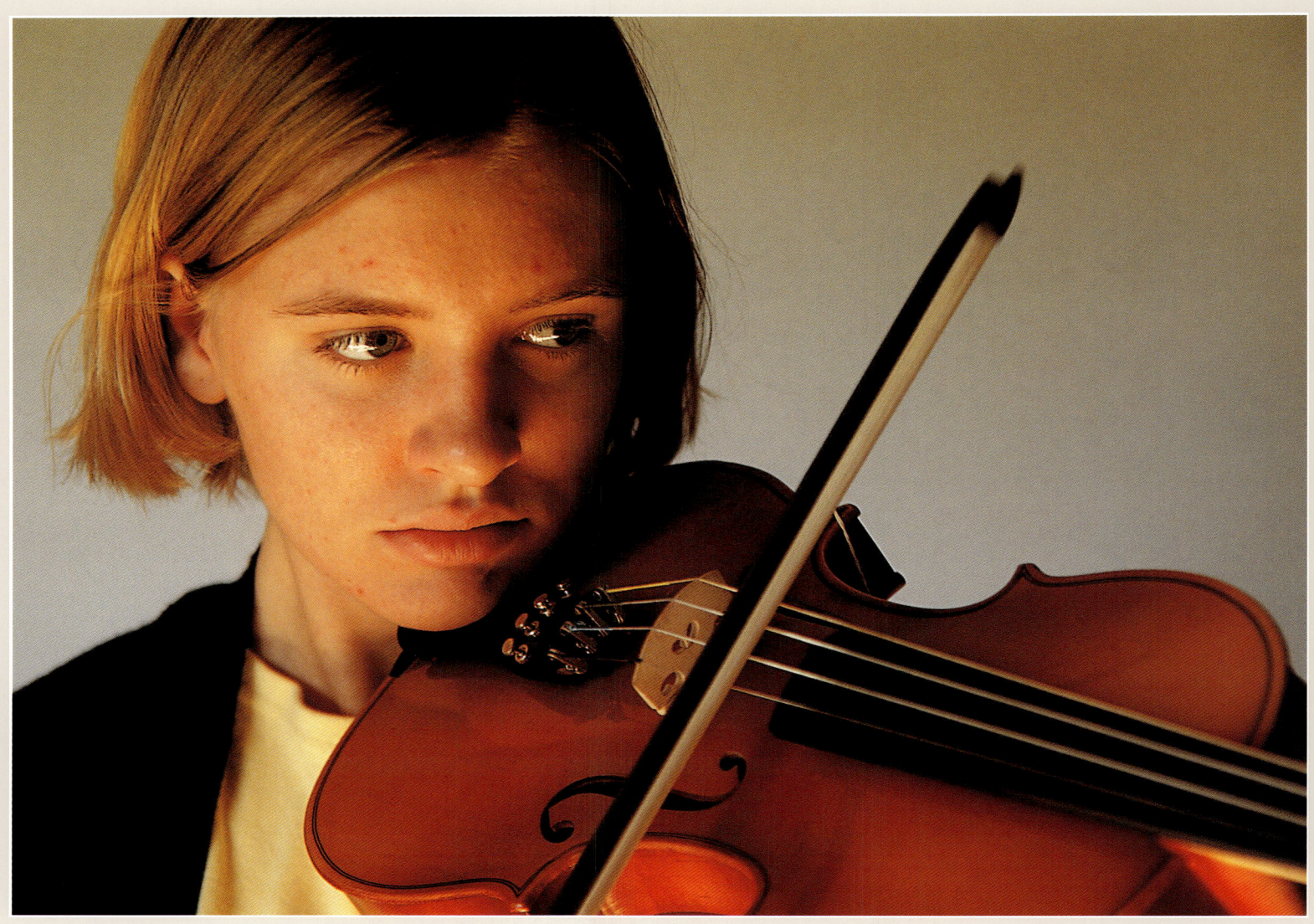

Above: An Iowan nurtures musical culture with violin practice. LARSH K. BRISTOL

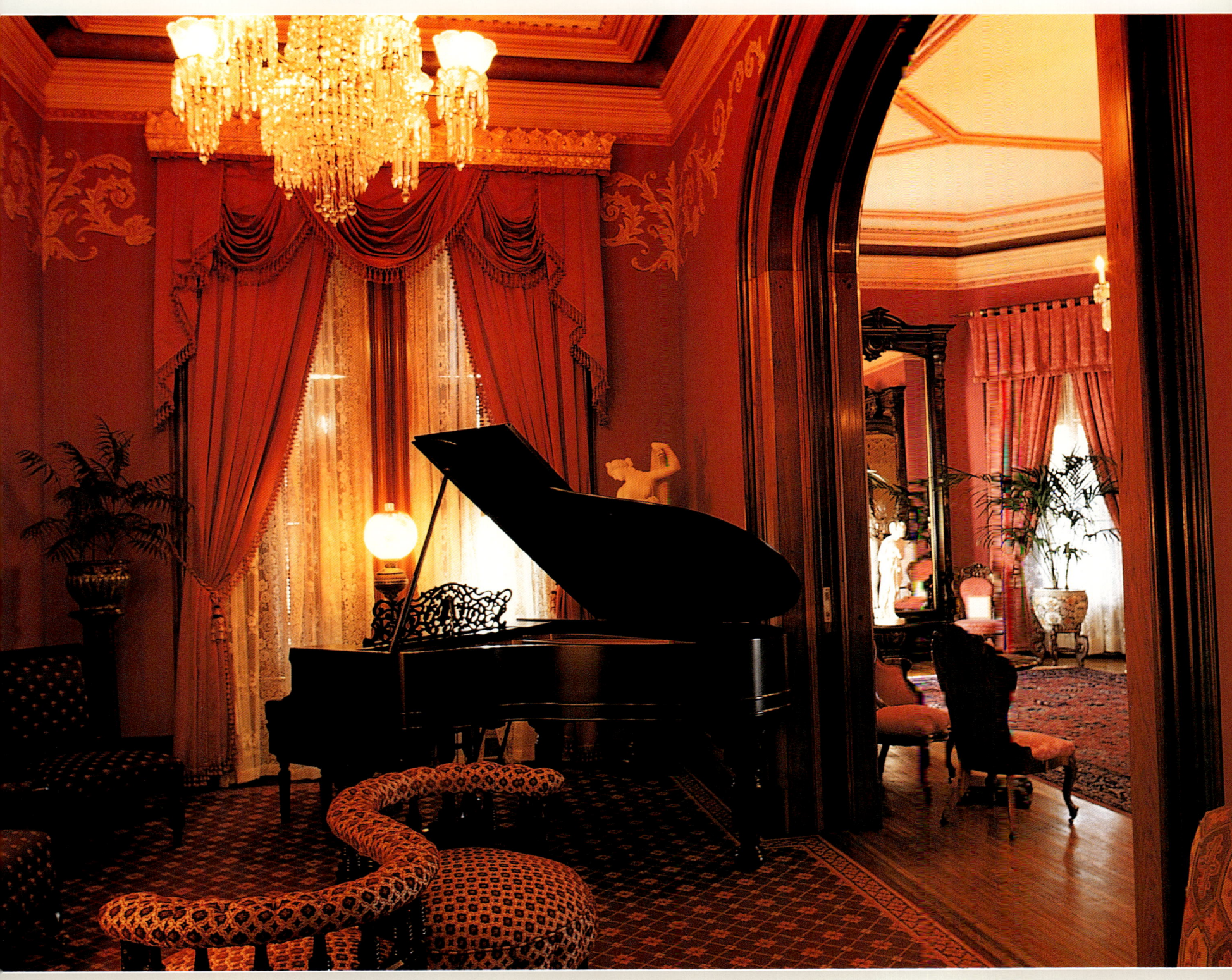

Above: The stunning red music room in Terrace Hill Governor's Mansion, Des Moines. KENT FOSTER

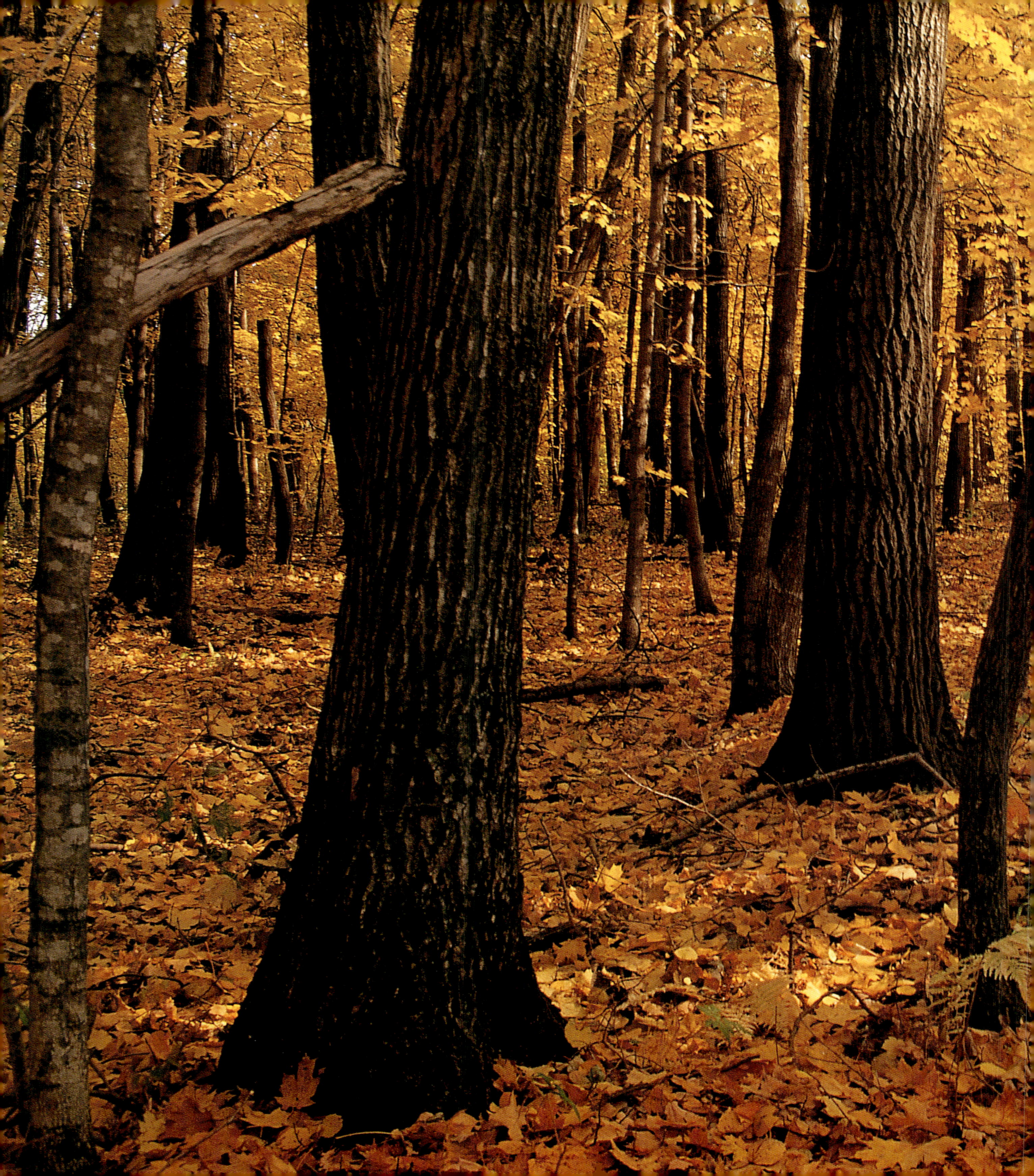

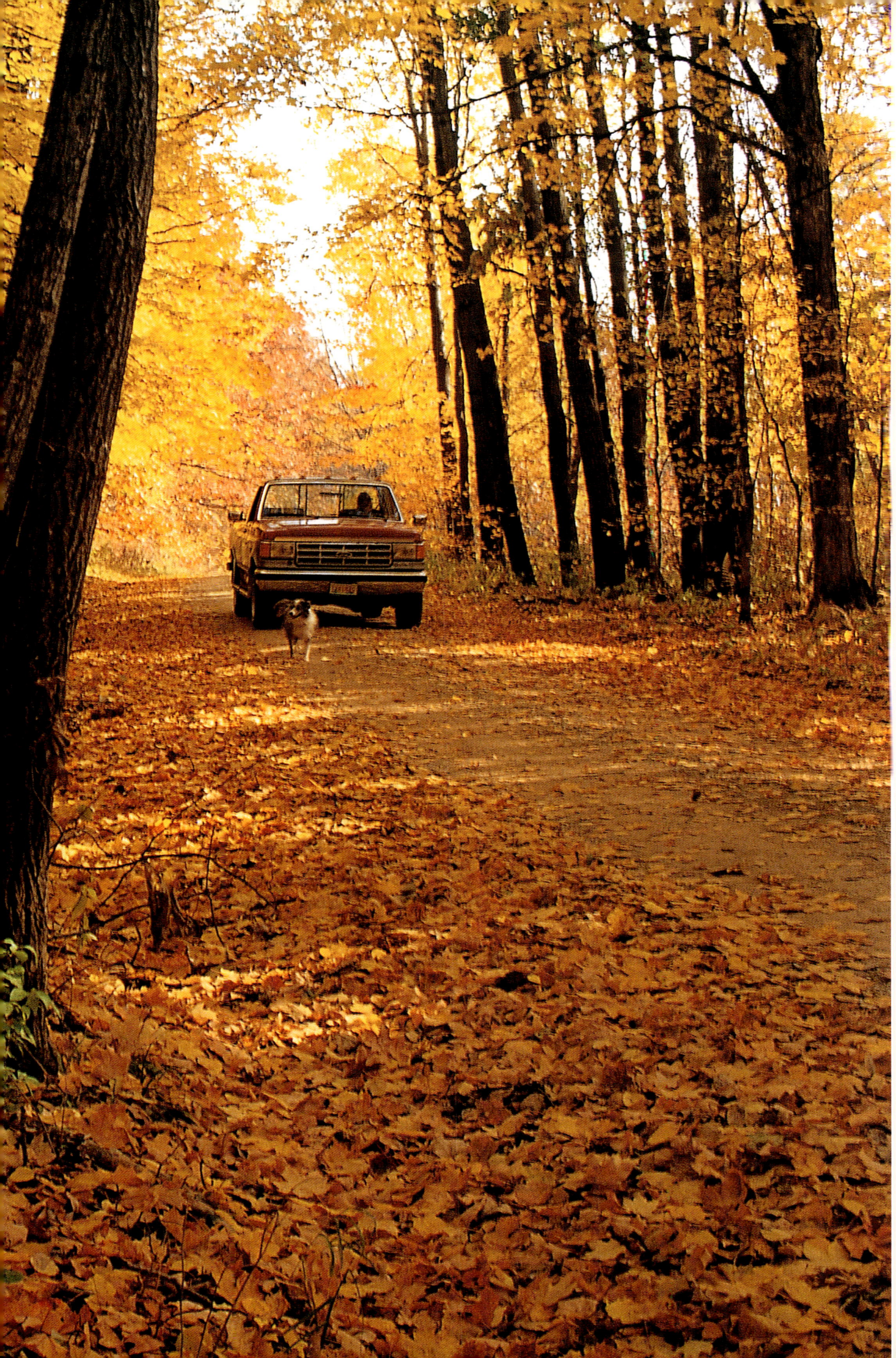

An inspiring drive through gilded woods in the Yellow River Forest of northeastern Iowa. LARSH K. BRISTOL

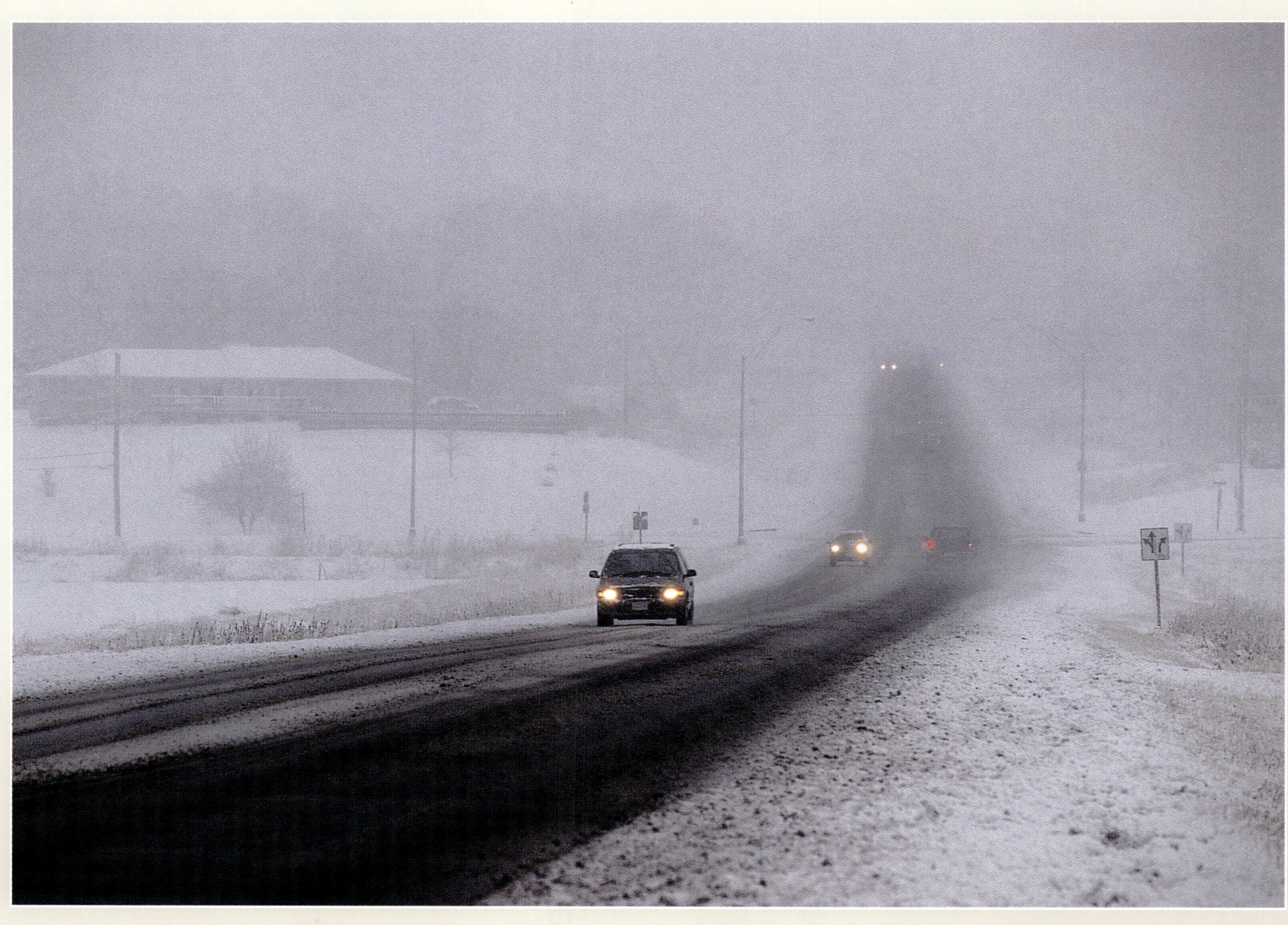

Above: A chilly morning commute from Ankeny to Des Moines. CURT MAAS

Facing page: A freight train barrels through a snowstorm in Lansing. LARSH K. BRISTOL

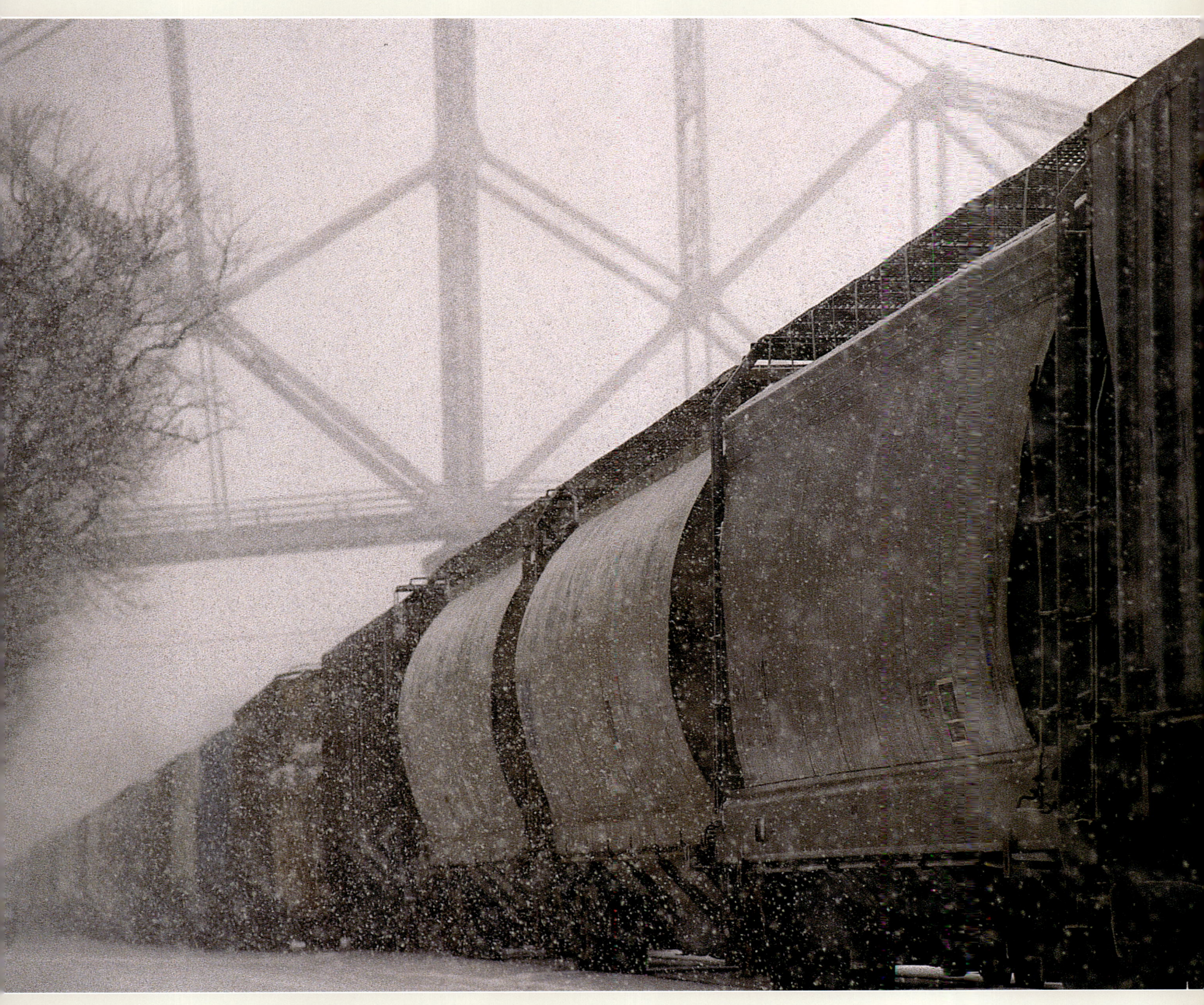

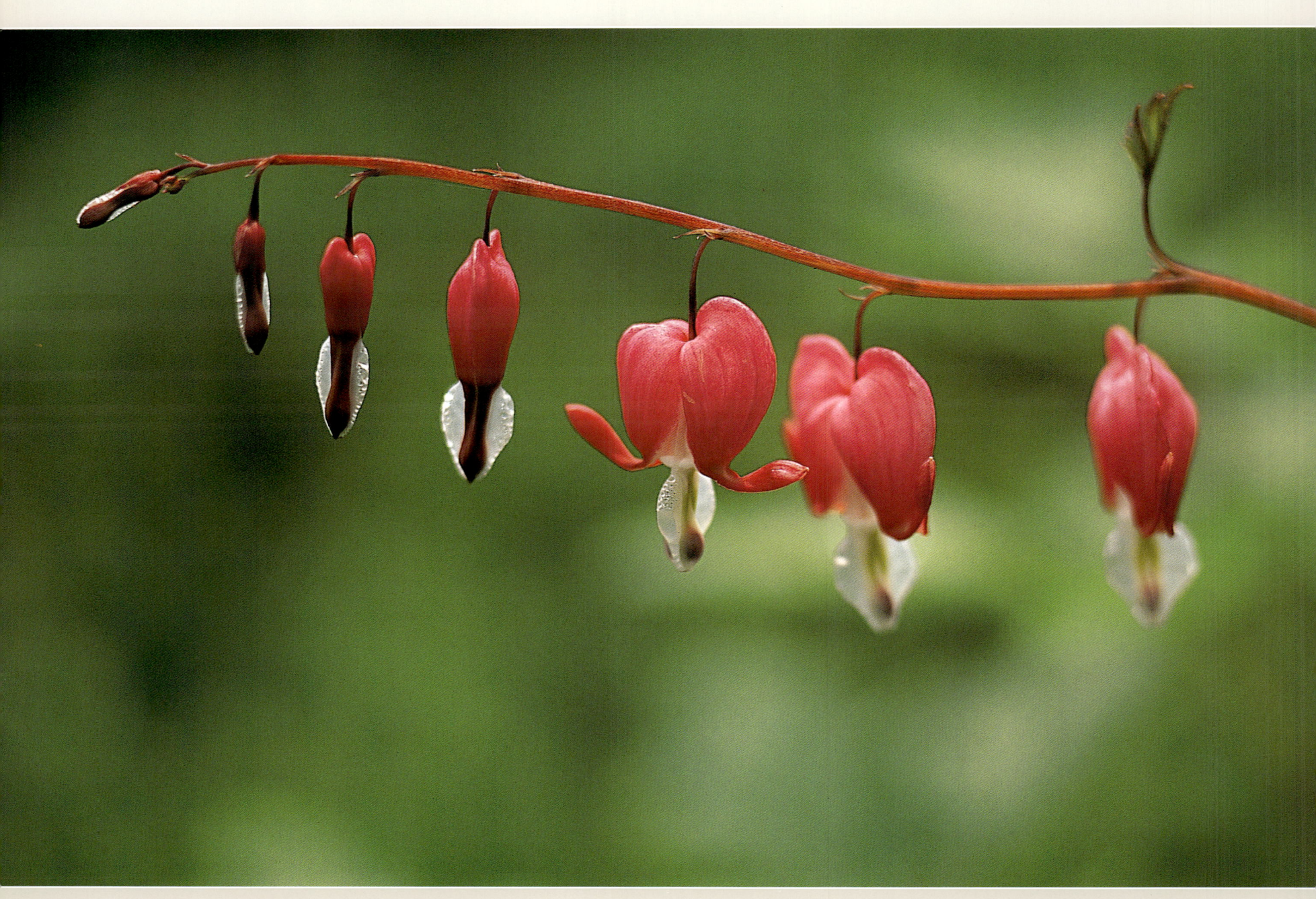

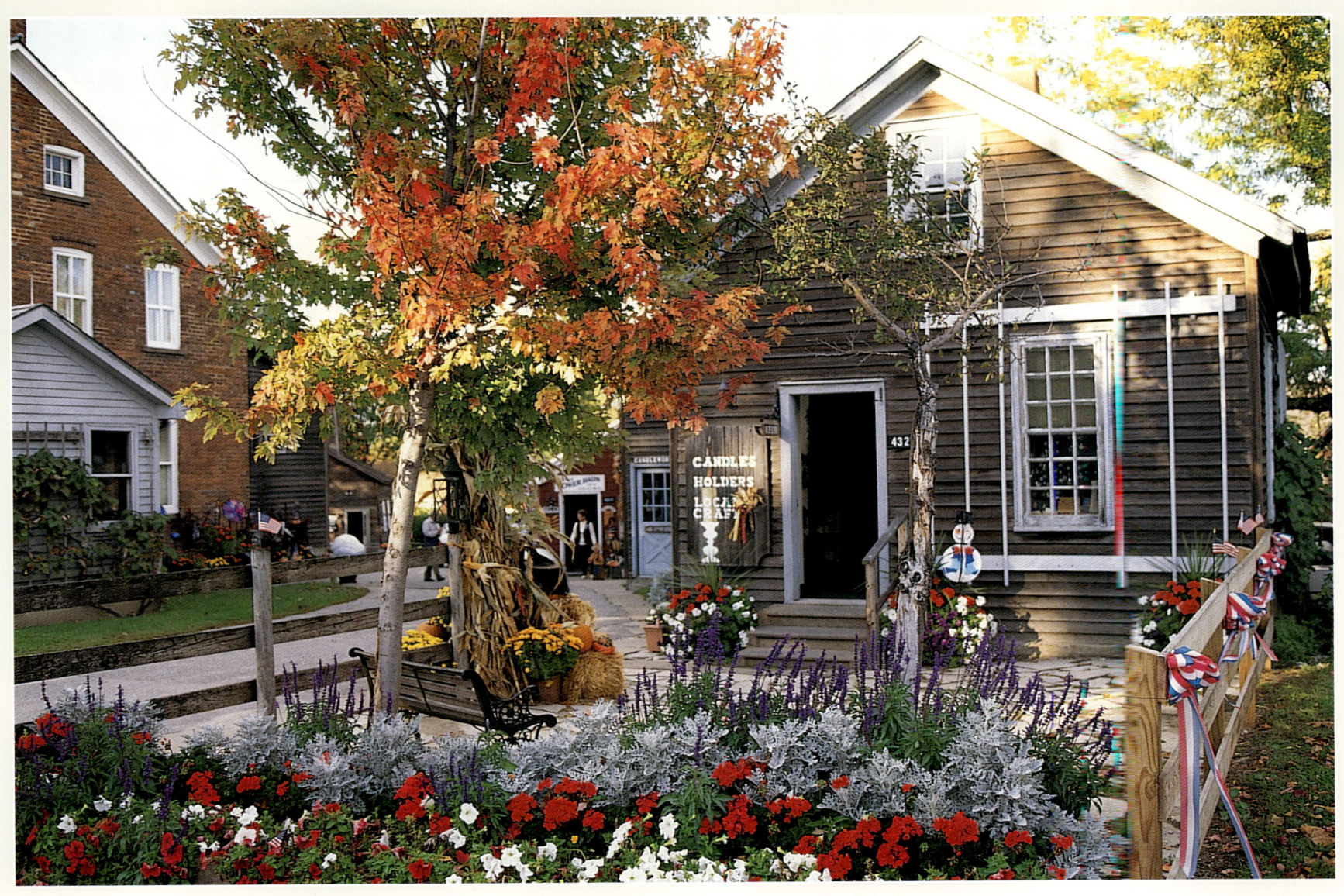

Above: The festive colors of Octoberfest at the Amana Colonies. KENT FOSTER

Facing page: A delicate stem of bleeding heart. KENT FOSTER

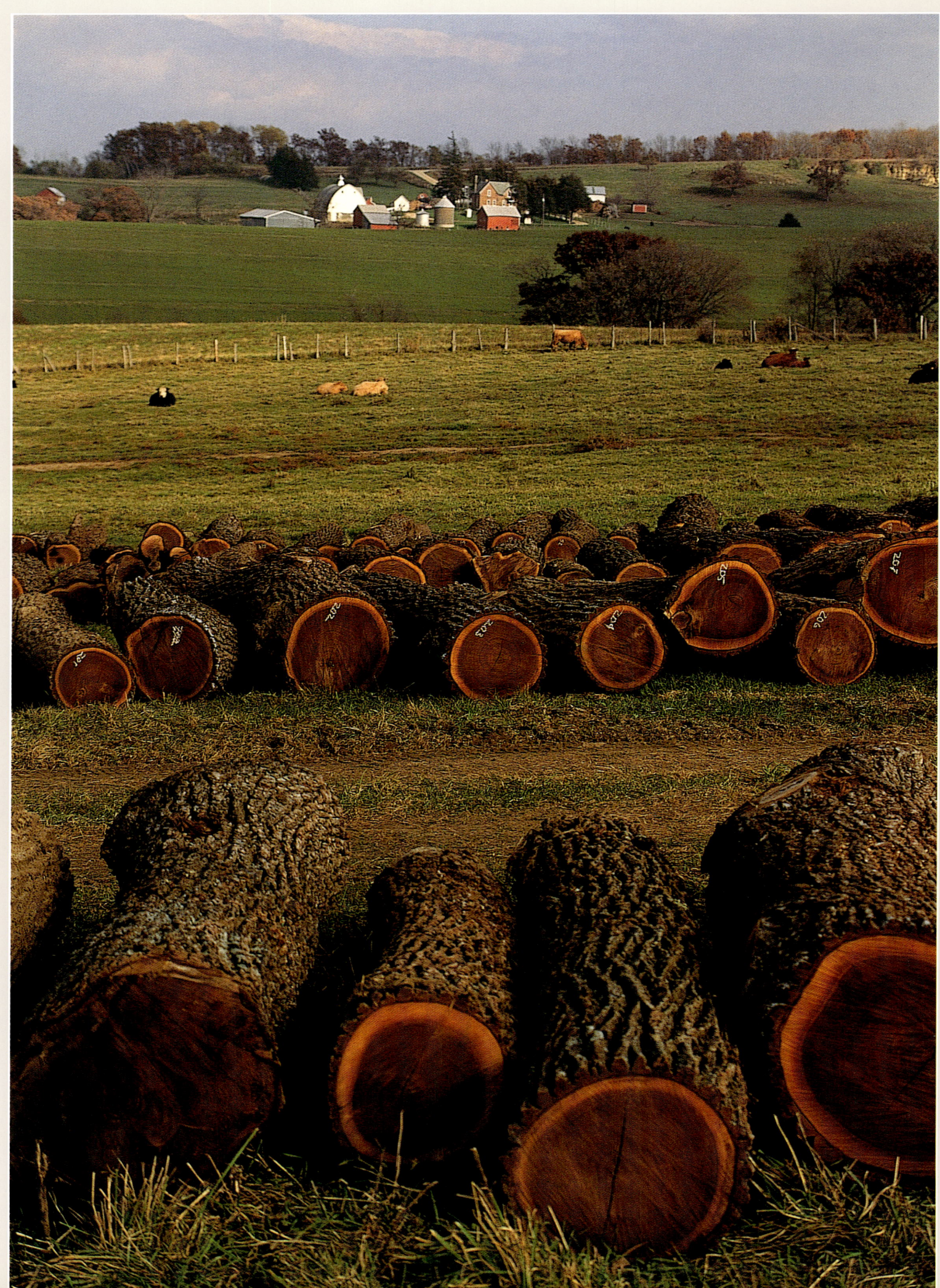

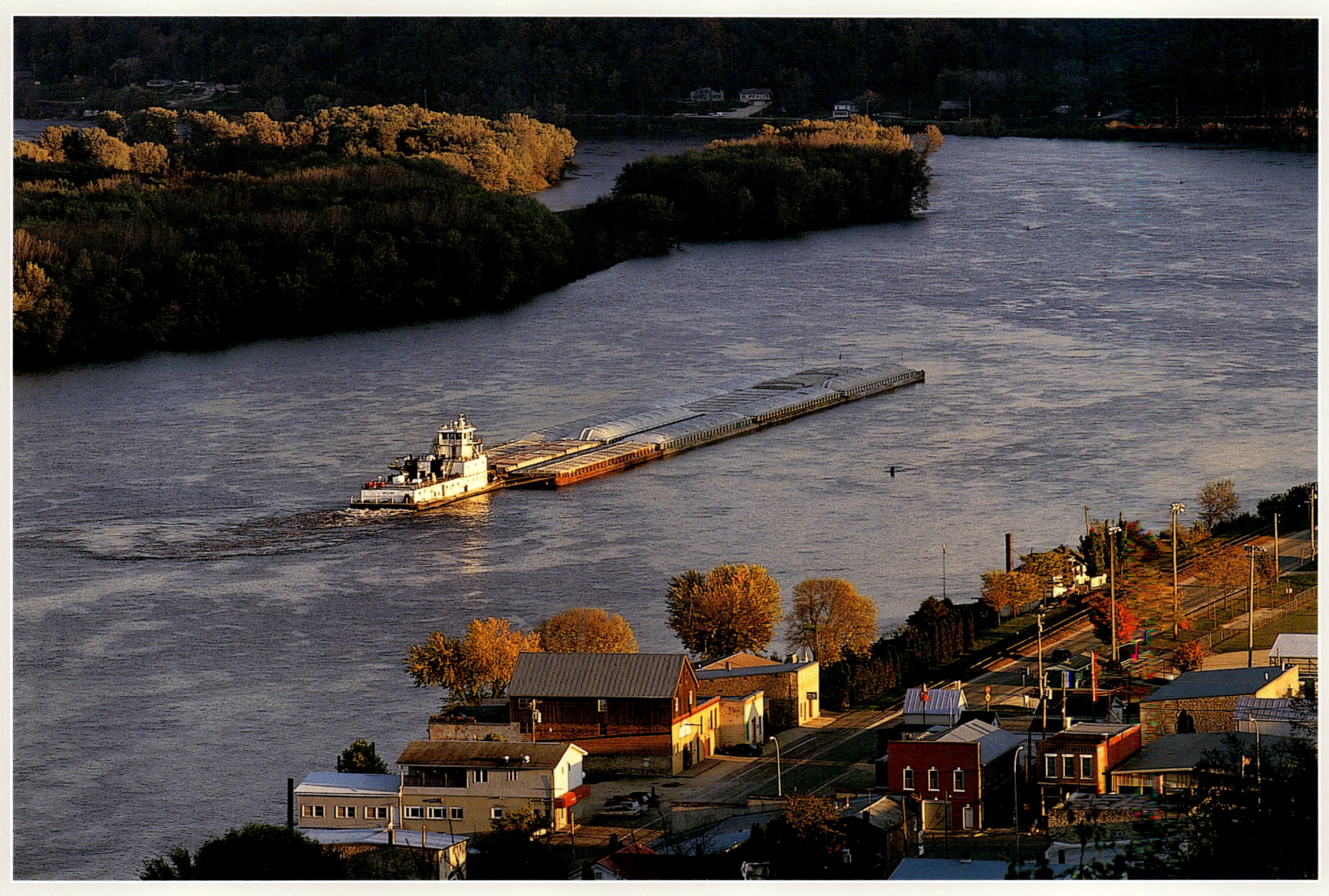

Above: A grain barge glides down the Mississippi near Lansing. LARSH K. BRISTOL

Facing page: Veneer walnut lumber is harvested in northeastern Iowa. LARSH K. BRISTOL

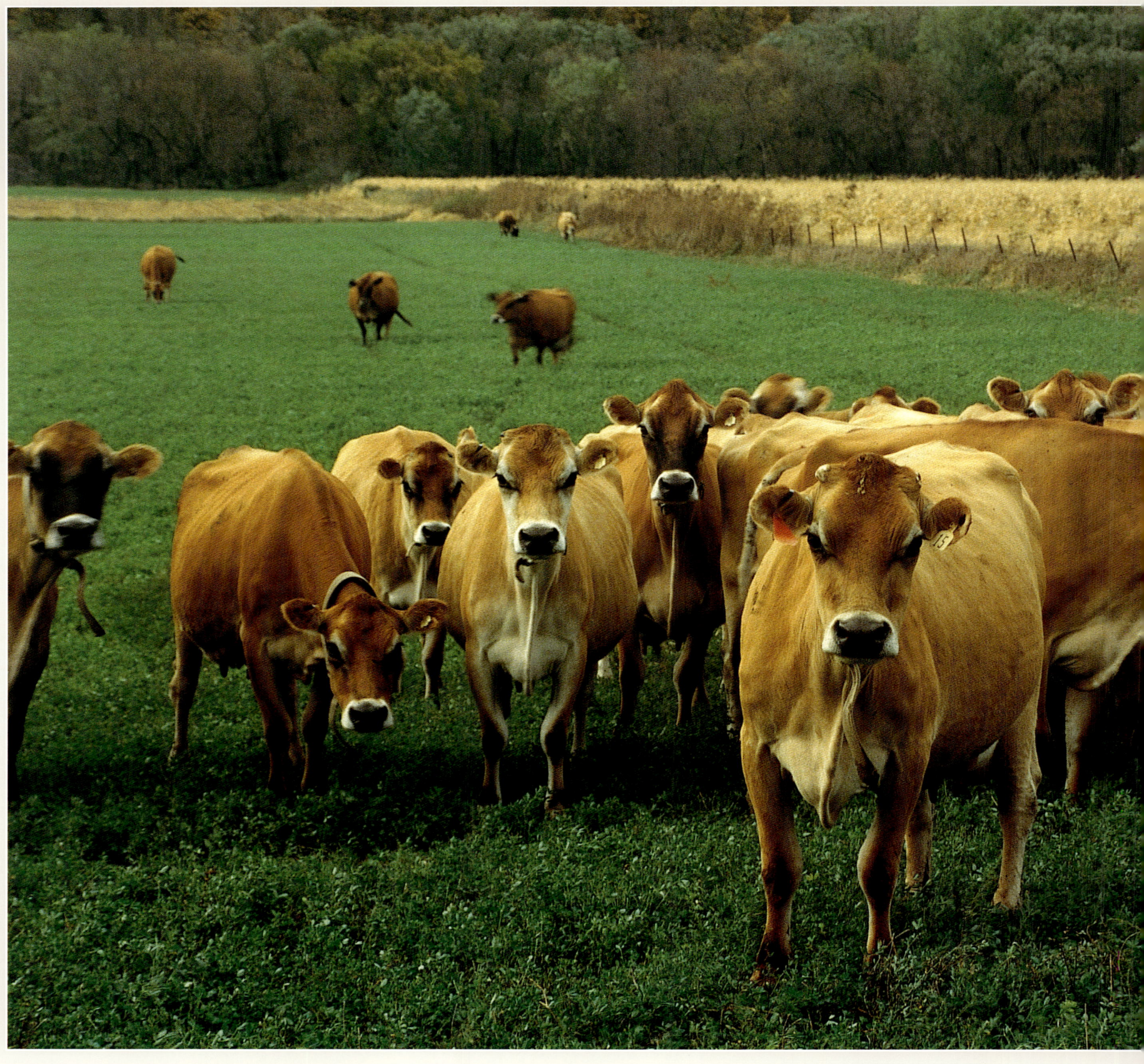

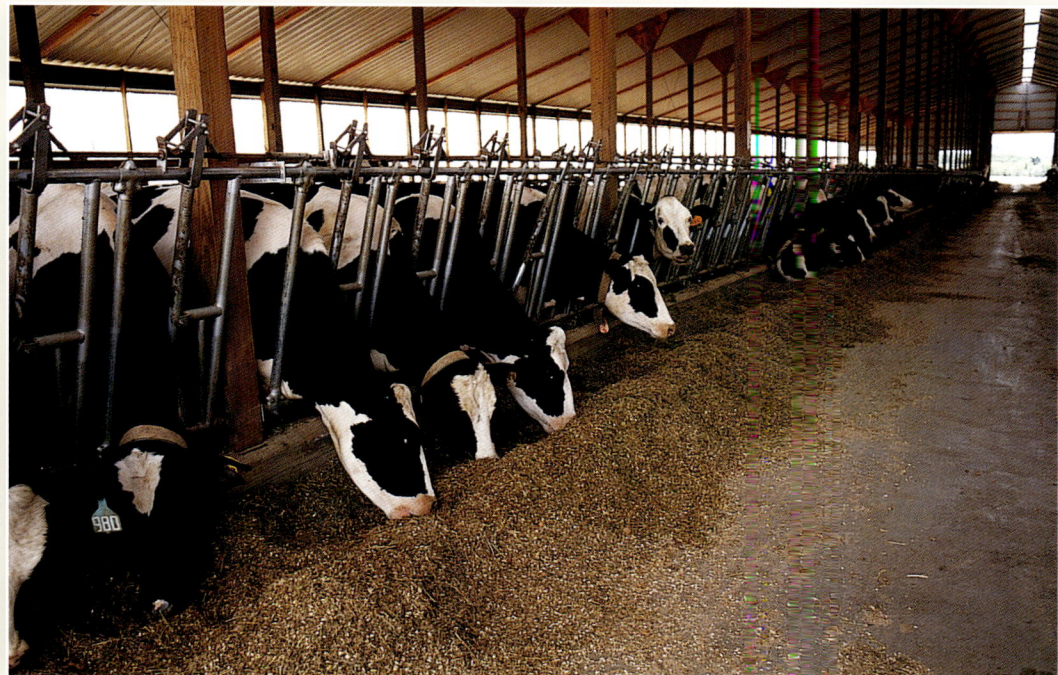

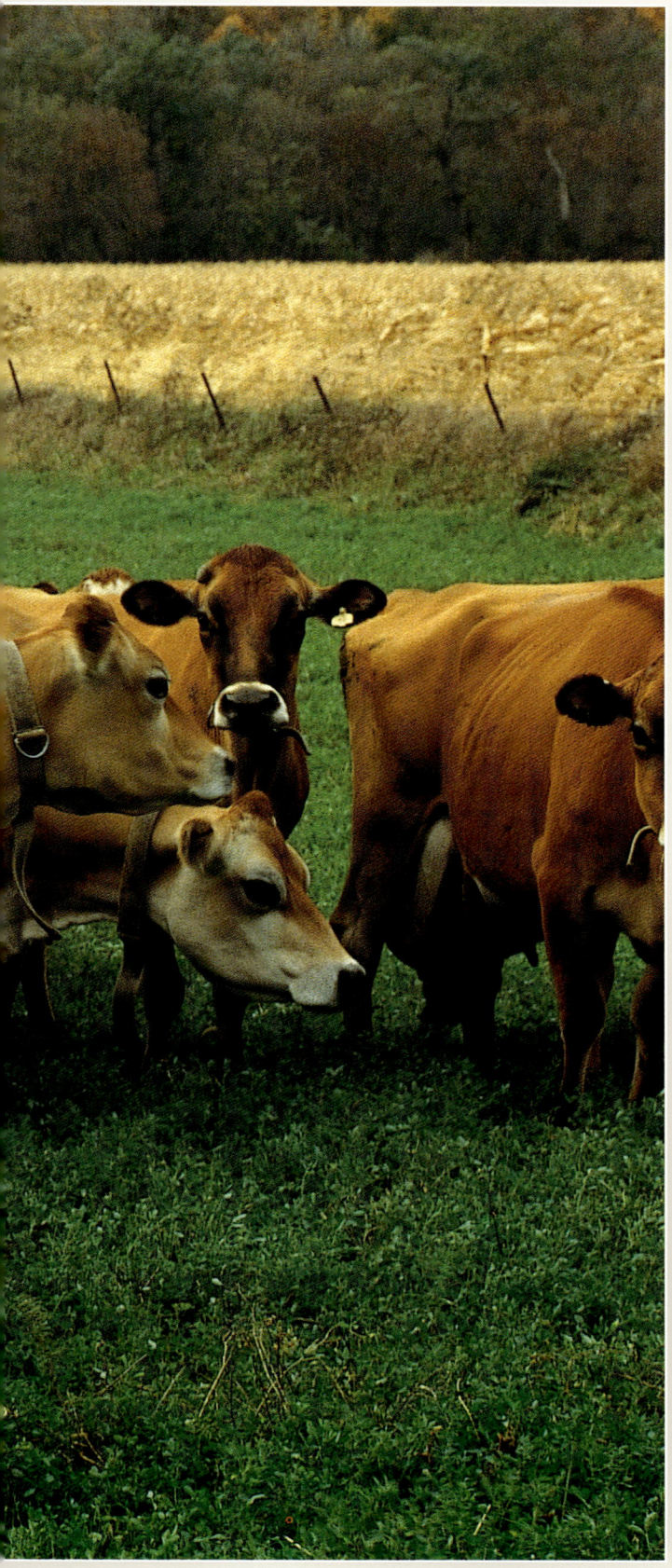

Above: A modern dairy farm in operation in southeastern Iowa. LARSH K. BRISTOL

Left: Brown Swiss cows come in for a closer look. It is believed that the Brown Swiss is the oldest of the dairy breeds. LARSH K. BRISTOL

Below: In Granger, beef cattle bask in the sunrise. CURT MAAS

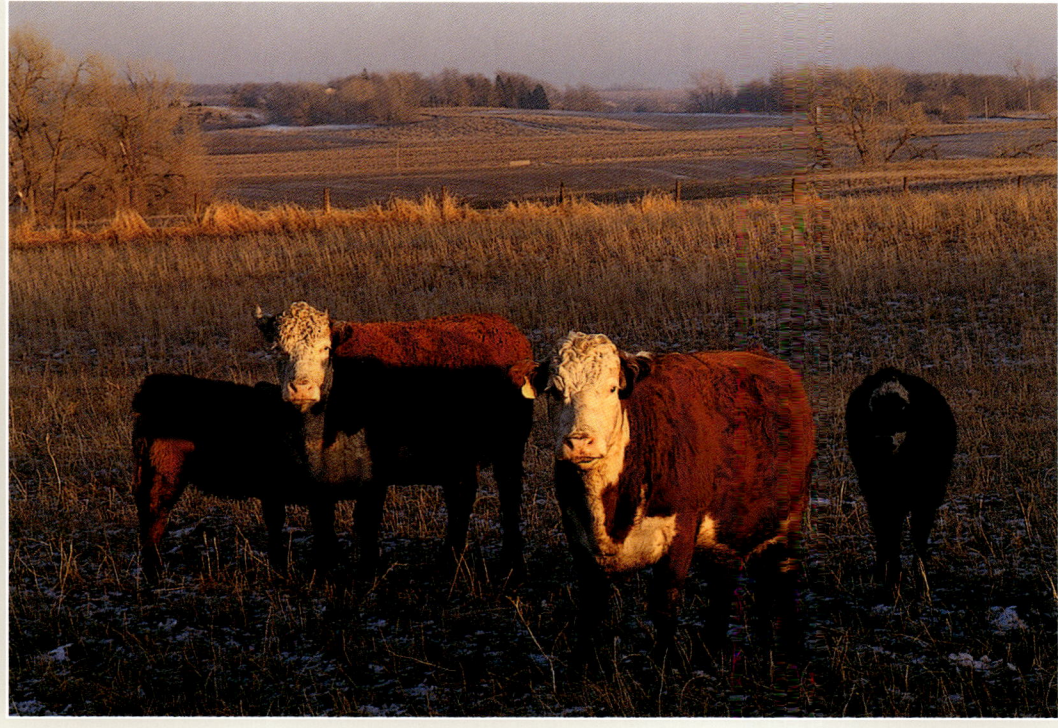

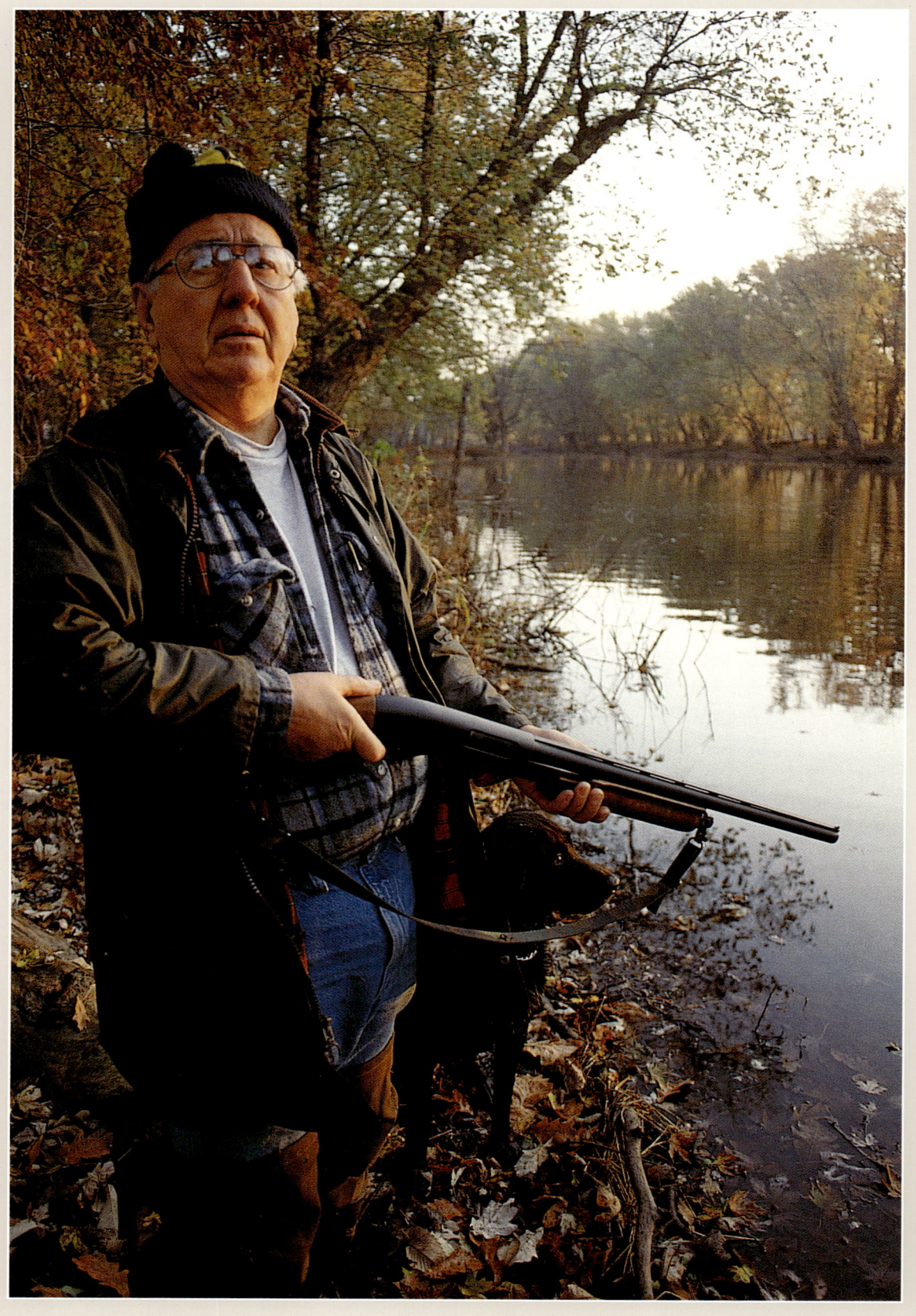

Above: Duck hunting in a slough at Harpers Ferry. LARSH K. BRISTOL

Facing page: A farm pond is framed in fall tones. LARSH K. BRISTOL

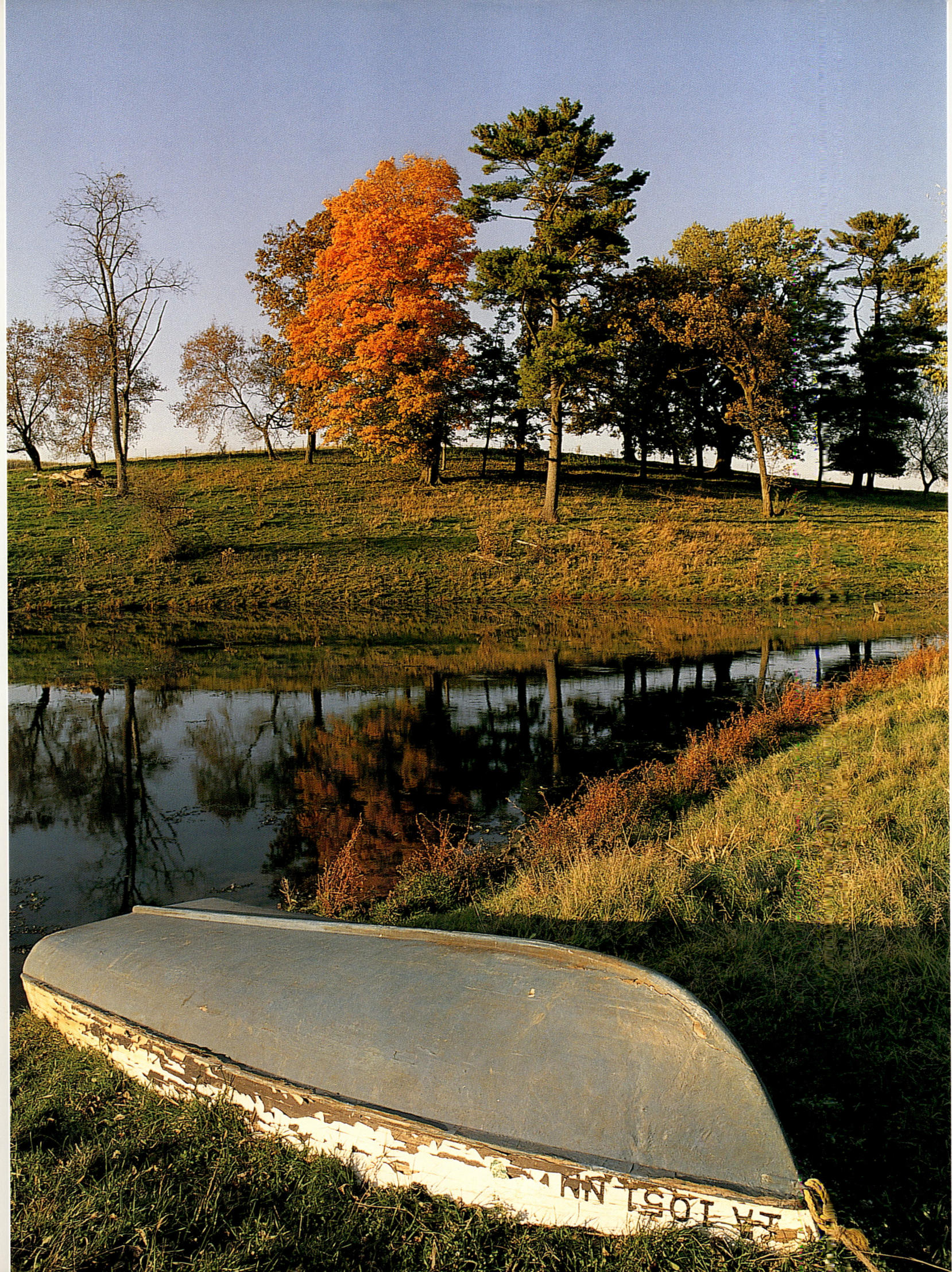

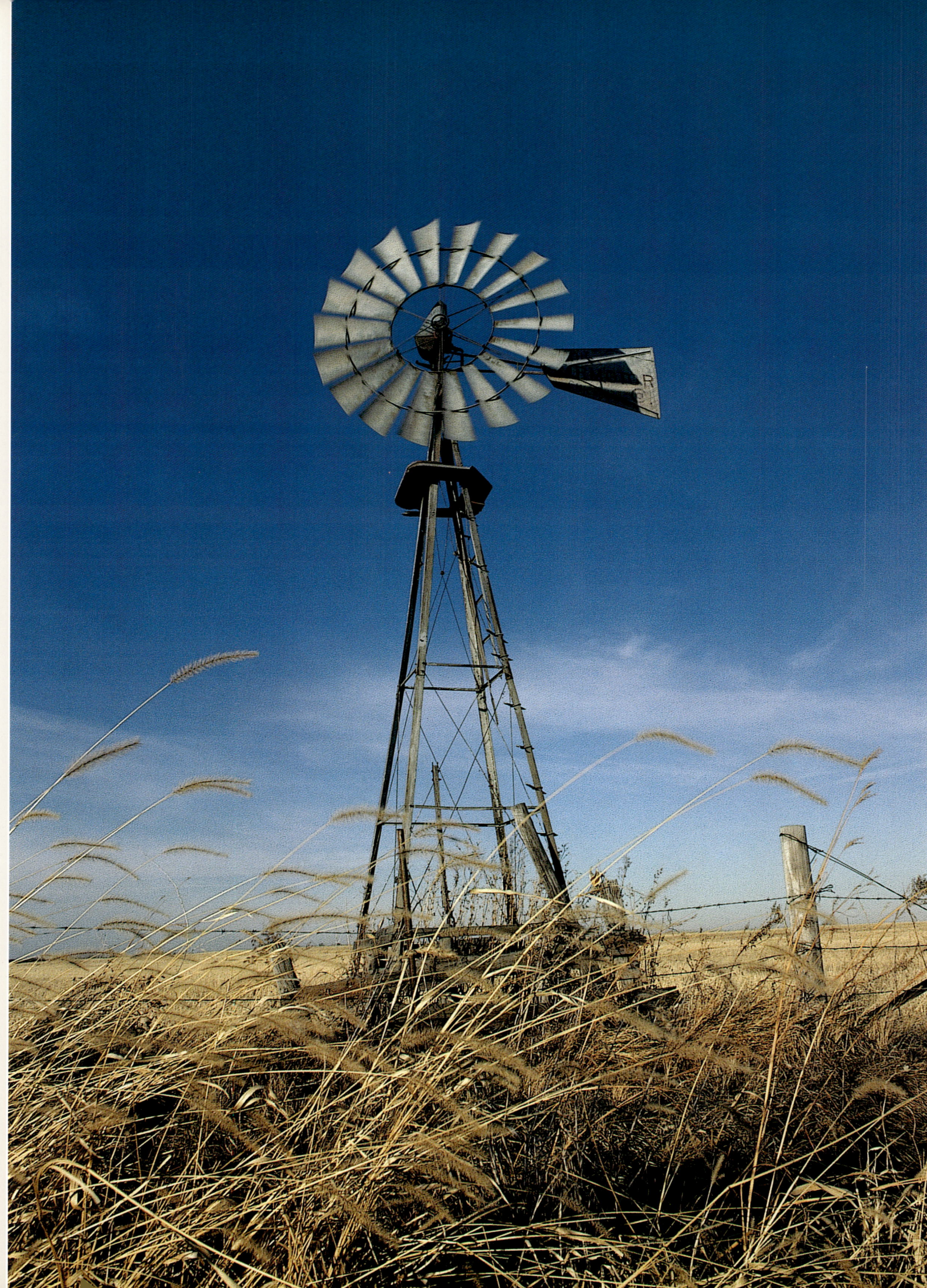

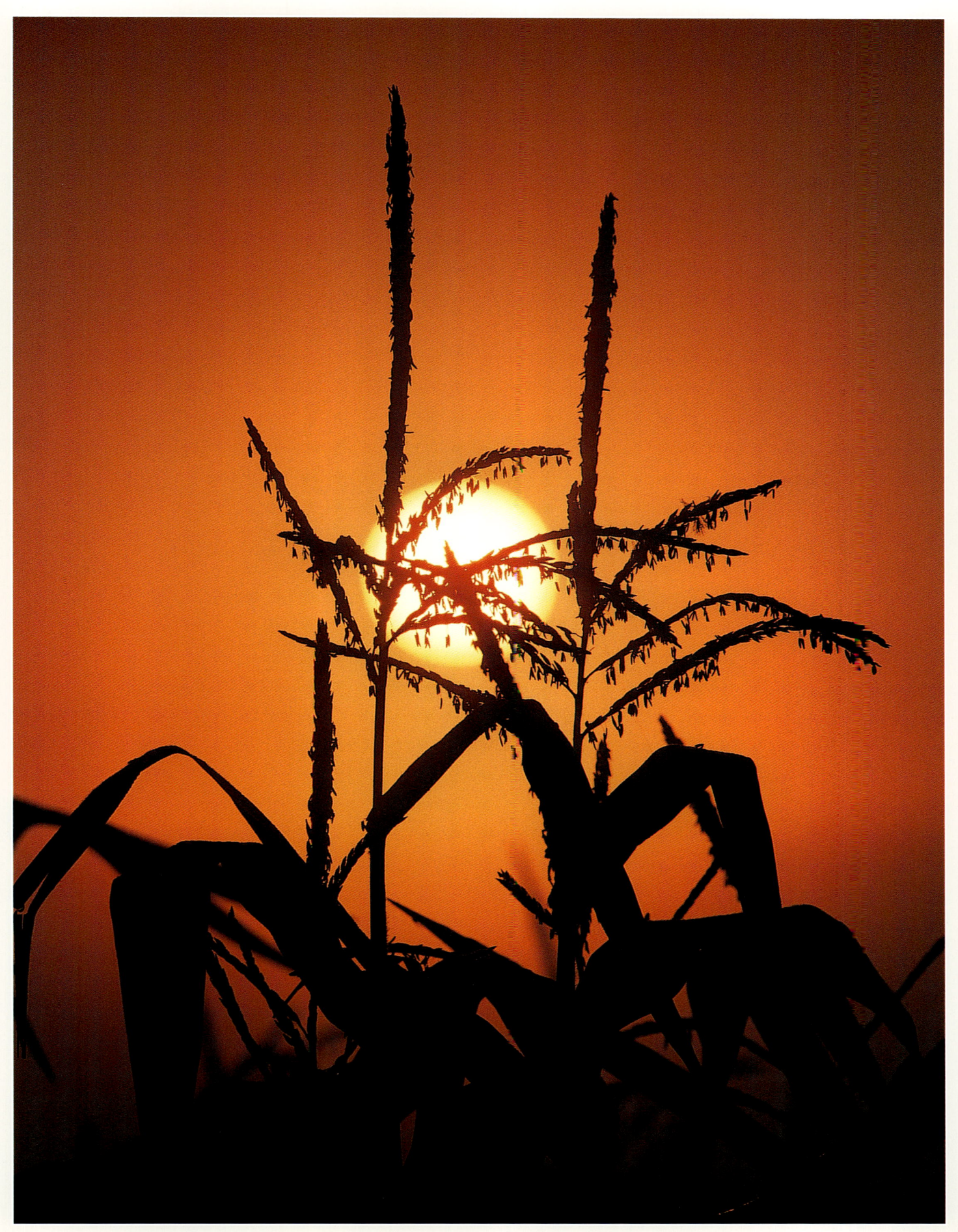

Above: Setting sun casts a dramatic light on Iowa corn. CURT MAAS

Facing page: A windmill stands tall over a field near Jefferson. CURT MAAS

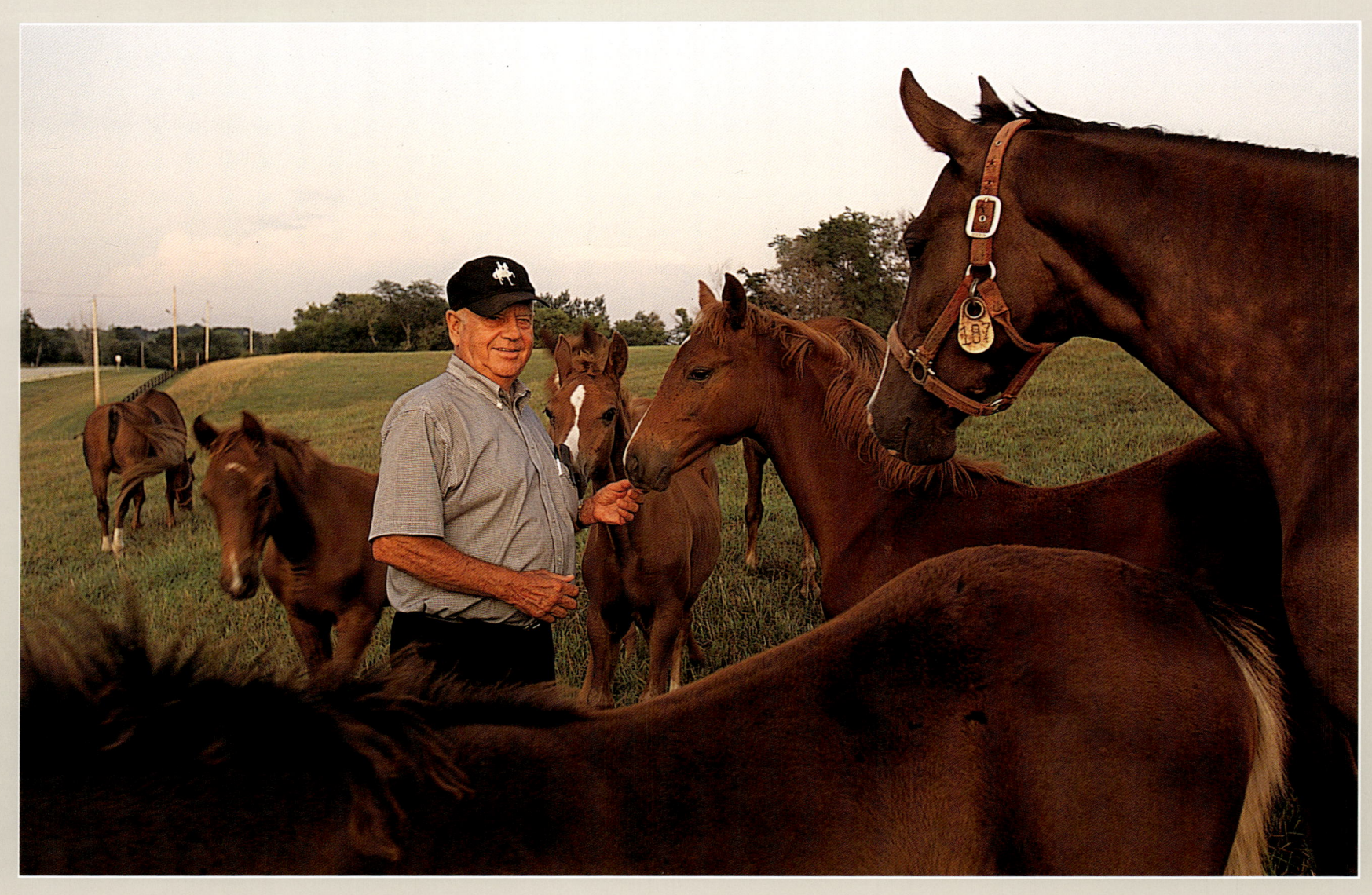

Above and facing page: Veterinarian "Doc Raun" proudly displays his American Saddlebred horses near Norwalk. CURT MAAS

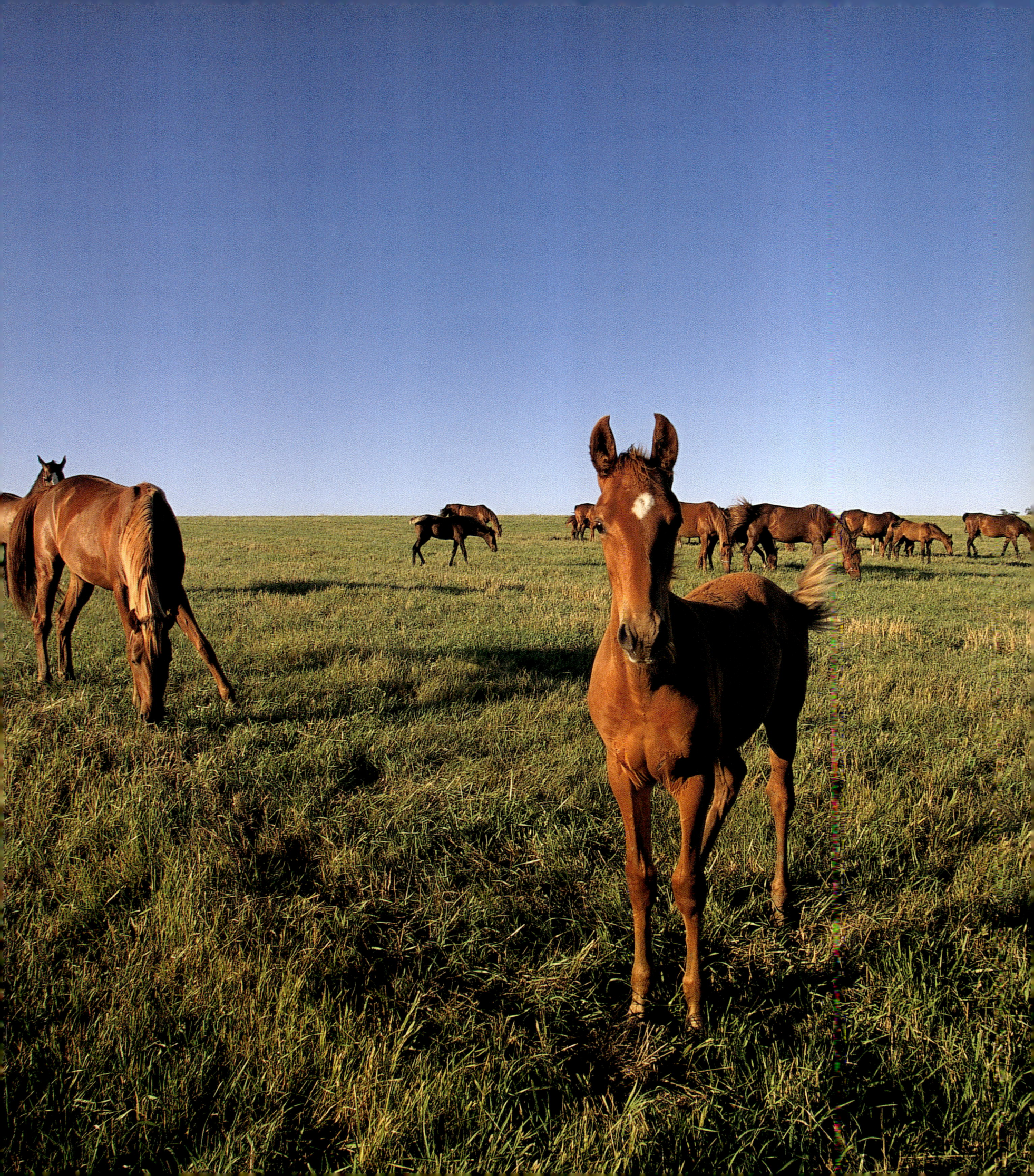

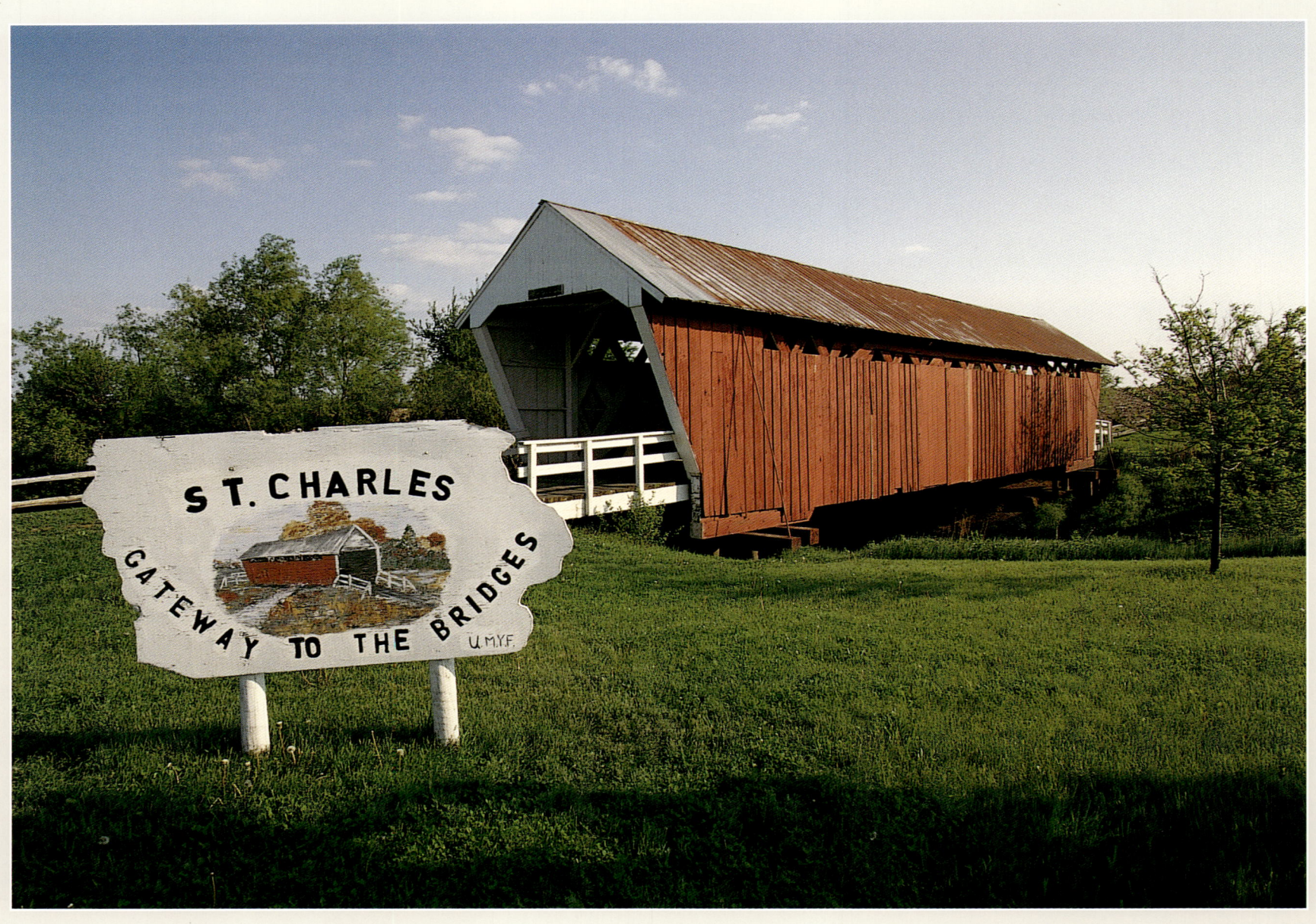

Above: Imes Bridge, built in 1870, extends a pastoral welcome to visitors to Madison County. CURT MAAS

Facing page: Literal signs of yesteryear cover this old gas station. KENT FOSTER

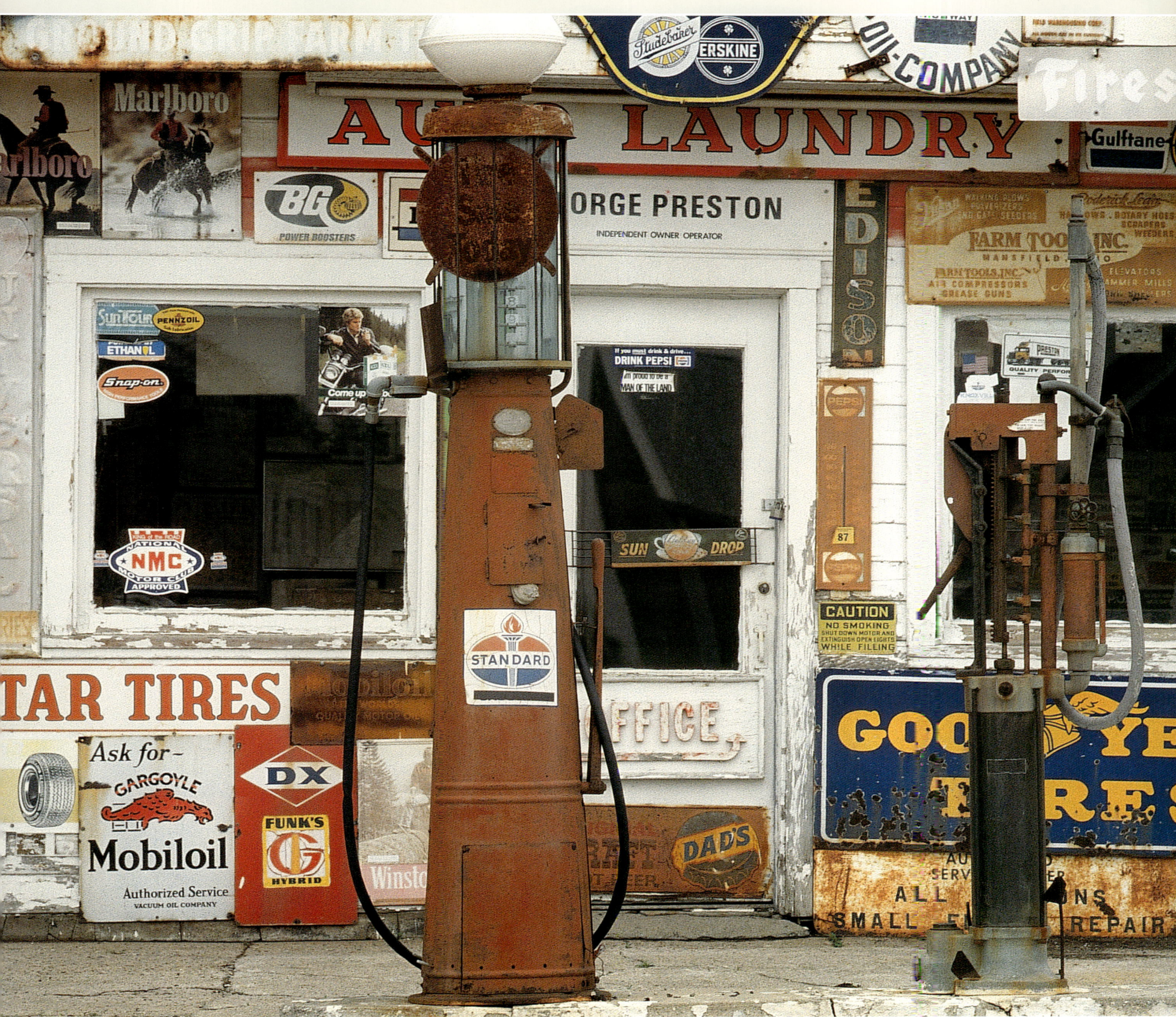

Right: The *Mississippi Queen* riverboat embarks north on a trip to Lansing.
LARSH K. BRISTOL

Below: A blue heron perches atop gnarled branches at twilight. LARSH K. BRISTOL

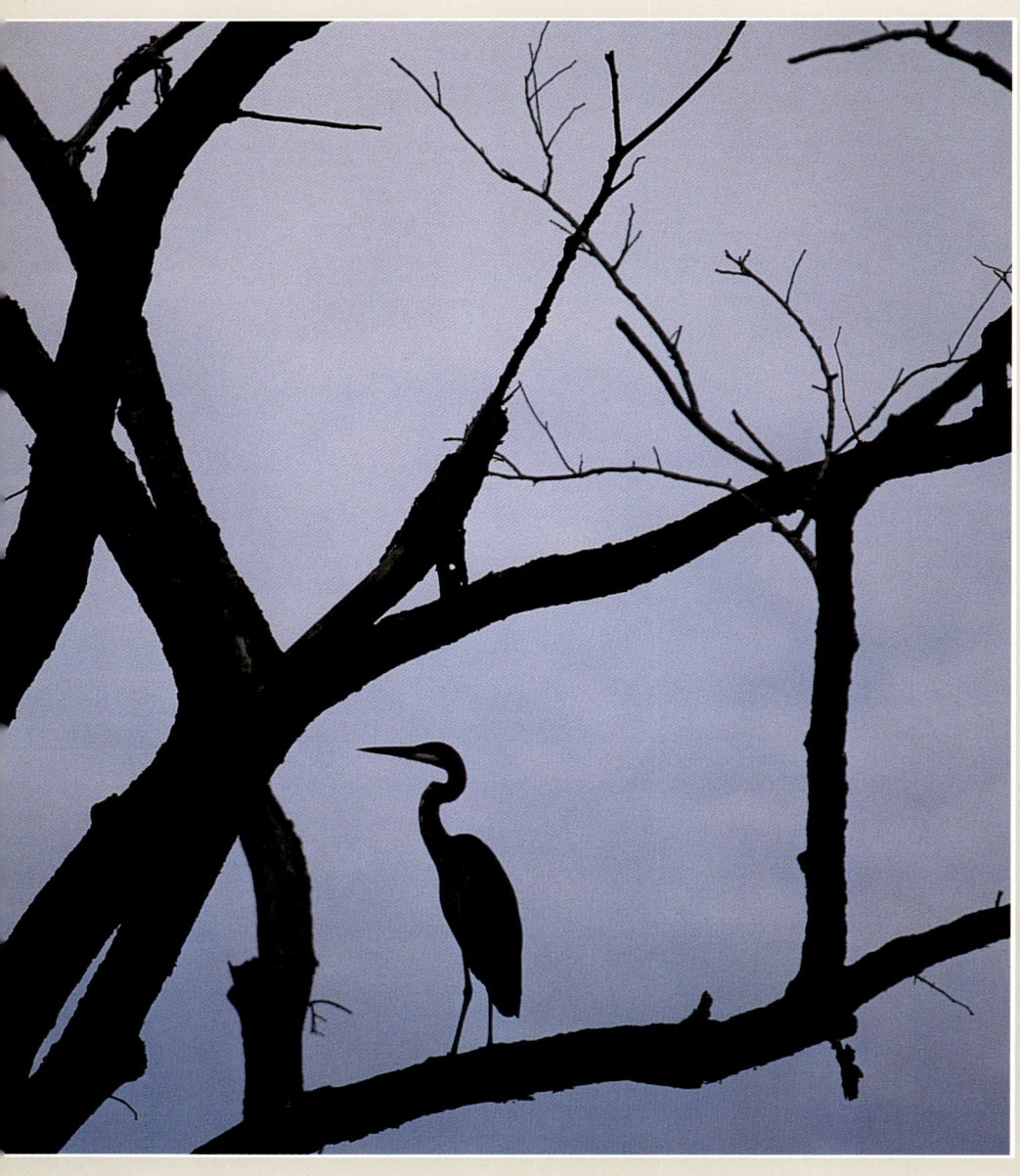

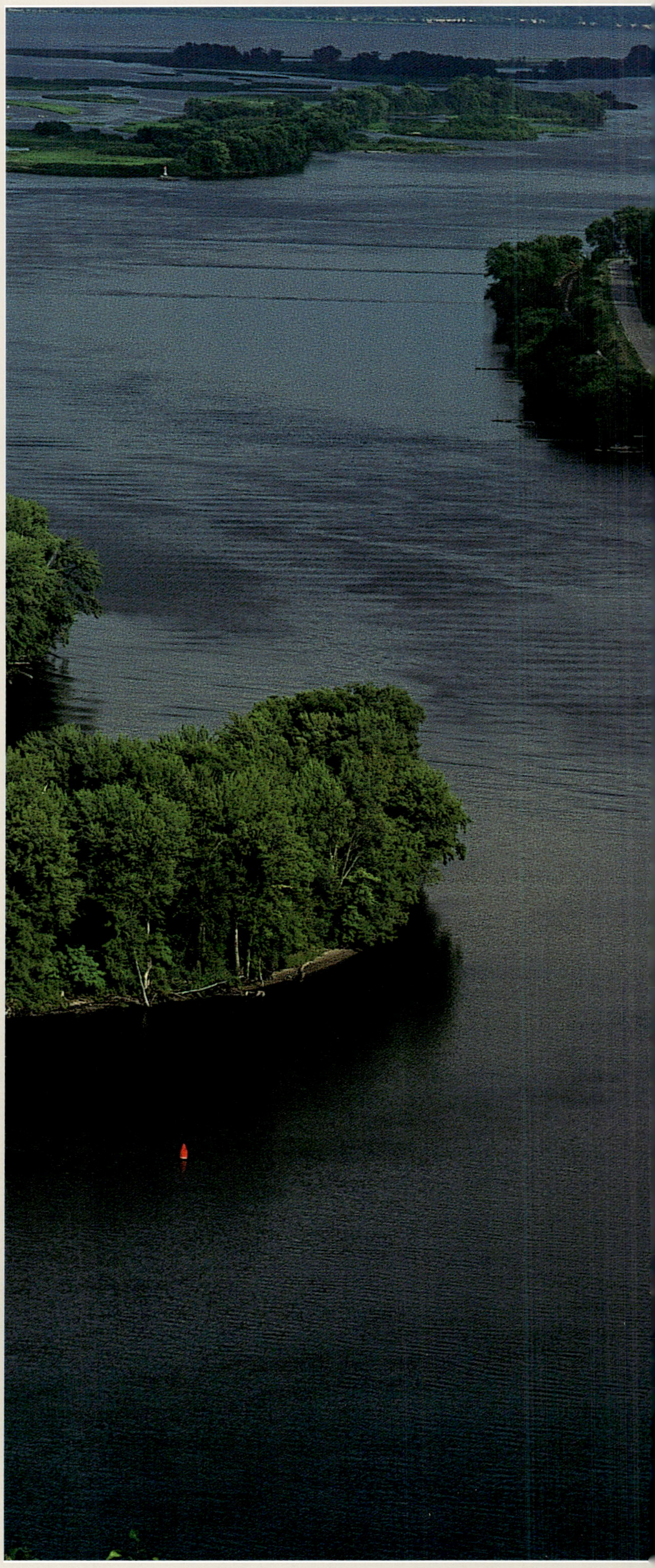

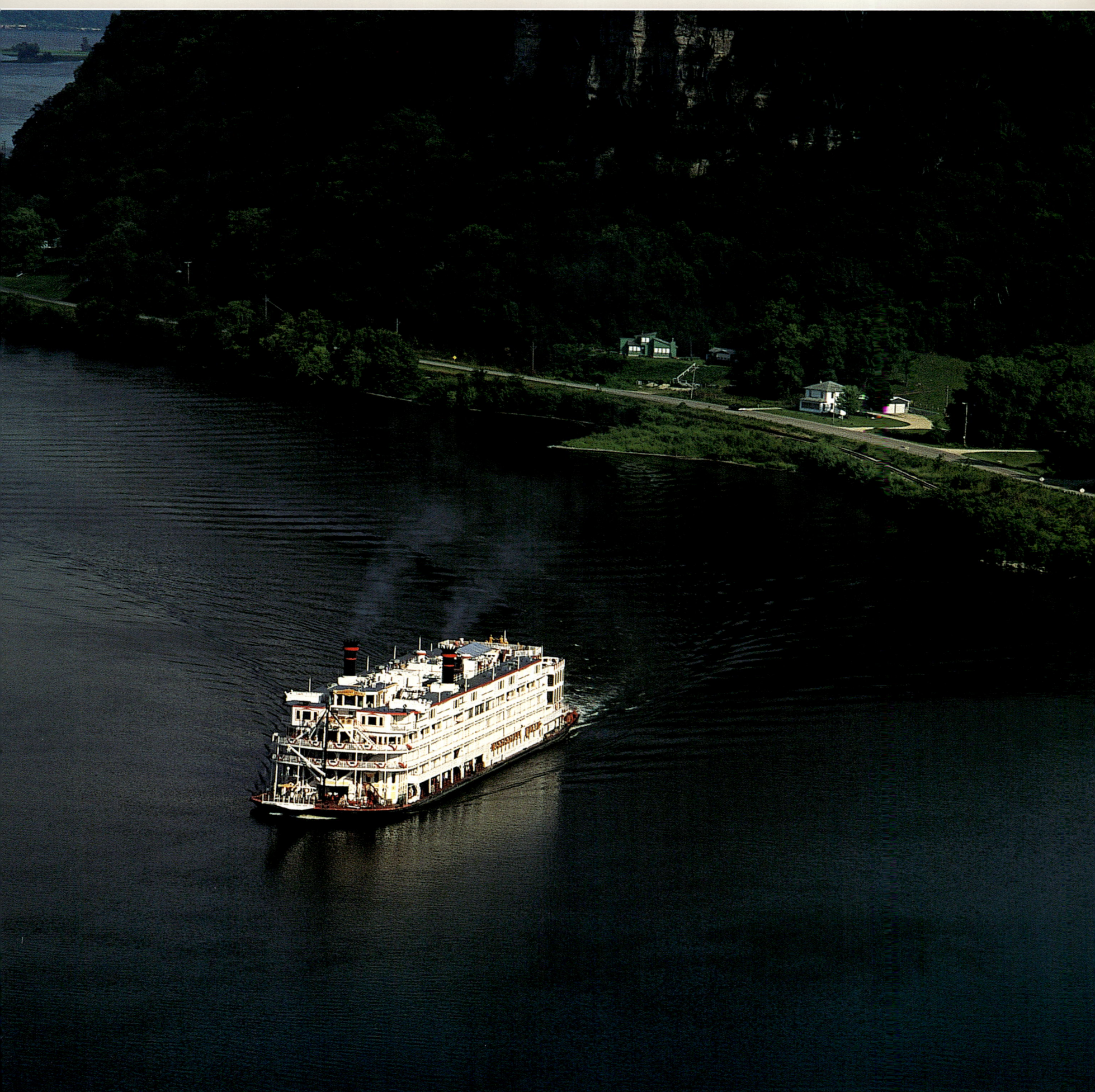

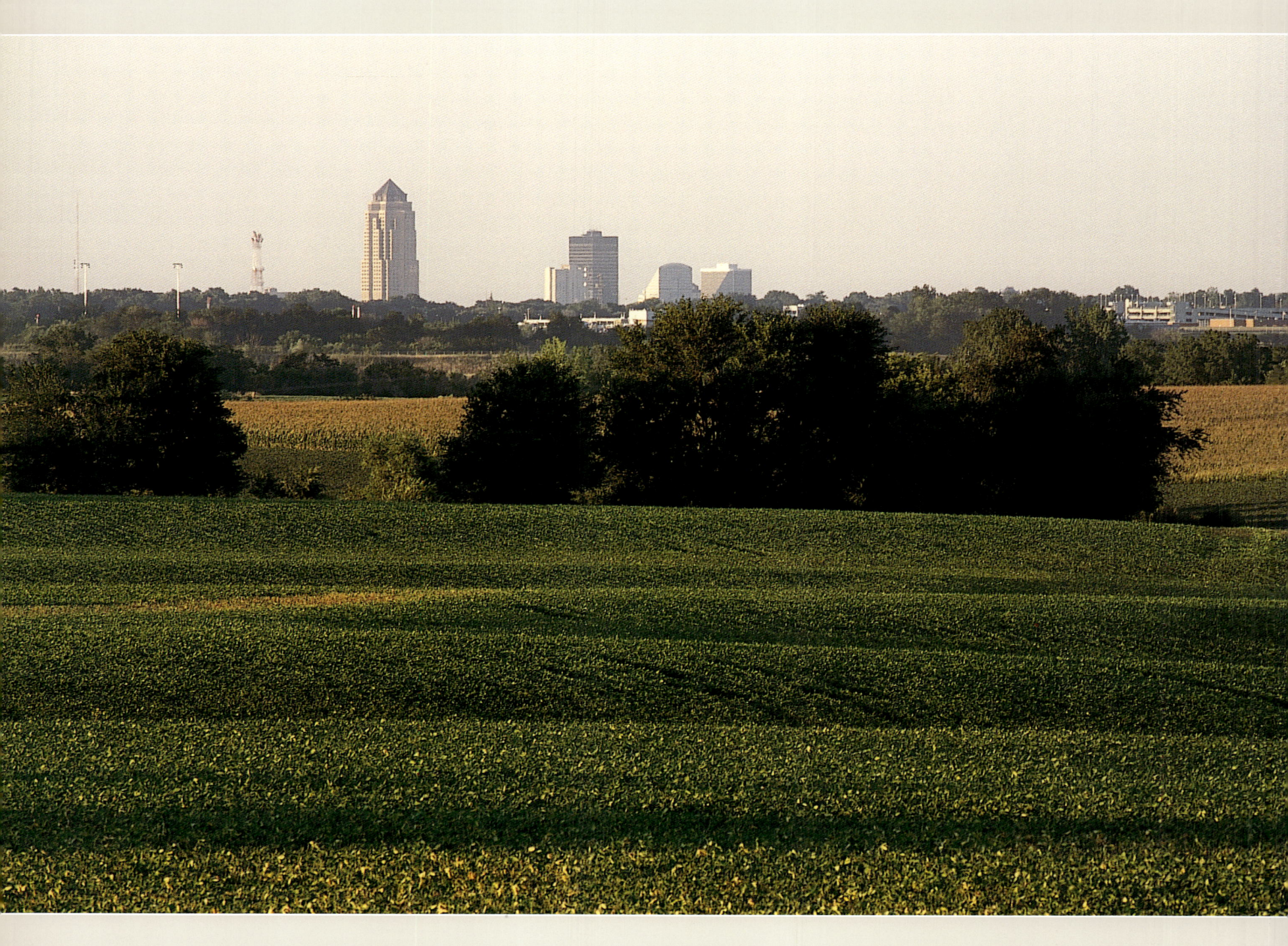

Above: Where the country meets the city—the Des Moines skyline with soy beans and corn in the foreground. CURT MAAS

Facing page: Checking the health of this year's crop. CURT MAAS

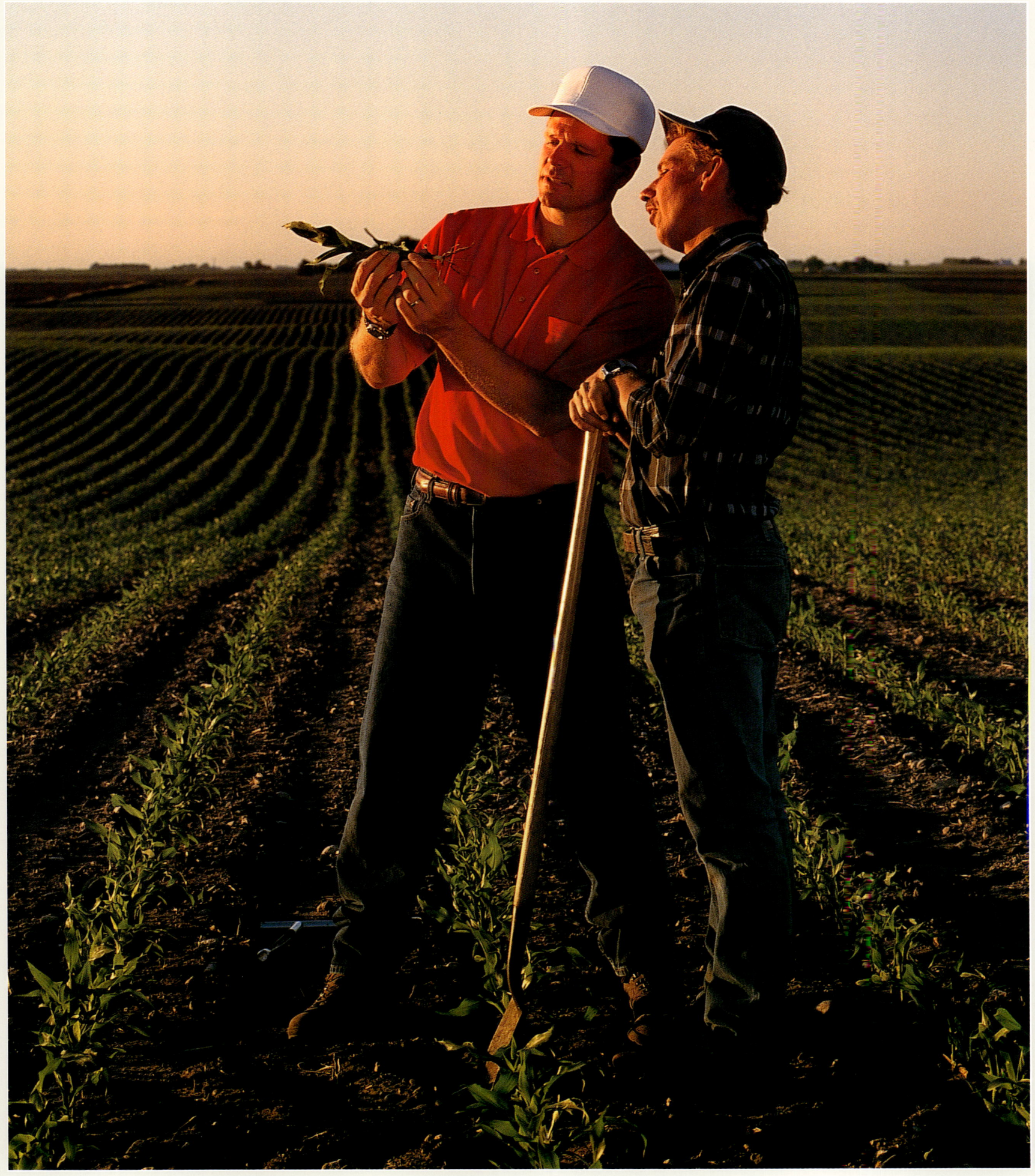

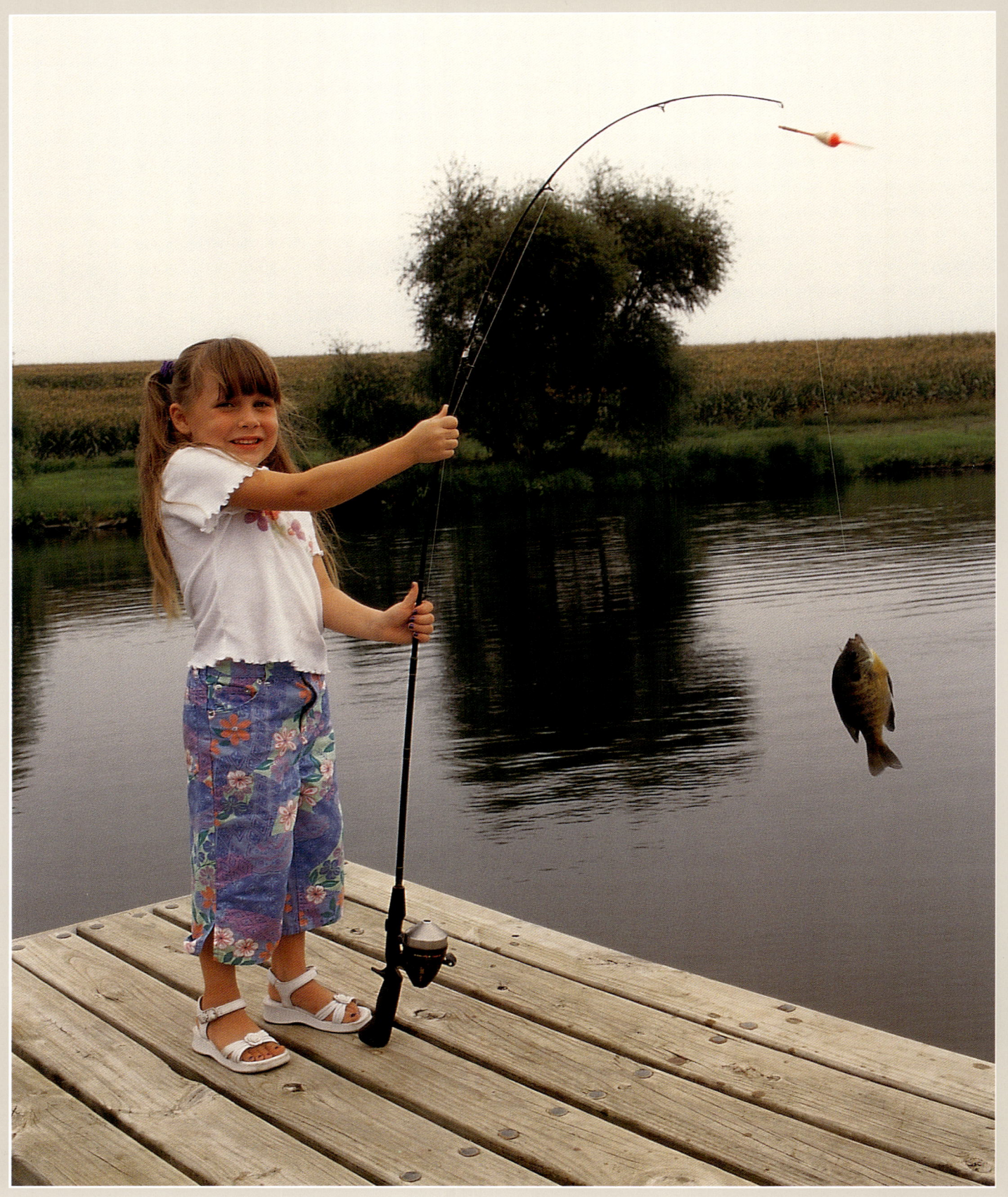

Above: A girl catches her first bluegill. CURT MAAS

Facing page: The Upper Iowa River at sunset near New Albin. LARSH K. BRISTOL

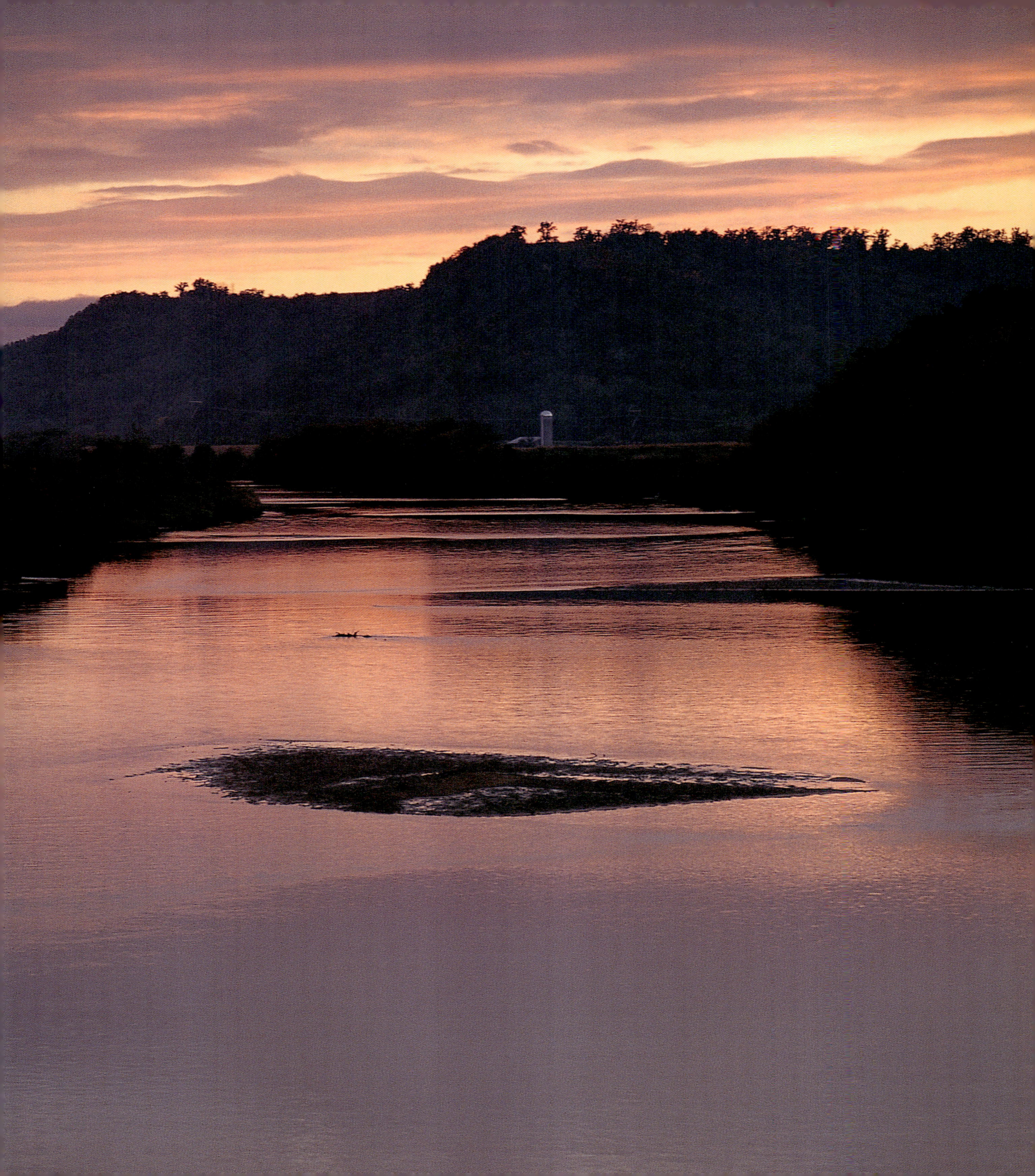

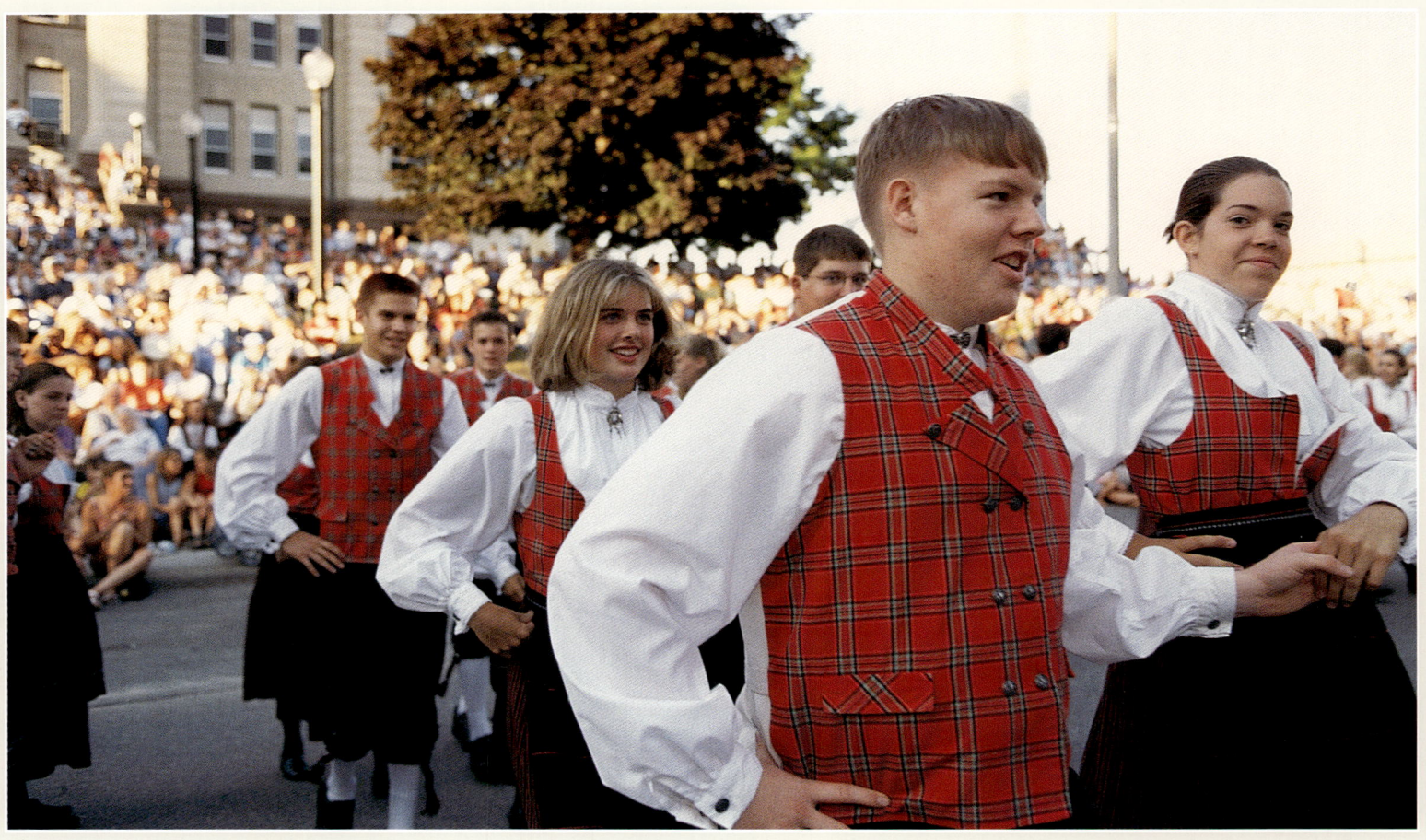

Above: Performers demonstrate Scandinavian dancing during the opening ceremony of Nordic Fest in Decorah. KENT FOSTER

Right: A rendezvous in late September at historic 1840s Fort Atkinson.
LARSH K. BRISTOL

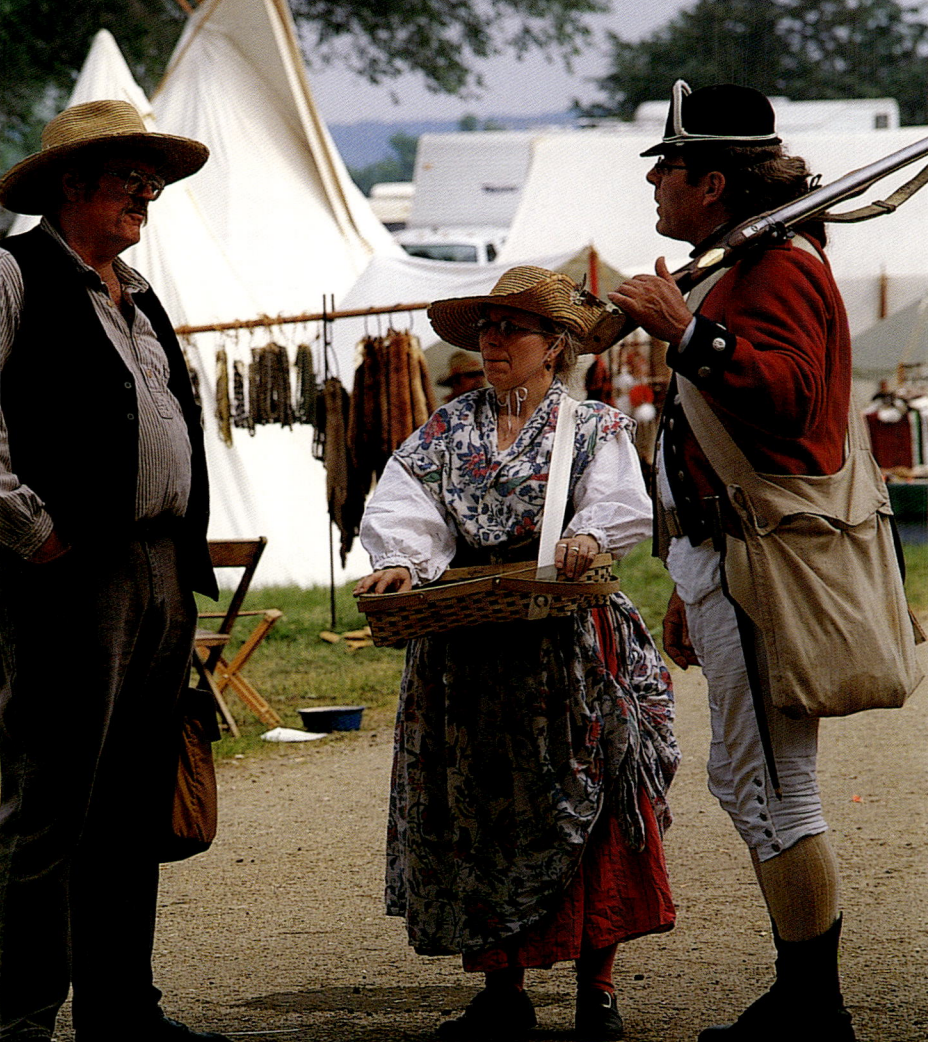

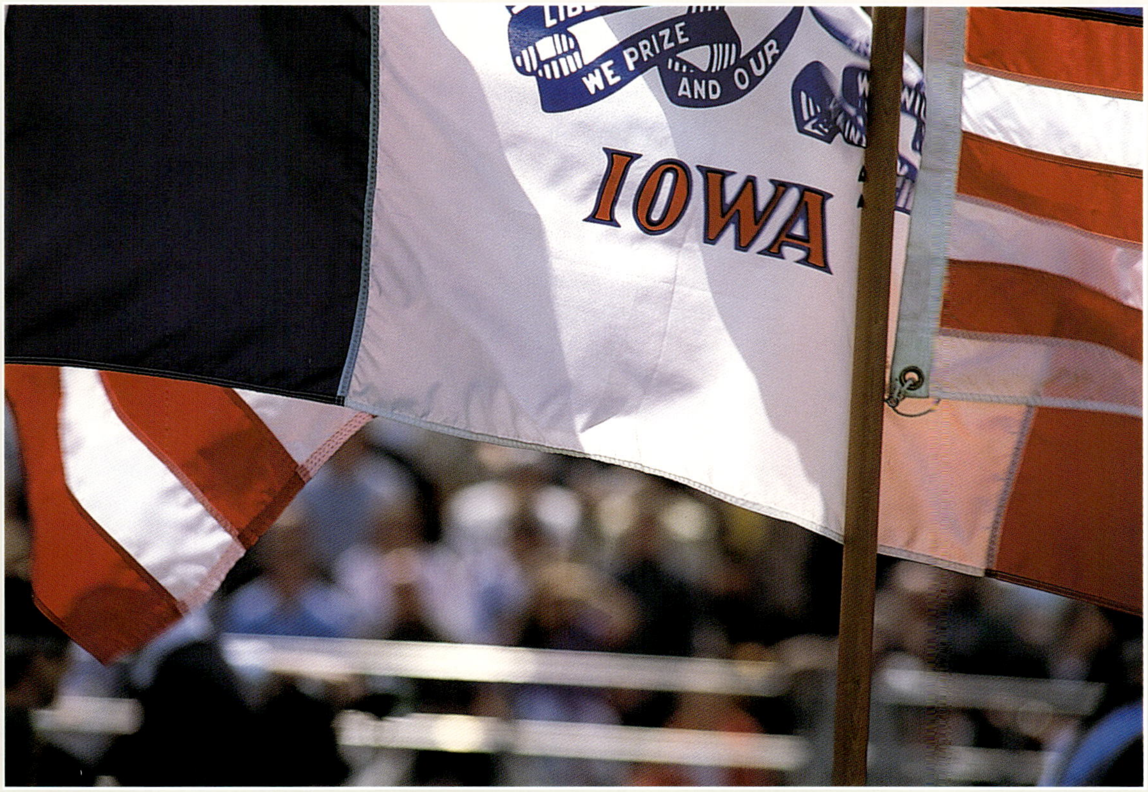

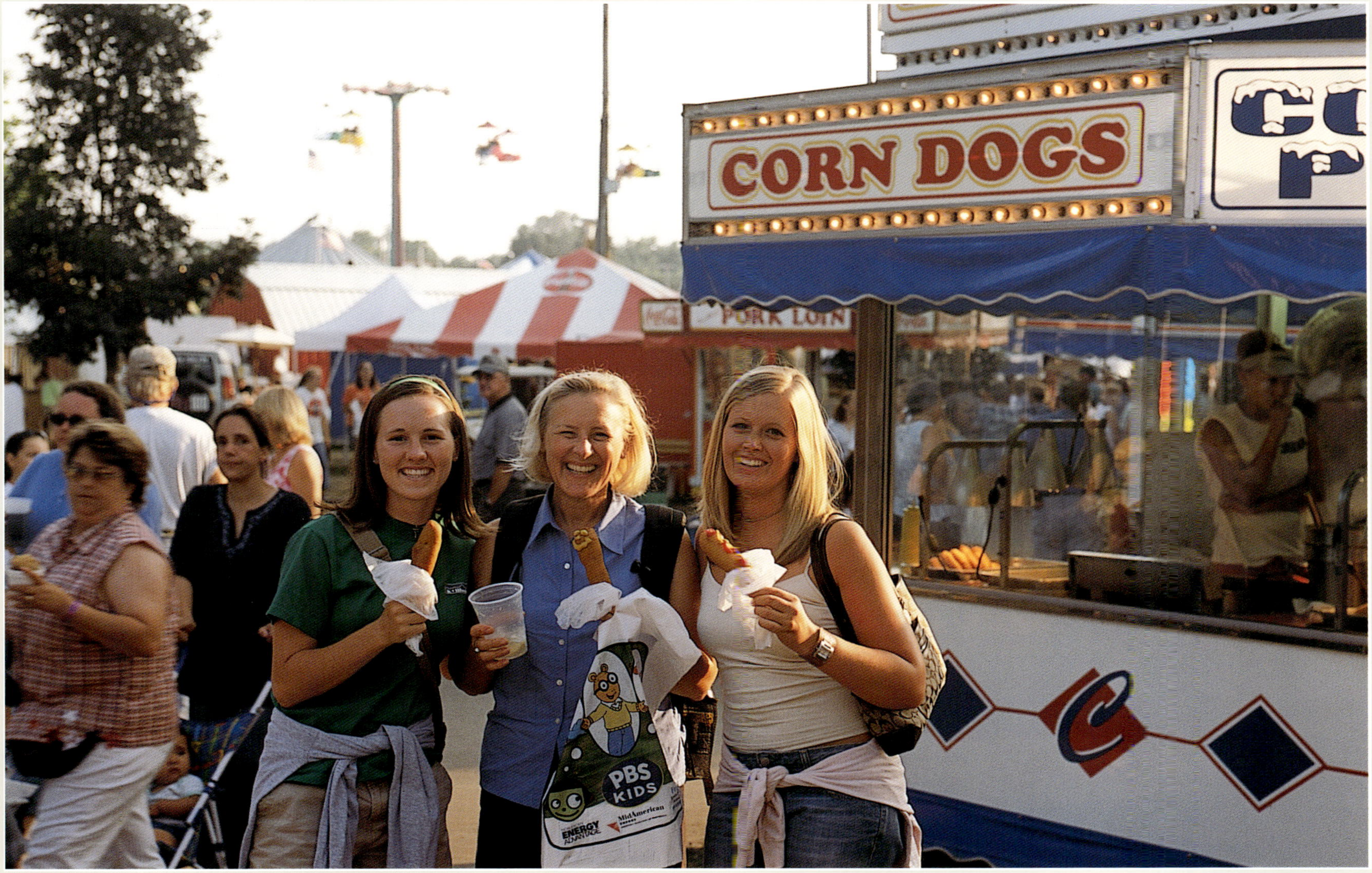

Left: The Iowa state flag flies proudly during a beef sale at the State Fair.
LARSH K. BRISTOL

Below: Enjoying snacks on the midway of the Iowa State Fair, which draws nearly a million visitors a year. CURT MAAS

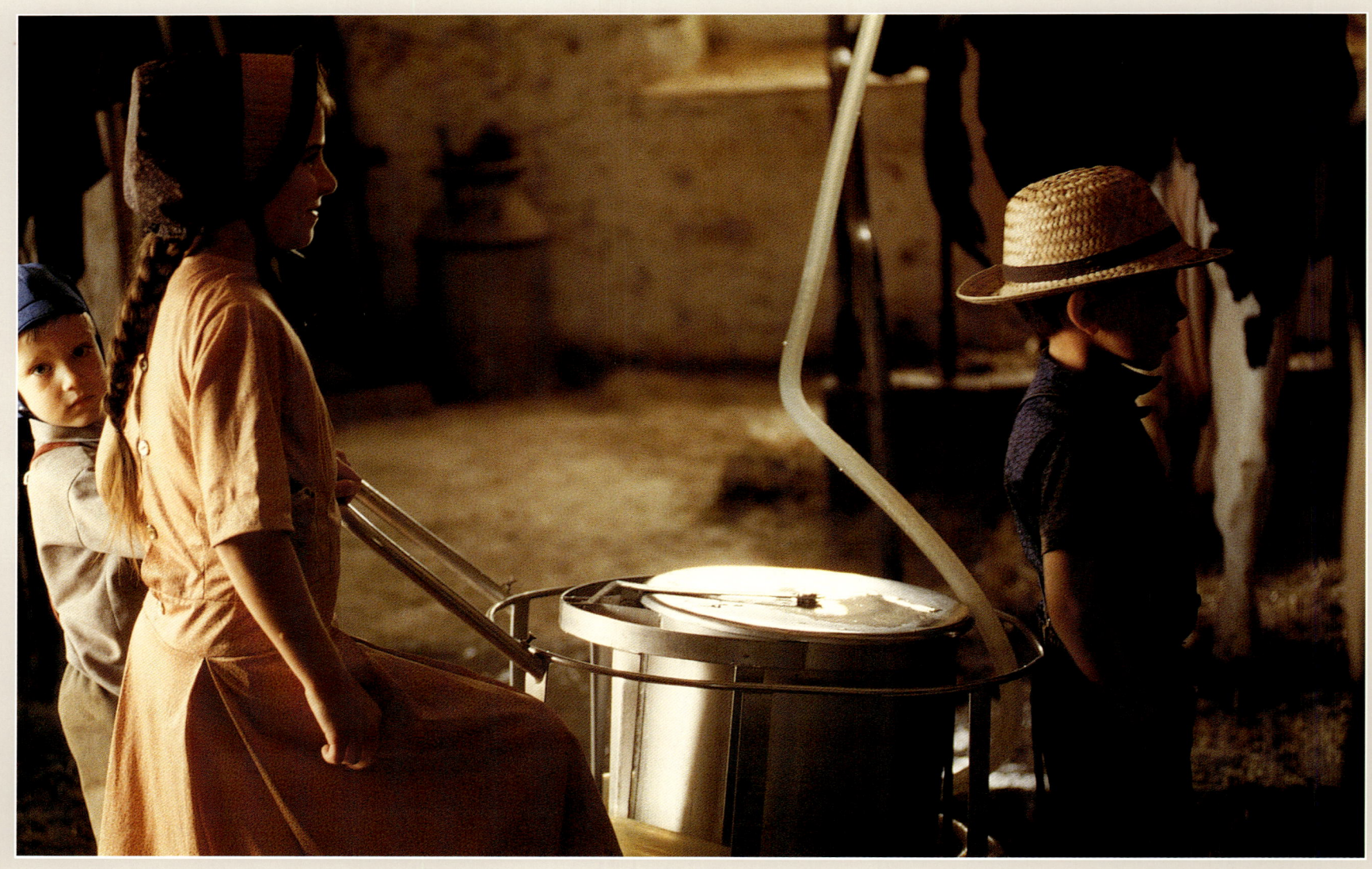

Above: Young Mennonites tend to dairy cows at their farm. LARSH K. BRISTOL

Facing page: Rolling, verdant farm country between Dubuque and Guttenburg. LARSH K. BRISTOL

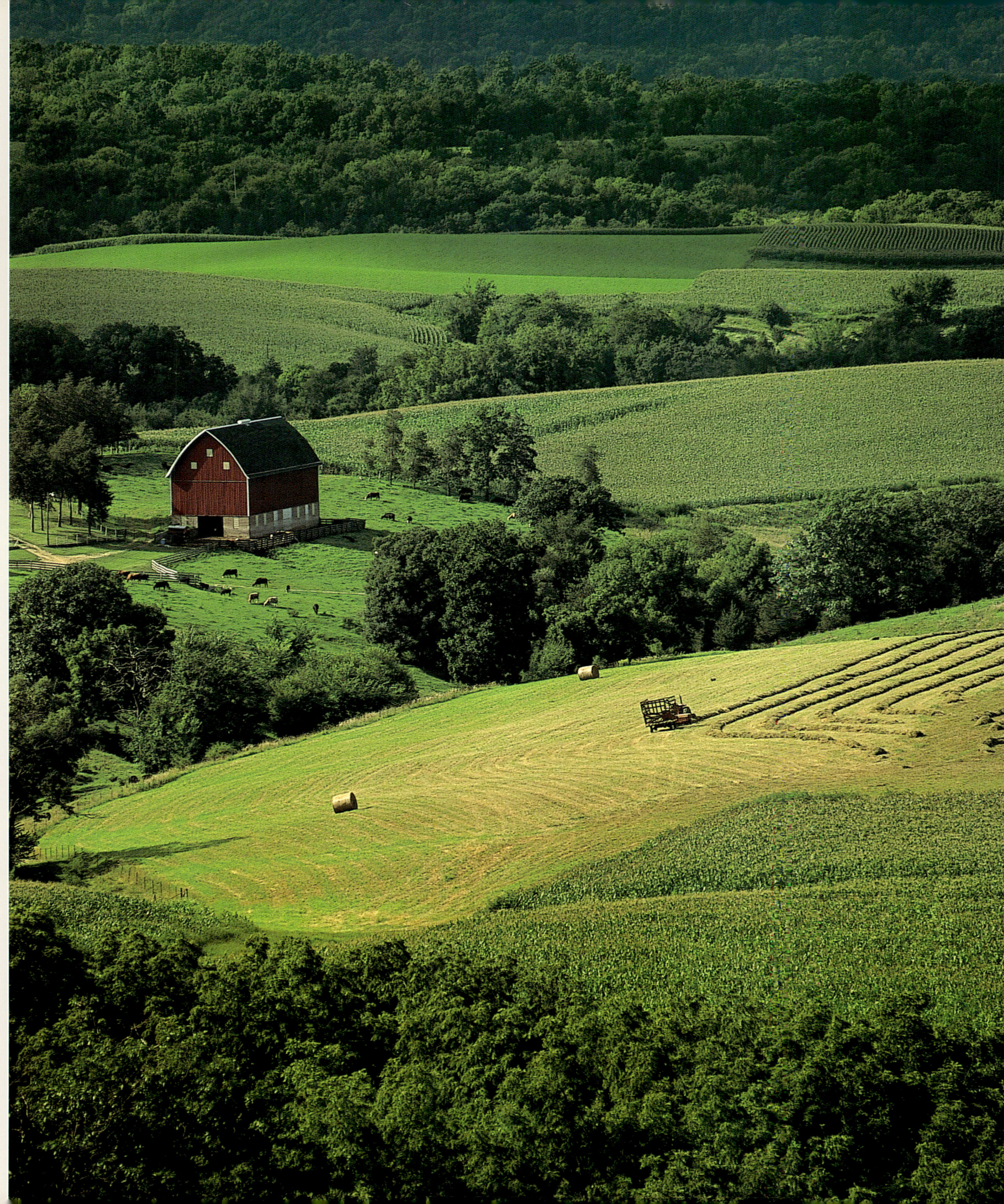

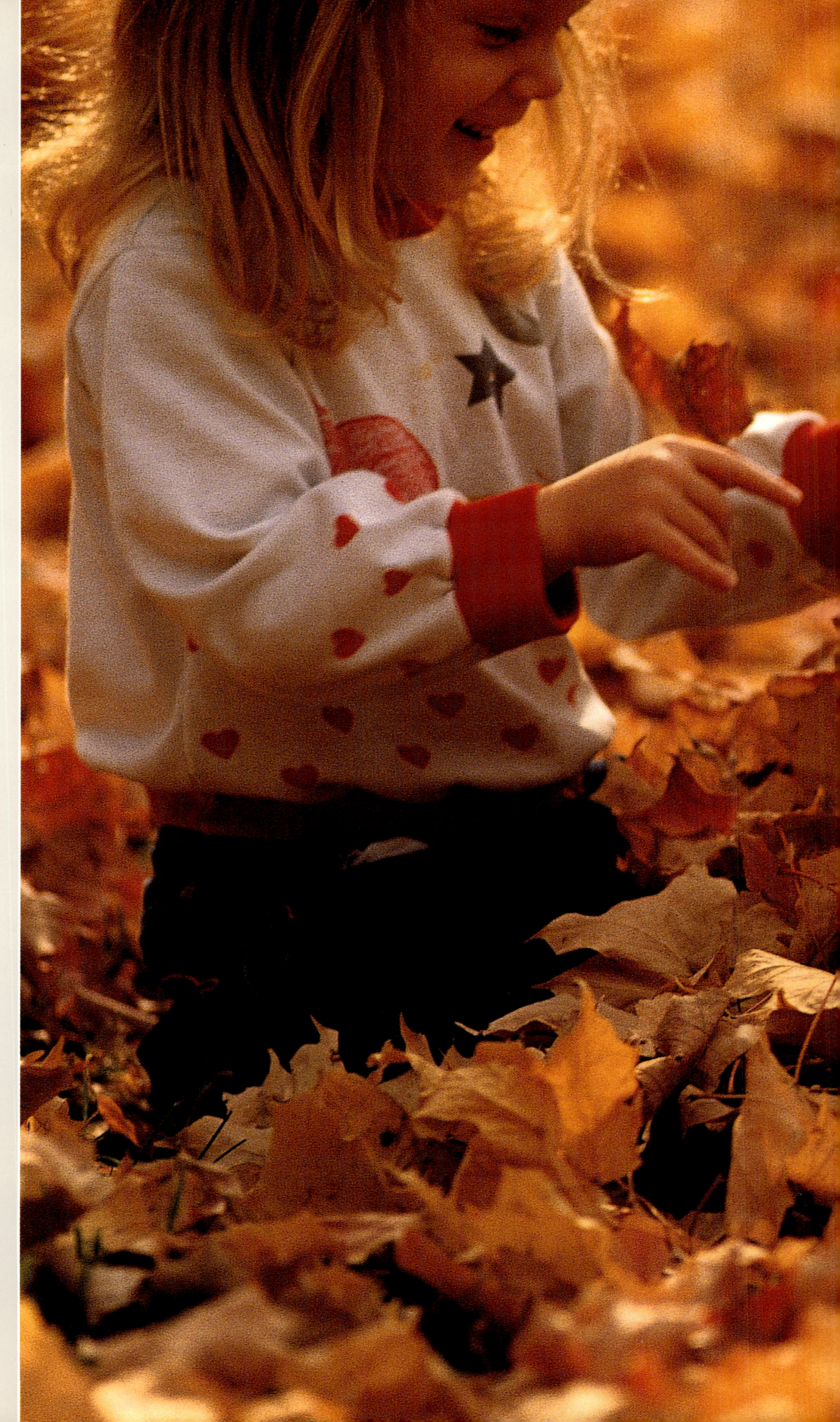

Fall leaves are a great source of autumn fun. LARSH K. BRISTOL

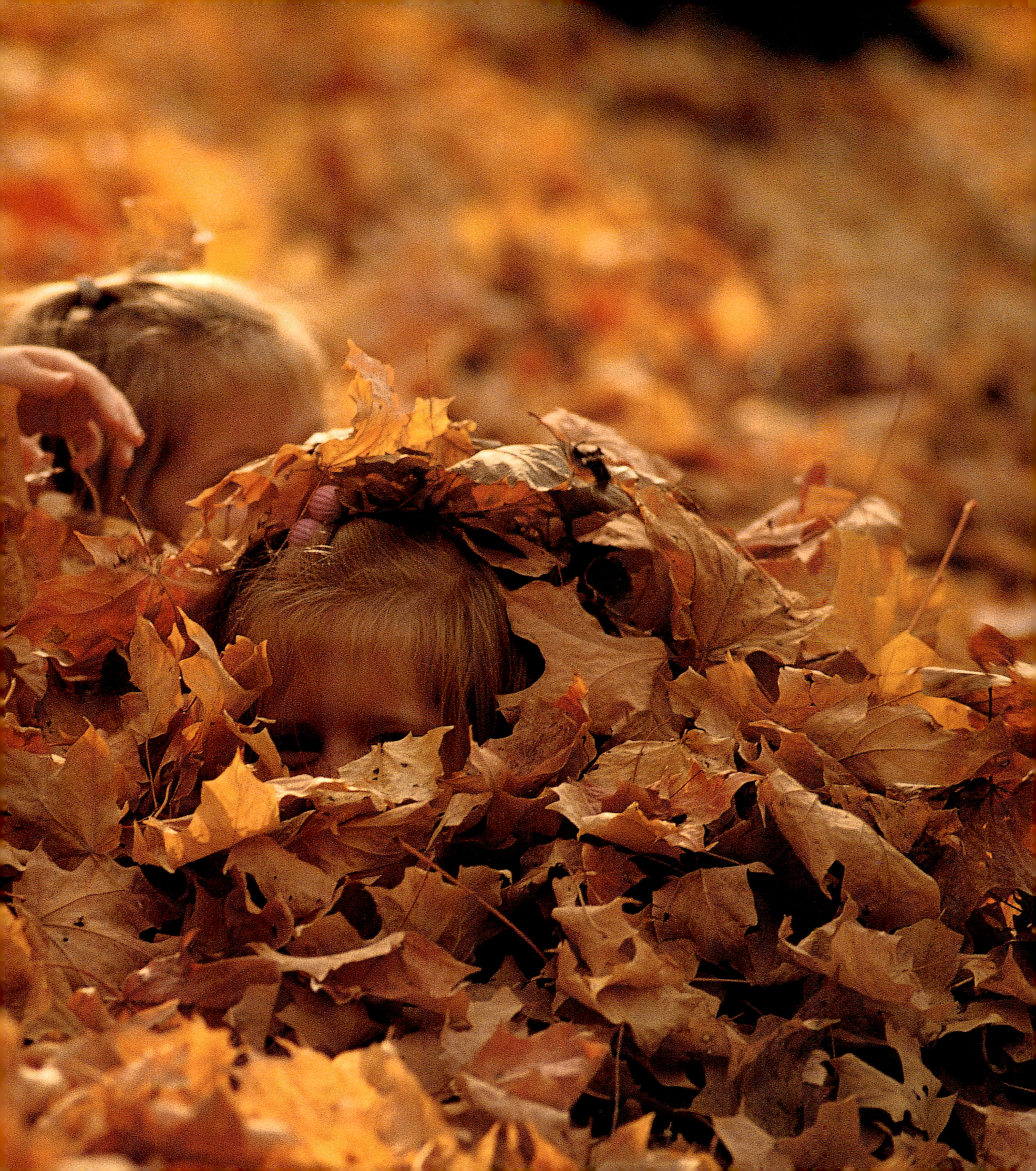

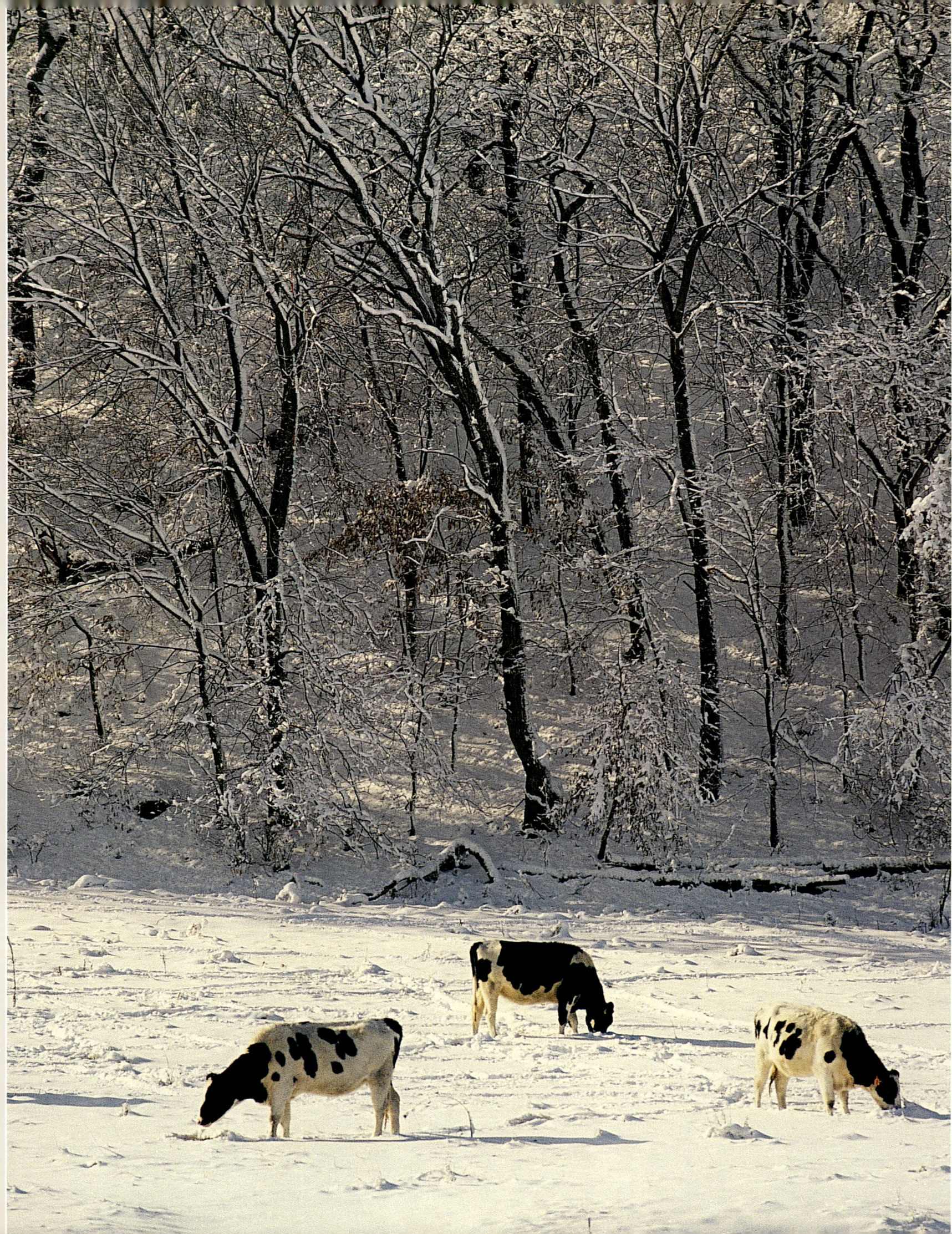

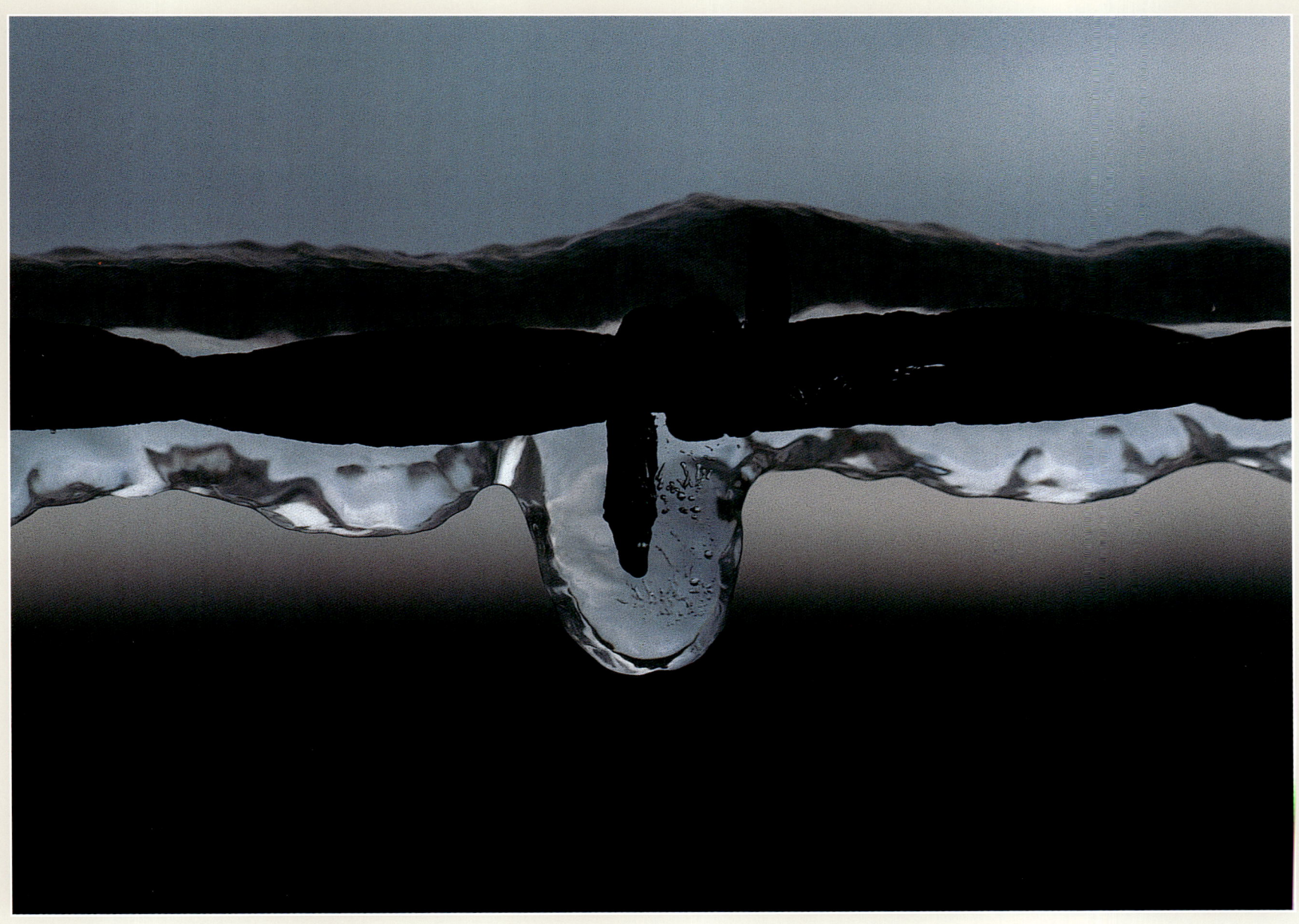

Above: Winter ice encases barbed-wire fencing. CURT MAAS

Facing page: Holstein dairy cows search snow-blanketed pastures for food. LARSH K. BRISTOL

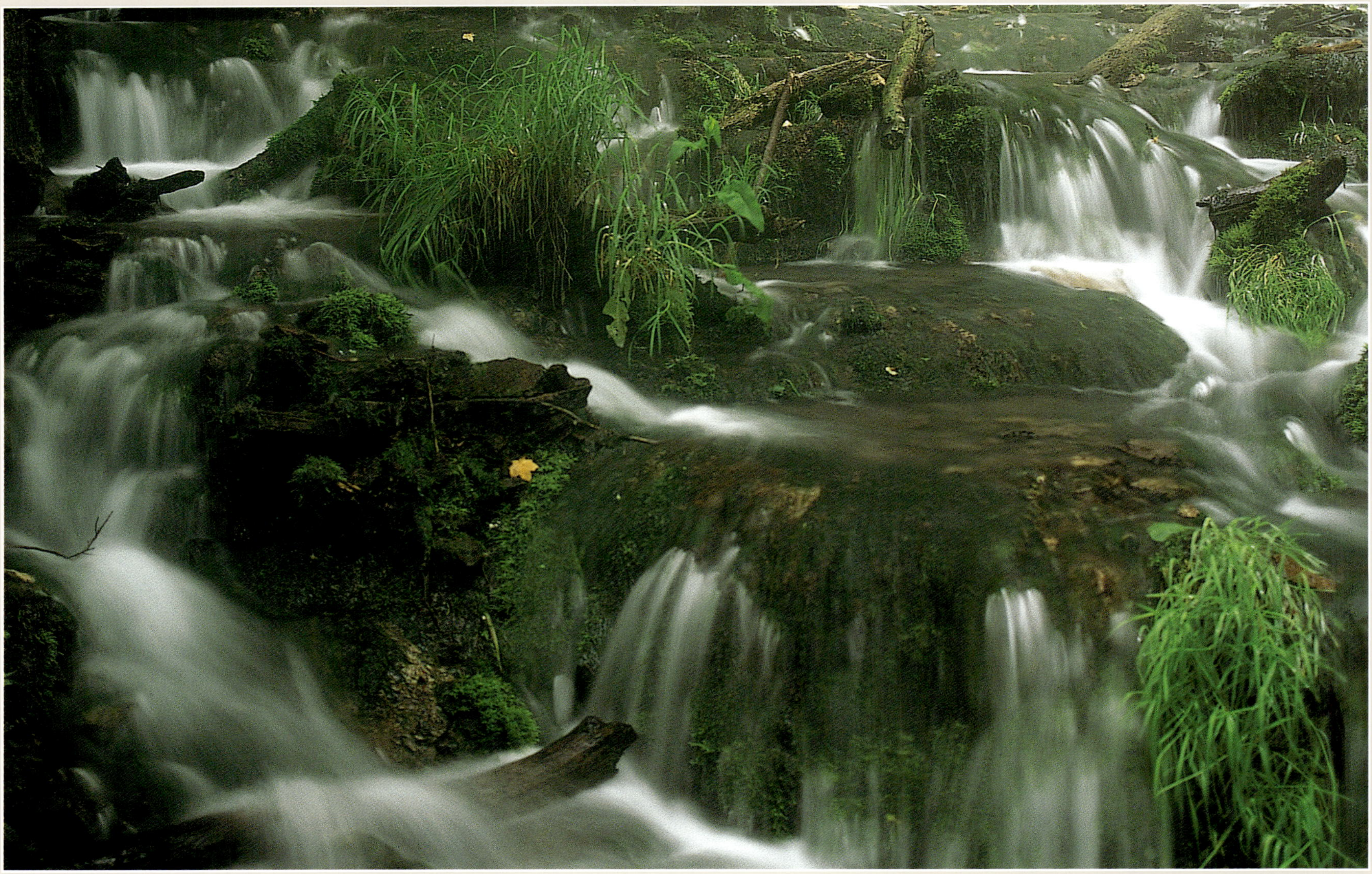

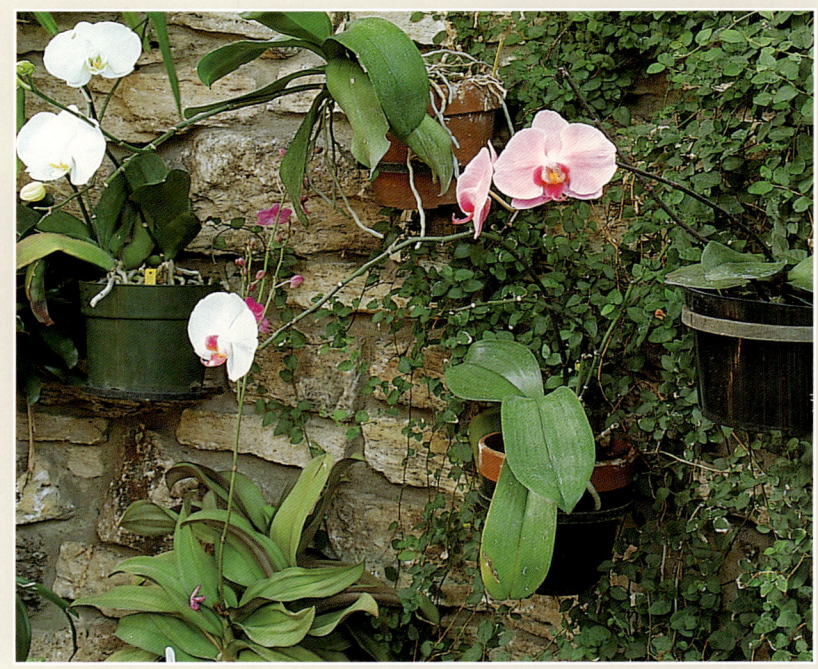

Above: The gentle cascades of Dunning Springs in early spring.
KENT FOSTER

Right: An orchid display at the Des Moines Botanical Center.
KENT FOSTER

Facing page: The Des Moines Botanical Center also features a tranquil Japanese-style water garden. KENT FOSTER

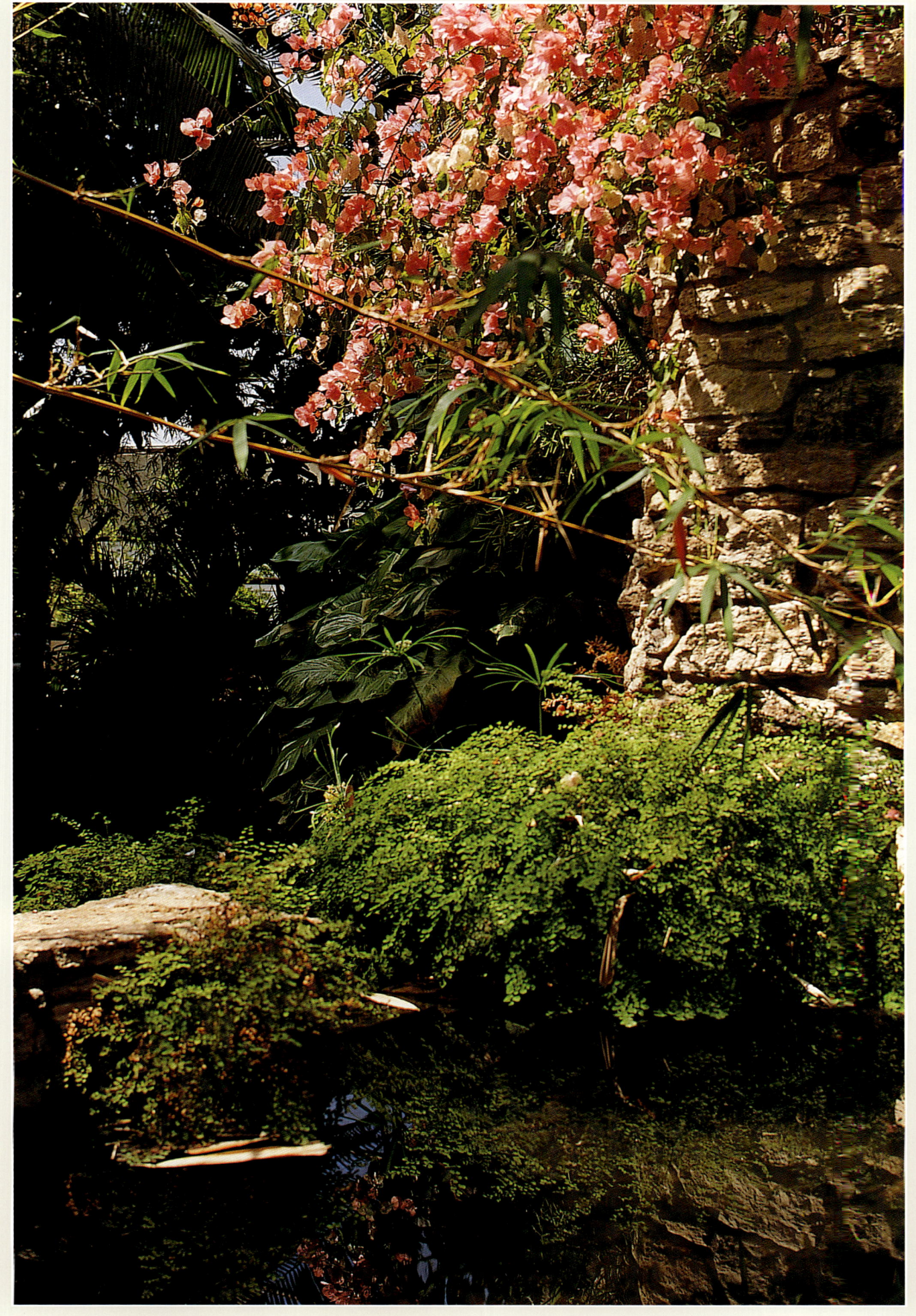

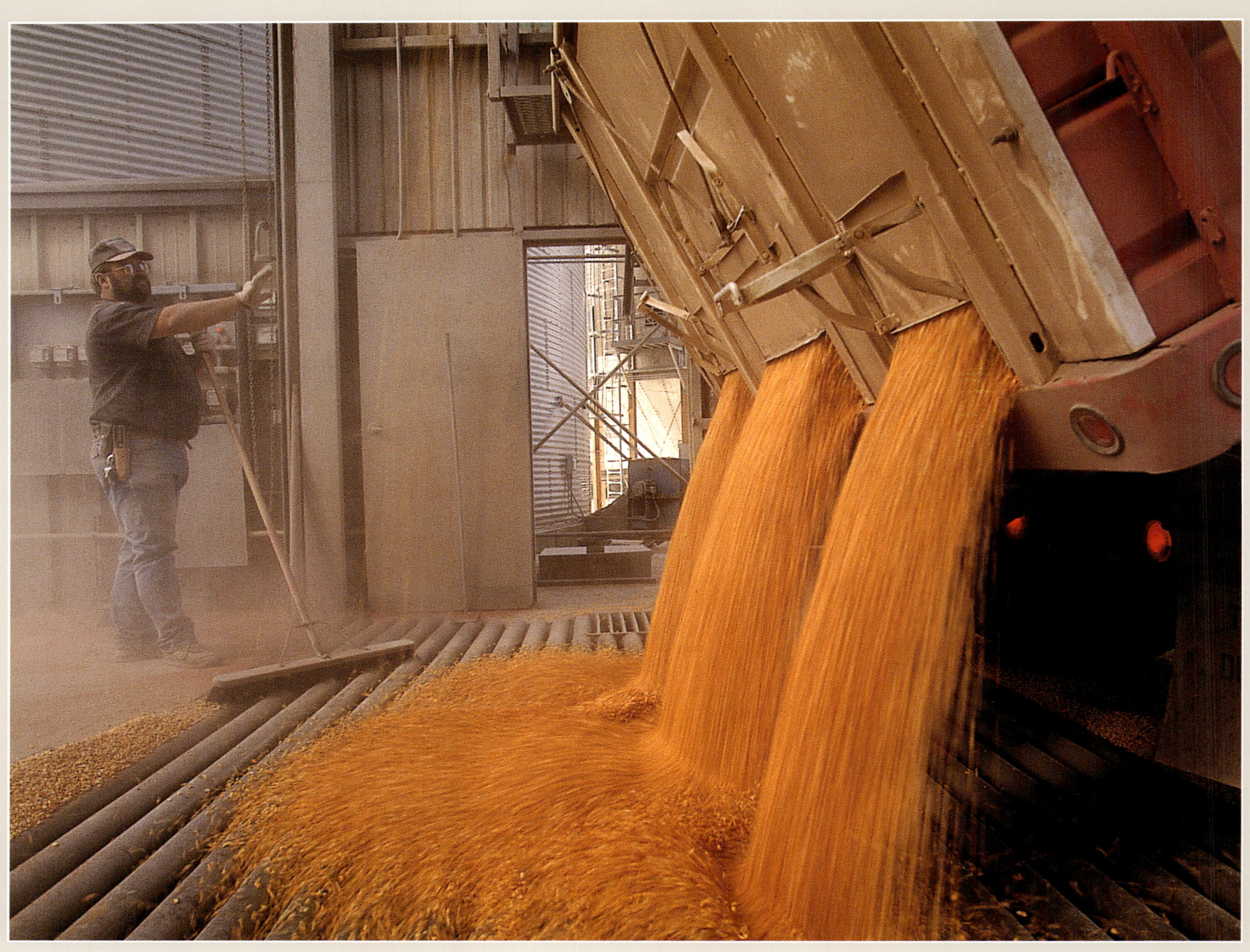

Above: Unloading corn at a Rippey grain elevator. CURT MAAS

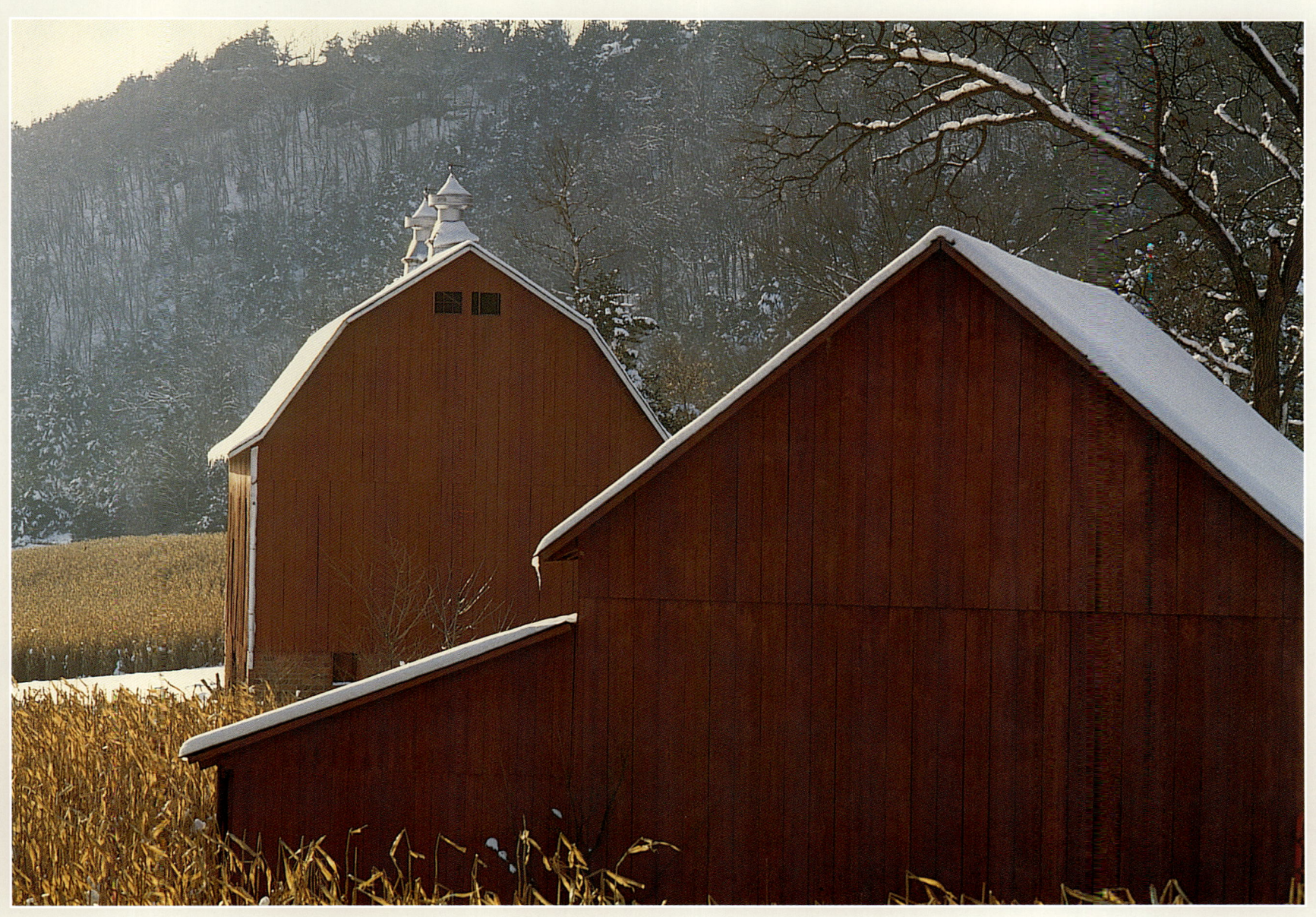

Above: A dusting of snow gives the look of cake frosting on these traditional barns. LARSH K. BRISTOL

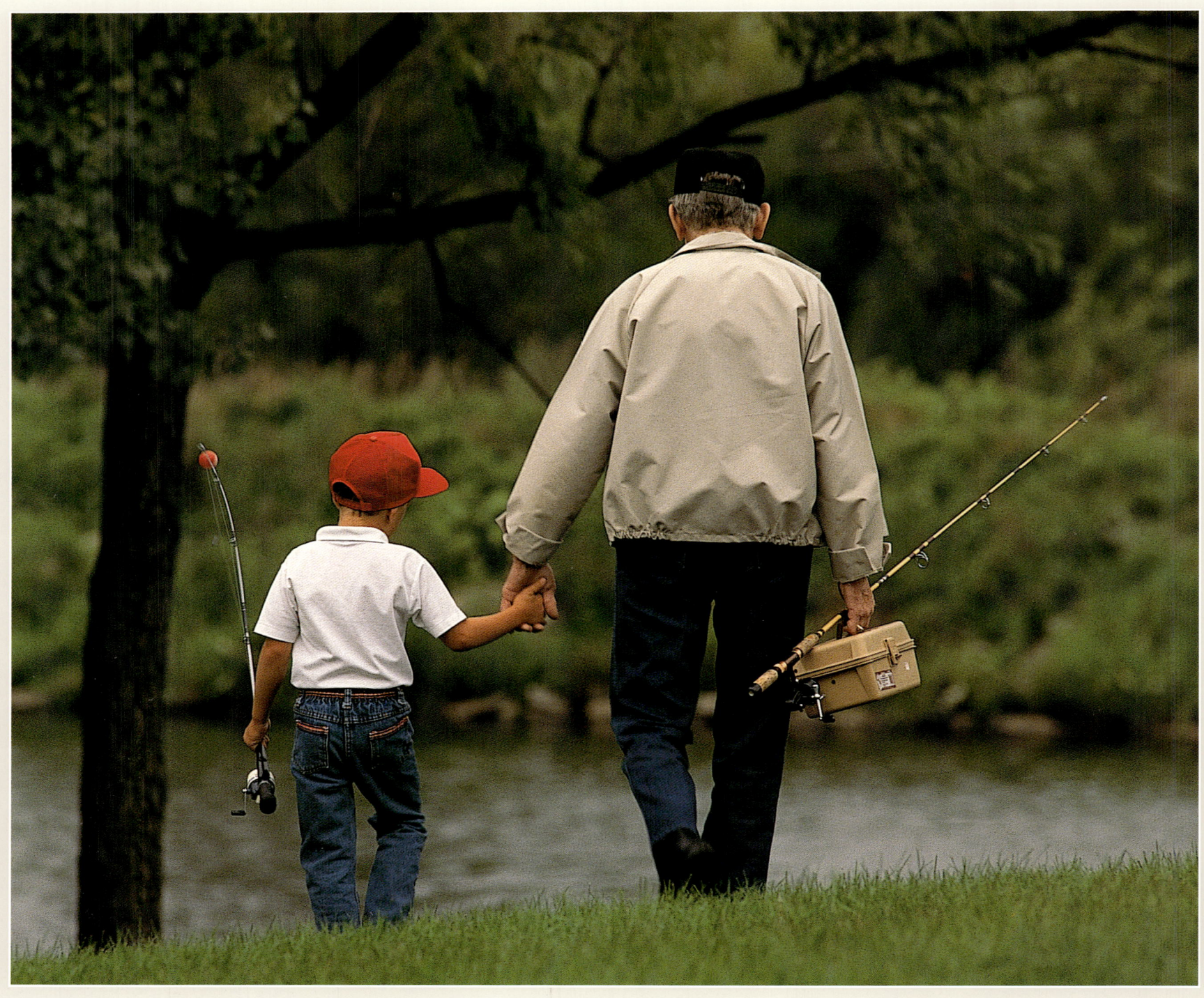

A boy and his grandfather head to the river for a little fishing. CURT MAAS